Richard Hooper, George Chapman

Homer's Batrachomyomachia : Hymns and Epigrams

Hesiod's Works and days. Musaeus' Hero and Leander. Juvenal's Fifth satire.

Second Edition

Richard Hooper, George Chapman

Homer's Batrachomyomachia : Hymns and Epigrams
Hesiod's Works and days. Musaeus' Hero and Leander. Juvenal's Fifth satire. Second Edition

ISBN/EAN: 9783337077679

Printed in Europe, USA, Canada, Australia, Japan

Cover: Foto ©ninafisch / pixelio.de

More available books at **www.hansebooks.com**

HOMER'S BATRACHOMYOMACHIA,

HYMNS AND EPIGRAMS.

HESIOD'S WORKS AND DAYS.
MUSÆUS' HERO AND LEANDER.
JUVENAL'S FIFTH SATIRE.

TRANSLATED

BY GEORGE CHAPMAN

WITH INTRODUCTION AND NOTES,

BY THE

REV. RICHARD HOOPER, M.A
VICAR OF UPTON AND ASTON UPTHORPE, BERKS.

SECOND EDITION,

TO WHICH IS ADDED A GLOSSARIAL INDEX TO THE WHOLE OF
CHAPMAN'S CLASSICAL TRANSLATIONS.

LONDON:
JOHN RUSSELL SMITH.
1888.

TO

SAMUEL WELLER SINGER, ESQ., F.S.A.

THROUGH WHOSE LABOURS

THE EDITOR WAS INTRODUCED

TO THE KNOWLEDGE OF

GEORGE CHAPMAN AND HIS WORKS,

THIS VOLUME IS INSCRIBED.

ADVERTISEMENT.

In accordance with a promise made in the Advertisement to the Second Edition of Chapman's Odyssey, the Editor here adds a Glossarial Index to the whole of Chapman's Classical Translations, which he trusts will give a valuable completeness to a set of volumes which appear to have established themselves in public favour.

UPTON, BERKS,
   May 12, 1888.

INTRODUCTION.

AT length, reader, you have the fifth, and concluding, volume of George Chapman's Translations. Besides its literary value, it is a bibliographical curiosity; and I cannot permit it to appear without expressing my admiration of the spirit and enterprise of the Publisher. He has spared no expense in endeavouring to give to the world, *for the first time*, a complete collection of the labours of one of the greatest Translators of the Elizabethan period. Hitherto Chapman's Translations, from their rarity, were known to a few only, and were supposed by the multitude to be so antiquated—nay, obsolete—and obscure, as to be hardly worth the labour of search. I trust, now that they are within the reach of all, that it will be found that they are of genuine value; and amongst the noblest monuments of a pre-eminently great age. I am quite sensible of their many defects—nay, I am free to confess that they are frequently harsh and rugged; but at the same time, as I have carefully read through the originals with them, I am wonderfully struck with their many exquisite beauties. When I *first* saw the sentence of William Godwin, that "the

Translation of Homer, published by George Chapman in the reigns of Q. Elizabeth and K James, is *one of the greatest treasures the English language has to boast*," I confess I was inclined to demur; but when I attentively read it, and marked the spirit, the roughness and simplicity, the singular sweetness of the epithets, the richness of the language in many of the lines, the grandeur of many of the scenes, and when I compared these with **Pope**, Cowper, and Sotheby, and with the new translation by Professor F. W. Newman (whose metre, by the bye, however adapted for short passages, sadly wearies in a long perusal*), I could not but be impressed with the superiority of Chapman, and not only with his work as a representation of the Homeric mind, but as a most valuable contribution to our English poetry.

I am sometimes inclined to think that his readers are not apt to realize (to use a modern term) the metre of his Iliads, that it is in truth simply our common ballad-metre. I am quite conscious that he has not a complete mastery over it—such, for instance, as Arthur Golding has in his "Ovid's Metamorphoses"—but still if we would read his long lines throughout as two—thus:

> John Gilpin **was** a citizen, of credit and renown;
> A trained-band captain eke was he, of famous London town;

the measure would soon accustom itself to our ear, and we should see, with Lamb, that it is "capable of all sweetness and grandeur," and that "Chapman gallops off with you his own free pace, &c." That Chapman requires study, I consider one of his merits. So do all our best old writers. It is this study that makes them

---

* Mr. Newman's version may be accurate and valuable, but we can hardly call it poetical.

INTRODUCTION.

valuable, that instils into us their nerve and vigour, that enables us to draw from them freshness and health in ideas and language. But it must not be supposed that I wish to offer an apology or defence for good old George. He is perfectly able to defend himself; and the reader must beware lest (as hearty Christopher North warns him) he rouse the ghost of Master Chapman, who will assuredly call him "a certain envious windsucker, that hovers up and down, laboriously engrossing all the air with his luxurious ambition, and buzzing into every ear my detraction"—and again, "a castrill with too hot a liver, and lust after his own glory, and, to devour all himself, discouraging all appetites to the fame of another."* But as I have spoken so much on this subject in the "Introductions" to the Iliad and Odyssey, it is time to return to the present volume.

It is a bibliographical curiosity, inasmuch as all the pieces in it are of more or less rarity Chapman seems to have been determined to translate every possible, or probable, portion of Homer. Hence, having finished the Iliad and Odyssey, he published "*The Crowne of all Homer's Workes, Batrachomyomachia; or the Battaile of Frogs and Mise. His Hymnes and Epigrams. Translated according to the originall, by George Chapman. London. Printed by John Bill, his Maiestie's Printer.*"† This very rare volume is a thin folio, the contents of which are here presented to the reader. It has an exquisitely engraved title, by William Pass; of which we have endeavoured to give a

---
* See Preface to Iliads, pp. LXVII-VIII.
† He considers it his destiny,—
"The work that I was born to do is done!"

facsimile. It is not necessary to inquire into the authenticity of the (so-styled) Homeric Hymns. It will be sufficient to inform the reader that Chapman is the *only* writer who has translated the *whole* of the works ascribed to Homer.

The original **folio** has been entirely followed in the present edition. Copies are now only to be purchased by **those who** can indulge in the luxuries of literature, if **books of** extreme rarity may be so called. Of this **folio, a LARGE PAPER** copy is in the Archiepiscopal Library at Lambeth; the only one I have seen. Messrs. Boone of Bond Street, **whose** collection of fine books is as well known as **the** liberality with which they communicate information **on** them, have permitted me to transcribe a dedication, in Chapman's autograph, from a beautiful copy in their possession (since sold). It is as follows:—"*In love & honor of ye Righte virtuouse and worthie Gent : Mr Henry Reynolds, and to crowne all his deservings with eternall memorie, Geo. Chapman formes this Crowne & conclusion of all the Homericall* **meritts** *wth his accomplisht Improvements ; advising* **that if** *at first sighte he seeme darcke or too fierie, He will yet holde him fast (like Proteus) till he appere in his propper similitude, and he will then shewe himselfe*

> —*vatem egregium, cui non cit publica vena,*
> *Qui nihil expositum soleat deducere ; nec qui*
> *Communi feriat carmen triviale moneta.*"*

This book has been wrongly described in a former "Introduction," as having a presentation *Sonnet*. Chapman has with his pen made an alteration in his portrait, as possessing too much beard; and in the Preface, in

* Juvenal. Sat. VII. 53.

INTRODUCTION

the passage "all for *devouring* a mouse," he writes *drowning ;* and in the final Poem (line 17) for

All is extuberance and *excretion* all,

he reads "and *tumor* all."

The date of the folio is probably about 1624. In the year 1818, my friend Mr. Singer* (to whom I dedicate this volume with the sincerest gratification) published an elegant edition of these Hymns, &c. at Chiswick. It contained two fine original poems by Chapman (first printed 1594) entitled "*The Shadowe of Night: containing two poetical hymnes, devised by G. C. Gent.*" It formed one of Mr. Singer's series of "Select Early English Poets," and has long since been numbered amongst scarce books, as but a limited impression was given. The original edition of "*The Shadowe of Night*" is very rare.

The version of the "*Georgics of Hesiod*" was so difficult to find in Warton's time, that he doubted its existence, (see Hist. of English Poetry, III. 360. ed. 1840,) although he discovered its entry in the Stationers' Registers. It is a small 4to. of 40 pp. As may be presumed from its extreme rarity, its price is usually very

---

* I avail myself of this opportunity of congratulating this veteran in Elizabethan Literature on his having lived to see the day when *all* Chapman's Translations have been republished. His many reprints of early books (all testifying, by the eagerness with which they are sought, to his ability and accuracy) led the public to look back to our sterling old writers. Nor should we forget that Mr. Singer was the associate of Sir Egerton Brydges, Haslewood, and others, who loved these writers when they were comparatively unknown. Mr. Singer expressed a wish in the preface to the above-cited work, "that sufficient encouragement might be given to print Chapman's entire translation of Homer in a compressed and unostentatious portable form."

great. A good copy may be worth ten guineas; it has reached *eighteen*. The largest I have seen is that in the Malone Collection in the Bodleian. There is a fair one in the General Library **of the** British Museum; that in the Grenville (as has my own) **has** been much injured by the binder cutting into the notes, which are in the margin. Of this work, which is sadly misprinted in the original 4to., the present edition is the first reprint; **and I have** spared no pains to make it as *accurate as possible*. **Its** value as a Translation has been acknowledged by **our** best Translator of Hesiod, Elton. I trust, both from its rarity, and its intrinsic merits, it will **be** found an acceptable addition to the present volume. The title is a facsimile of the original edition.

The "*Hero and Leander*" of Musæus is perhaps *one of the rarest books in the whole range of English Literature*. I have never heard of any copy but that in the Bodleian Library at Oxford; and I presume it to be *unique*. Dr. Bliss has given a full account of this very diminutive volume in vol. II. col. 9. of his edition of Wood's "Athenæ Oxonienses." It is about two inches long, **and one** broad. I *most carefully* transcribed it, and *twice* **visited** Oxford to ensure the accuracy of this reprint. Chapman, it will be remembered, had continued Marlow's poem on the same subject; but this is a translation from the Greek of (the so-called) Musæus. The original edition being so extremely small, the lines are printed thus:—

> "Goddess, relate
> The witnesse-bearing light
> Of loves, that would not beare
> A human sight,

The sea-man
    That transported marriages,
Shipt in the night,
    His bosom ploughing the seas."

The title prefixed to this present edition is a facsimile (in a larger size) of the original.

The translation of the *Fifth Satire of Juvenal* is appended to "*A Justification of a Strange* action of Nero *in burying with a* solemne Funerall one of the cast hayres *of his Mistress* Poppœa; *also a just Reproofe of a Romane Smellfeast, being the* fifth Satyre of Juvenall." 4to. 1629. The Tract was not worth reprinting. The Juvenal has been given to complete Chapman's Classical Translations. It is very scarce, and fetches a high price.

Thus, reader, are you presented with this Chapmanni garland of rarities. In your hands I leave them.

By the usual kindness of J. Payne Collier, Esq. I am enabled to give a copy of the Sonnet to Sir Thomas Walsingham, prefixed to one or two copies of Chapman's "All Fools." (See Odyssey, p. XXII.) It is printed verbatim.

TO MY LONG LOU'D AND HONOURABLE FRIEND, SIR THOMAS WALSINGHAM, KNIGHT.

Should I expose to euery common eye,
    The least allow'd birth of my shaken braine;
And not entitle it perticulerly
    To your acceptance, I were wurse then vaine.
And though I am most loth to passe your sight
    with any such light marke of vanitie,

INTRODUCTION.

Being **markt with** Age for Aimes of greater weight,
  and drownd in darke Death-vshering melancholy,
Yet least by others stealth it be imprest,
  without my pasport, patcht with others wit,
Of two enforst ills I elect the least ;
  and so desire your loue will censure it ;
    Though my old fortune keepe me still obscure,
    The light shall still bewray my ould loue sure.

The **reader** is requested **to** correct the following " Faults escaped," before perusing the volume.

FAULTS ESCAPED.

HYMN TO VENUS, l. 121, place comma after *past*, and destroy it after *beast* in next line. P. 136, l. 10, destroy comma after *nostrorum*.

HESIOD, p. 172, notes, l. 2, read *partum;* p. 178, l. 1, after *hir'd* place semicolon; p. 184, notes, l. 5, for *bother* r. *brother;* p. 186, l. 5, after *Hellenians* place semicolon; p. 188, l. 6, put comma after *observing*, and destroy it after *remain;* p. 189, l. 4, destroy comma after *beds;* p. 191, l. 4, r. *seasons'*.

MUSÆUS, in title put full-stop after *originall;* l. 29, *then Love*, is the true reading in the original, therefore destroy note; 198, r. *earthly;* 234, for *should* speed, r. *shall;* 244, r. " At last this sweet voice past, and out did break;" 259, for *loose* to scandal, r. *friend;* annotations, p. 235, last line but two, r. *tam* for *jam*.

ADDITIONAL NOTES.

BATRACHOMYOMACHIA, line 100, for *thither* the true reading is doubtless *th' other*, notwithstanding the authority of the folio.

HYMN TO HERMES, 442, *shrouds*, i. e. recesses, see line 695.

HESIOD. In consequence of Chapman's own notes being so numerous, I was unwilling to interpolate explanations of words (save here and there), but the following may be noted.

Drayton's Introd. Poem, line 1, *fraught*, i. e. freight. 5, I print *travell*, as it is in the original, as it may bear either meaning of *travail* or *travel*. Bk. I. 570, *rode*, I do not remember the word, but, if genuine, it would appear to mean *supply*. Bk. II. 111, *clanges;* the original 4to. has *changes*, but Chapman twice uses the word *clanges* for the cry of the crane, see Iliad, III. 5, X. 244. 310, *horn'd house-bearer*—snail. 382, *imp*—add to, assist. A term in falconry, when a new feather is inserted in place of a broken one.

In Chapman's Iliad, V. 498-9, occur the words *dites* and *diters* in reference to winnowing. Nares gives them in his Glossary citing Chapman as the only authority. It will be found, however, that the word is nothing more than *dights*. See Hesiod, Georgics, Bk. II. 343, and Days, 67.

TABLE OF CONTENTS.

	Page
EPISTLE Dedicatory	xxi.
The Batrachomyomachia	1
Hymn to Apollo	18
Hymn to Hermes	46
First Hymn to Venus	79
Second Hymn to Venus	95
Bacchus or the Pirates	96
Hymn to Mars	100
—— to Diana	101
Third Hymn to Venus	102
Hymn to Pallas	102
—— to Juno	103
—— to Ceres	103
—— to Cybele	103
—— to Hercules	104
—— to Æsculapius	105
—— to Castor and Pollux	105
—— to Mercury	106
—— to Pan	106
—— to Vulcan	109
—— to Phœbus	110
—— to Neptune	110
—— to Jove	111
—— to Vesta	111
—— to the Muses and Apollo	112
—— to Bacchus	112
—— to Diana	113
—— to Pallas	114
—— to Vesta and Mercury	115
—— To Earth	116

b

CONTENTS.

	Page
Hymn to the Sun	118
——— to the Moon	119
——— to Castor and Pollux	120
——— to Men of Hospitality	121

EPIGRAMS AND OTHER POEMS.

To Cuma	122
In his Return to Cuma	122
Upon the Sepulchre of Midus	123
Cuma, refusing to eternize their State, &c.	123
An Essay of his begun Iliads	125
To Thestor's Son inquisitive about the Causes of Things	125
To Neptune	125
To the City of Erythræa	126
To Mariners	126
The Pine	127
To Glaucus	128
Against the Samian Ministress or Nun	128
Written on the Council Chamber	129
The Furnace called in to sing by Potters	129
Eiresione, or the Olive Branch	131
To Certain Fisher-Boys pleasing him with Riddles	132
The Translator's Epilogue	133

END OF THE TRANSLATIONS OF HOMER.

The Georgics of Hesiod	137
Hesiod's Book of Days	201
The Hero and Leander of Musæus	207
The Fifth Satire of Juvenal	237

THE

CROWNE *of all* HOMER'S WORKES,

Batrachomyomachia;

OR,

The Battaile of Frogs and Mise.

HIS HYMNES AND EPIGRAMS.

Tranſlated according to y^e *Originall*

By George   Chapman.

London:
Printed by Iohn Bill, *his* MAIESTIE'S *Printer.*

TO MY EVER MOST-WORTHY-TO-BE-MOST HONOURED LORD,

THE EARL OF SOMERSET, &c.

OT *forc'd by fortune, but since your free
mind
(Made by affliction) rests in choice re-
sign'd*
*To calm retreat, laid quite beneath the wind
Of grace and glory, I well know, my Lord,
You would not be entitled to a word* 5
*That might a thought remove from your repose,
To thunder and spit flames, as greatness does,
For all the trumps that still tell where he goes.
Of which trumps Dedication being one,
Methinks I see you start to hear it blown.* 10
    *But this is no such trump as summons lords
'Gainst Envy's steel to draw their leaden swords,
Or 'gainst hare-lipp'd Detraction, Contempt,
All which from all resistance stand exempt,
It being as hard to sever wrong from merit,* 15
*As meat-indu'd from blood, or blood from spirit.
Nor in the spirit's chariot rides the soul
In bodies chaste, with more divine control,*

*Nor virtue shines more in a lovely face,
Than true desert is stuck off with disgrace.
And therefore Truth itself, that had to bless
The merit of it all, Almightiness,
Would not protect it from the **bane** and ban
Of all moods most distraught and Stygian;
As counting it the crown of all desert,
Borne to heaven, to take of earth, no part
Of false joy here, for joys-there-endless troth,
Nor sell his birthright for a mess of broth.
But stay and still sustain, and his bliss bring,
Like to the hatching of the blackthorn's spring,
With bitter frosts, and smarting hailstorms, forth.
Fates love bees' labours; only Pain crown's Worth.
This Dedication calls no greatness, then,
To patron this greatness-creating pen,
Nor you to add to your dead calm a breath,
For those arm'd angels, that in spite of death
Inspir'd those flow'rs that wrought this Poet's wreath,
Shall keep it ever, Poesy's steepest star,
As in Earth's flaming walls, Heaven's sevenfold Car,
From all the wilds of Neptune's wat'ry sphere,
For ever guards the Erymanthian bear.*

  *Since then your Lordship settles in **your** shade
A life retir'd, and no retreat is made
But to some strength, **(for else** 'tis no retreat,
But rudely running from your battle's heat)
I give this as your strength; your strength, my Lord,
In counsels and examples, that afford
More guard than whole hosts of corporeal pow'r,
And more deliverance teach the fatal hour.*

  Turn not your med'cine then to your disease,

THE EPISTLE DEDICATORY. xxiii

By your too set and slight repulse of these,
The adjuncts of your matchless Odysses;
Since on that wisest mind of man relies
Refuge from all life's infelicities.
    Nor sing these such division from them,   55
But that these spin the thread of the same stream
From one self distaff's stuff; for Poesy's pen,
Through all themes, is t' inform the lives of men;
All whose retreats need strengths of all degrees;
Without which, had you even Herculean knees,   60
Your foes' fresh charges would at length prevail,
To leave your noblest suff'rance no least sail.
Strength then the object is of all retreats;
Strength needs no friends' trust; strength your foes
      defeats.
Retire to strength, then, of eternal things,   65
And y'are eternal; for our knowing springs
Flow into those things that we truly know,
Which being eternal, we are render'd so.
And though your high-fix'd light pass infinite far
Th' adviceful guide of my still-trembling star,   70
Yet hear what my discharg'd piece must foretel,
Standing your poor and perdue sentinel.
Kings may perhaps wish even your beggar's-voice
To their eternities, how scorn'd a choice
Soever now it lies; and (dead) I may   75
Extend your life to light's extremest ray.
If not, your Homer yet past doubt shall make
Immortal, like himself, your bounty's stake
Put in my hands, to propagate your fame;
Such virtue reigns in such united name.   80
    Retire to him then for advice, and skill,

xxiv THE EPISTLE DEDICATORY.

To know things call'd worst, best; and best, most ill,
Which known, **truths best choose**, and retire to still.
And as our English general, (whose name
Shall equal interest find in th' house of fame   85
With all Earth's great'st commanders,) *in* retreat
To Belgian Gant, stood all Spain's armies' heat
By Parma led, though but one thousand strong;
Three miles together thrusting through the throng
Of th' enemy's horse, still pouring on their fall   90
'**Twixt** him and home, and thunder'd through them all.
The Gallic Monsieur standing on the wall,
And wond'ring at his dreadful discipline,
Fir'd with a valour that spit spirit divine;
In *five* battallions ranging all **his** *men*,   95
Bristl'd with pikes, and flank'd with flankers ten;
Gave fire still in his rear; retir'd, and wrought
Down to his fix'd strength still; retir'd and fought;
All the battallions of the enemy's horse
Storming **upon** him still their fieriest force;   100
Charge upon charge laid fresh; he, fresh as day,
Repulsing all, and forcing glorious way
Into *the* gates, that gasp'd, (as swoons for air,)
And took **their life in**, **with** untouch'd repair:—
So fight out, **sweet** Earl, your retreat in peace;   105
No ope-war equals that where privy prease
Of never-number'd odds of enemy,
Arm'd all by envy, in blind ambush lie,
To rush out like an opening threatning sky,
Broke all in meteors round about your ears.   110

₈₄ A simile illustrating the most renowned service of General Norris in his retreat before Gant, never before made sacred to memory.—CHAPMAN.

'Gainst which, though far from hence, through all your
    rears,
Have fires prepar'd ; wisdom with wisdom flank,
And all your forces range in present rank ;
Retiring as you now fought in your strength,
From all the force laid, in time's utmost length,
To charge, and basely come on you behind.
The doctrine of all which you here shall find,
And in the true glass of a human mind.
Your Odysses, the body letting see
All his life past, through infelicity,
And manage of it all. In which to friend,
The full Muse brings you both the prime and end
Of all arts ambient in the orb of man ;
Which never darkness most Cimmerian
Can give eclipse, since, blind, he all things saw,
And to all ever since liv'd lord and law.
And though our mere-learn'd men, and modern wise,
Taste not poor Poesy's ingenuities,
Being crusted with their covetous leprosies,
But hold her pains worse than the spiders' work,
And lighter than the shadow of a cork,
Yet th' ancient learn'd, heat with celestial fire,
Affirms her flames so sacred and entire,
That not without God's greatest grace she can
Fall in the wid'st capacity of man.
  If yet the vile soul of this verminous time
Love more the sale-muse, and the squirrel's chime,
Than this full sphere of poesy's sweetest prime,
Give them unenvied their vain rein and vent,

[135] Ut non sine maximo favore Dei comparari queat.
                              PLATONIS IN IONE.

*And rest your wings in his approv'd ascent
That yet was never reach'd, nor ever fell
Into affections bought with things that sell,
Being the sun's flow'r, and wrapt so in his sky
He cannot yield to every candle's eye.*

> Whose most worthy discoveries, to your lordship's
> judicial perspective, in most subdue humility
> submitteth,

GEORGE CHAPMAN.

NOTE.

On this Epistle Dedicatory, Coleridge remarks: "Chapman's identification of his fate with Homer's, and his complete forgetfulness of the distinction between Christianity and idolatry, under the general feeling of some religion, is very interesting. It is amusing to observe, how familiar Chapman's fancy has become with Homer, his life and circumstances, though the very existence of any such individual, at least with regard to the Iliad and Hymns, is more than problematic."

THE OCCASION OF THIS IMPOSED CROWNE.

AFTER this not only Prime of Poets, but Philosophers, had written his two great poems of Iliads and Odysseys; which (for their first lights born before all learning) were worthily called the Sun and Moon of the Earth; finding no compensation, he writ in contempt of men this ridiculous poem of Vermin, giving them nobility of birth, valorous elocution not inferior to his heroes. At which the Gods themselves, put in amaze, called councils about their assistance of either army, and the justice of their quarrels, even to the mounting of Jove's artillery against them, and discharge of his three-forked flashes; and all for the drowning* of a mouse. After which slight and only recreative touch, he betook him seriously to the honour of the Gods, in Hymns resounding all their peculiar titles, jurisdictions, and dignities; which he illustrates at all parts, as he had been continually conversant amongst them; and whatsoever authentic Poesy he omitted in the episodes contained in his Iliads and Odysseys, he comprehends and concludes in his

* This is Chapman's MS. correction for *devouring* in the folio.

Hymns and Epigrams. All his observance and honour of the Gods, rather moved their envies against him, than their rewards, or respects of his endeavours. And so like a man *verecundi ingenii* (which he witnesseth of himself) he lived unhonoured and needy till his death; and yet notwithstanding all men's servile and manacled miseries, to his most absolute and never-equalled merit, **yea** even bursten profusion to imposture and impiety, **hear our** ever-the-same intranced, and never-sleeping, **Master of the** Muses, to his last accents, incomparably singing.

BATRACHOMYOMACHIA.

ENT'RING the fields, first let my vows
    call on
The Muses' whole quire out of Helicon
Into my heart, for such a poem's sake,
As lately I did in my tables take,
And put into report upon my knees.   5
A fight so fierce, as might in all degrees
Fit Mars himself, and his tumultuous hand,
Glorying to dart to th' ears of every land
Of all the voice-divided; and to show
How bravely did both Frogs and Mice bestow   10
In glorious fight their forces, even the deeds
Daring to imitate of Earth's Giant Seeds.
Thus then men talk'd; this seed the strife begat:
    The Mouse once dry, and 'scaped the dangerous cat,
Drench'd in the neighbour lake her tender beard,   15
To taste the sweetness of the wave it rear'd.

    ⁹ Intending *men:* being divided from all other creatures by the voice; μέροψ, being a periphrasis, signifying *voce divisus,* of μείρω (μείρομαι) *divido,* and ὄψ, ὀπός, *vox.*—CHAPMAN.
    The notes marked C. are Chapman's.

The far-famed Fen-affecter, seeing him, said:
"Ho, stranger! What are you, and whence, that tread
This shore of ours? Who brought you forth? Reply
What truth may witness, lest I find you lie.   20
If worth fruition of my love and me,
I'll have thee home, and hospitality
Of feast and gift, good and magnificent,
Bestow on thee; for all this confluent
Resounds my royalty; my name, the great   25
In blown-up-count'nances and looks of threat,
ᵃ Physignathus, adored of all Frogs here
All their days' durance, and the empire bear
Of all their beings; mine own being begot
By royal ᵇ Peleus, mix'd in nuptial knot   30
With fair ᶜ Hydromedusa, on the bounds
Near which Eridanus his race resounds.
And thee mine eye makes my conceit inclined
To reckon powerful both in form and mind,
A sceptre-bearer, and past others far   35
Advanc'd in all the fiery fights of war.
Come then, thy race to my renown commend."

The Mouse made answer "Why inquires my friend?
For what so well know men and Deities,
And all the wing'd affecters of the skies?   40
ᵈ Psicharpax I am call'd; ᵉ Troxartes' seed,
Surnamed the mighty-minded. She that freed
Mine eyes from darkness was ᶠ Lichomyle,

---

²⁷ ᵃ Φυσίγναθος, *Genas et buccas inflans.* C.
³⁰ ᵇ Πηλεύς, *qui ex luto nascitur.* C.
³¹ ᶜ 'Υδρομέδουσα. *Aquarum regina.* C.
³² The river Po, in Italy. C.
⁴¹ ᵈ Ψιχάρπαξ. Gather-crum, or ravish-crum. C.
⁴¹ ᵉ Shear-crust. C.   ⁴³ ᶠ Lick-mill. C.

King ^a Pternotroctes' daughter, showing me,
Within an aged hovel, the young light,   45
Fed me with figs and nuts, and all the height
Of varied viands. But unfold the cause,
Why, 'gainst similitude's most equal laws
Observed in friendship, thou mak'st me thy friend?
Thy life the waters only help t' extend;   50
Mine, whatsoever men are used to eat,
Takes part with them at shore; their purest cheat,
Thrice boulted, kneaded, and subdued in paste,
In clean round kymnels, cannot be so fast
From my approaches kept but in I eat;   55
Nor cheesecakes full of finest Indian wheat,
That crusty-weeds wear, large as ladies' trains;
Liverings, white-skinn'd as ladies; nor the strains
Of press'd milk, renneted; nor collops cut
Fresh from the flitch; nor junkets, such as put   60
Palates divine in appetite; nor any
Of all men's delicates, though ne'er so many
Their cooks devise them, who each dish see deckt
With all the dainties all strange soils affect.
Yet am I not so sensual to fly   65
Of fields embattled the most fiery cry,

⁴⁴ ^a Bacon-flitch-devourer, or gnawer. C.
⁵² *Cheat*—the second sort of wheaten bread, according to Halliwell, who has well illustrated the word. See also NARES.
⁵⁴ *Kymnels*—household tubs. Chaucer has *kemelin*.
⁵⁷ Τανύπεπλος. *Extenso et promisso peploamictus.* A metaphor taken from ladies' veils, or trains, and therefore their names are here added. C.
⁵⁸ "Ηπατα λευκοχίτωνα. Livering puddings, white-skinn'd. C. *Livering*, i. e. made of liver.
⁶⁰ *Junkets*—cheese pressed on rushes. Ital. *giuncata*. See Odyssey, Bk. VI. 107.
⁶¹ Παντοδαποῖσιν. Whose common exposition is only *variis*, when it properly signifies *ex omni solo*. C.

BATRACHOMYOMACHIA.

But rush out straight, and with the first in fight
Mix in adventure. No man with affright
Can daunt my forces, though his body be
Of never so immense a quantity, 70
But making up, even to his bed, access,
His fingers' ends dare with my teeth compress,
His feet taint likewise, and so soft seize both
They shall not taste th' impression of a tooth.
Sweet sleep shall hold his own in every eye 75
Where my tooth takes his tartest liberty.
But two there are, that always, far and near,
Extremely still control my force with fear,
The Cat, and Night-hawk, who much scathe confer
On all the outrays where for food I err. 80
Together with the straits-still-keeping trap,
Where lurks deceitful and set-spleen'd mishap.
But most of all the Cat constrains my fear,
Being ever apt t' assault me everywhere;
For by that hole that hope says I shall 'scape, 85
At that hole ever she commits my rape.
The best is yet, I eat no pot-herb grass,
Nor radishes, nor coloquintidas,
Nor still-green beets, nor parsley; which you make
Your dainties still, that live upon the lake." 90
The Frog replied: "Stranger, your boasts creep all
Upon their bellies; though to our lives fall
Much more miraculous meats by lake and land,
Jove tend'ring our lives with a twofold hand,
Enabling us to leap ashore for food, 95

[73] *Taint.*—i. e. touch, assault. See Iliad, Bk. III. 374.
[80] *Outrays*—see Iliad, Bk. v. 793.
[81] Στονοίσσαν, of στενὸς, *angustus*. C.
[88] *Coloquintidas*—pumpkins.

And hide us straight in our retreatful flood.
Which, if you will serve, you may prove with ease.
I'll take you on my shoulders; which fast seize,
If safe arrival at my house y' intend."
He stoop'd, and thither spritely did ascend,　　100
Clasping his golden neck, that easy seat
Gave to his sally; who was jocund yet,
Seeing the safe harbours of the king so near,
And he a swimmer so exempt from peer.
But when he sunk into the purple wave,　　105
He mourn'd extremely, and did much deprave
Unprofitable penitence; his hair
Tore by the roots up, labour'd for the air
With his feet fetch'd up to his belly close;
His heart within him panted out repose,　　110
For th' insolent plight in which his state did stand;
Sigh'd bitterly, and long'd to greet the land,
Forced by the dire need of his freezing fear.
First, on the waters he his tail did stere,
Like to a stern; then drew it like an oar,　　115
Still praying the Gods to set him safe ashore;
Yet sunk he midst the red waves more and more,
And laid a throat out to his utmost height;
Yet in forced speech he made his peril slight,
And thus his glory with his grievance strove:　　120
"Not in such choice state was the charge of love
Borne by the bull, when to the Cretan shore
He swum Europa through the wavy roar,
As this Frog ferries me, his pallid breast

[106] *Deprave*—vilify, abuse. See Iliad, **Bk. VI.** 564.
[114] *Stere*—this is the old orthography for *stir* in Chapman, but it may probably mean *steer*.
[115] *Stern*—rudder.

BATRACHOMYOMACHIA.

Bravely advancing, and his verdant crest 125
(Submitted to my seat) made my **support,**
Through his white **waters, to his royal court."**
But on the sudden did apparance make
An horrid spectacle,—a Water-snake
Thusting his freckled neck above the **lake.** 130
Which seen to both, away Physignathus
Dived to his deeps, as no way conscious
Of whom he left to perish in his lake,
But shunn'd black fate himself, and let him **take**
The blackest of it; who amidst the fen 135
Swum with his breast up, hands held up in vain,
Cried *Peepe*, and perish'd; sunk the waters oft,
And often with his sprawlings came aloft,
Yet no way kept down death's relentless force,
But, full of water, made an heavy corse. 140
Before he perish'd yet, he threaten'd thus:
"Thou lurk'st not yet from heaven, Physignathus,
Though yet thou hid'st here, that hast cast from thee,
As from a rock, the shipwrack'd life of me,
Though thou thyself no better was than I, 145
O worst of things, at any faculty,
Wrastling **or race.** But, for thy perfidy
In this my wrack, Jove bears a wreakful eye;
And to the host of Mice thou pains **shalt pay,**
Past all evasion." This his life **let say,** 150
And left him to the waters. Him beheld
ᵃ Lichopinax, placed in the pleasing field,
Who shriek'd extremely, ran and told the Mice;
Who having heard his wat'ry destinies,

[126] *Submitted*—see **Iliad, Bk. xix. 258.**
[152] ᵃ Lickdish. C.

Pernicious anger pierced the hearts of all,   155
And then their heralds forth they sent to call
A council early, at Troxartes' house,
Sad father of this fatal shipwrack'd Mouse;
Whose dead corse upwards swum along the lake,
Nor yet, poor wretch, could be enforced to make   160
The shore his harbour, but the mid-main swum.
When now, all haste made, with first morn did come
All to set council; in which first rais'd head
Troxartes, angry for his son, and said:
"O friends, though I alone may seem to bear   165
All the infortune, yet may all met here
Account it their case. But 'tis true, I am
In chief unhappy, that a triple flame
Of life feel put forth, in three famous sons:
The first, the chief in our confusions,   170
The Cat, made rape of, caught without his hole:
The second, Man, made with a cruel soul,
Brought to his ruin with a new-found sleight,
And a most wooden engine of deceit,
They term a Trap, mere murth'ress of our Mice.   175
The last, that in my love held special price,
And his rare mother's, this Physignathus
(With false pretext of wafting to his house)
Strangled in chief deeps of his bloody stream.
Come then, haste all, and issue out on them,   180
Our bodies deck'd in our Dædalean arms."
This said, his words thrust all up in alarms,

[166] *Infortune*—Odyssey, Bk. xx. 119.
[175] 'Ολέτειρα. *Interfectrix, perditrix.* C. *Mere*—see Odyssey, Bk. viii. 115.
[181] *Dædalean*—simply *variegated*, (δαιδαλέοισι.)

*

And Mars himself, that serves the cure of war,
Made all in their appropriates circular.
First on each leg the green shales of a bean   185
They closed for boots, that sat exceeding clean ;
The shales they broke ope, boothaling by night,
And ate the beans; their jacks art exquisite
Had shown in them, being cats' skins, everywhere
Quilted with quills; their fenceful bucklers were   190
The middle rounds of can'sticks; but their spear
A huge long needle was, that could not bear
The brain of any but he Mars his own
Mortal invention; their heads' arming crown
Was vessel to the kernel of a nut.   195
And thus the Mice their powers in armour put.

   This the Frogs hearing, from the water all
Issue to one place, and a council call
Of wicked war; consulting what should be
Cause to this murmur and strange mutiny.   200
While this was question'd, near them made his stand
An herald with a sceptre in his hand,
"Embasichytrus call'd, that fetch'd his kind
From ᵇTyroglyphus with the mighty mind,
Denouncing ill-named war in these high terms: 205
"O Frogs! the Mice send threats to you of arms,

  ¹⁸⁴ *Appropriates*—proper arms.
  ¹⁸⁶ Εὖ τ' ἀσκήσαντες, ab ἀσκέω, *elaborate concinno.* C.
  ¹⁸⁷ *Boothaling*—foraging for booty, plundering. Halliwell has well explained it ; but this is a good example. Probably Chapman meant a pun on *boots* and *boot*-haling : they foraged for *booty* to make *boots.*
  ¹⁸⁸ *Jacks*—buff jerkins. See Chapman's Commentary on Iliad, XIII. 637
  ¹⁹¹ *Can'sticks*—candlesticks. See HALLIWELL.
  ²⁰³ ᵃ Enter-pot, or search-pot. C.
  ²⁰⁴ ᵇ Cheese-miner. *Qui caseum rodendo cavat.* C. (Tyroglyphus.)

And bid me bid ye battle and fix'd fight;
Their eyes all wounded with Psicharpax' sight
Floating your waters, whom your king hath kill'd.
And therefore all prepare for force of field, 210
You that are best born whosoever held."
This said, he sever'd: his speech firing th' ears
Of all the Mice, but freez'd the Frogs with fears,
Themselves conceiting guilty; whom the king
Thus answer'd, rising, "Friends! I did not bring 215
Psicharpax to his end; he, wantoning
Upon our waters, practising to swim,
Aped us, and drown'd without my sight of him.
And yet these worst of vermin accuse me,
Though no way guilty. Come, consider we 220
How we may ruin these deceitful Mice.
For my part, I give voice to this advice,
As seeming fittest to direct our deeds:
Our bodies decking with our arming weeds,
Let all our pow'rs stand rais'd in steep'st repose 225
Of all our shore; that, when they charge us close,
We may the helms snatch off from all so deckt,
Daring our onset, and them all deject
Down to our waters; who, not knowing the sleight
To dive our soft deeps, may be strangled straight, 230
And we triumphing may a trophy rear,
Of all the Mice that we have slaughter'd here."
  These words put all in arms; and mallow leaves
They drew upon their legs, for arming greaves.
Their curets, broad green beets; their bucklers were
Good thick-leaved cabbage, proof 'gainst any spear; 236

²¹⁸ Μιμούμενος. Aping, or imitating us. C.
²²⁴ *Weeds*—i. e. garments; a very common word.
²³⁴ Boots of War. C.

Their spears sharp bulrushes, of which were all
Fitted with long ones; their parts capital
They hid in subtle cockleshells from blows.
And thus all arm'd, the steepest shores they chose   240
T' encamp themselves; where lance with lance they lined,
And brandish'd bravely, each Frog **full** of mind.
    Then Jove call'd all Gods in his flaming throne,
And show'd all all this preparation
For resolute war; these able soldiers,   245
Many, **and great, all** shaking lengthful spears,
In show like **Centaurs,** or the Giants' host.
When, sweetly smiling, he inquired who, most
Of all th' Immortals, pleased **to add** their aid
To Frogs or Mice; and thus **to** Pallas said: 250
    "O Daughter! Must not your needs aid these Mice,
That, with the odours **and** meat sacrifice
Used in your temple, endless triumphs make,
And serve you for your sacred victuals' sake?"
    Pallas replied: "O Father, never I   255
Will aid the Mice in any misery.
So many mischiefs by them I have found,
Eating the cotton that my distaffs crown'd,
My **lamps still** haunting to devour the oil.
But that which most my mind eats, **is** their spoil   260
Made of a **veil,** that me in much did **stand,**
On which bestowing an elaborate hand,
A fine woof working of as pure a thread,
Such holes therein their petulancies fed
That, putting it to darning, when 'twas done,   265
The darner a most dear pay stood upon

    ²³⁹ Parts capital—heads.
    ²⁵⁸ Στέμματα, Lanas, eo quod colus cingunt seu coronent. Which
our learned sect translate eating the crowns that Pallas wore. C.

For his so dear pains, laid down instantly ;
Or, to forbear, exacted usury.
So, borrowing from my fane the weed I wove,
I can by no means th' usurous darner move   270
To let me have the mantle to restore.
And this is it that rubs the angry sore
Of my offence took at these petulant Mice.
Nor will I yield the Frogs' wants my supplies,
For their infirm minds that no confines keep ;   275
For I from war retired, and wanting sleep,
All leap'd ashore in tumult, nor would stay
Till one wink seized mine eyes, and so I lay
Sleepless, and pain'd with headache, till first light
The cock had crow'd up. Therefore, to the fight   280
Let no God go assistant, lest a lance
Wound whosoever offers to advance,
Or wishes but their aid, that scorn all foes,
Should any God's access their spirits oppose.
Sit we then pleased to see from heaven their fight."   285
   She said, and all Gods join'd in her delight.
And now both hosts to one field drew the jar,
Both heralds bearing the ostents of war.
And then the wine-gnats, that shrill trumpets sound,
Terribly rung out the encounter round ;   290
Jove thund'red ; all heaven sad war's sign resounded.
   And first ᵃ Hypsiboas ᵇ Lichenor wounded,
Standing th' impression of the first in fight.
His lance did in his liver's midst alight,
Along his belly. Down he fell ; his face   295

[268] Τόκος, *Partus, et id quod partu edidit mater. Metap. hic appellatur fœnus quod ex usurâ ad nos redit.* C.
[289] Κώνωψ. *Culex vinarius.* C.   [292] ᵃ Loud-mouth. C.
[292] ᵇ Kitchen-vessel licker. C.

His fall on that part sway'd, and all the grace
Of his soft hair fil'd with disgraceful dust.
  Then ᵃ Troglodytes his thick javelin thrust
In ᵇ Pelion's bosom, bearing him to ground,
Whom sad death seized ; his soul flew through his wound.
  ᶜ Seutlæus next Embasichytros slew,   301
His heart through-thrusting. Then ᵈ Artophagus threw
His lance at ᵉ Polyphon, and struck him quite
Through his mid-belly ; down he fell upright,
And from his fair limbs took his soul her flight.   305
  ᶠ Linnocharis, beholding Polyphon
Thus done to death, did, with as round a stone
As that the mill turns, Troglodytes wound,
Near his mid-neck, ere he his onset found ;
Whose eyes sad darkness seized. ᵍ Lichenor cast   310
A flying dart off, and his aim so placed
Upon Linnocharis, that sure he thought
The wound he wish'd him ; nor untruly wrought
The dire success, for through his liver flew
The fatal lance ; which when ʰ Crambophagus knew, 315
Down the deep waves near shore he, diving, fled ;
But fled not fate so ; the stern enemy fed
Death with his life in diving ; never more
The air he drew in ; his vermilion gore
Stain'd all the waters, and along the shore   320

---

²⁹⁶ ᵃ Hole-dweller. *Qui foramina subit.* C. Chapman, as is constantly the case, has altered the quantity of the word.
²⁹⁹ ᵇ Mud-born. C.   ³⁰¹ ᶜ Beet-devourer. C.
³⁰² ᵈ The great bread-eater. C.
³⁰³ ᵉ Πολύφωνον. The great-noise-maker, shrill or big-voiced. C.   ³⁰⁶ ᶠ The lake-lover. C.
³¹⁰ ᵍ *Qui lambit culinaria vasa.* C.
³¹² Τιτύσκομαι *intentissime dirigo ut certum ictum inferam.* C.
³¹⁵ ʰ The cabbage-eater. C.

He laid extended; his fat entrails lay
(By his small gut's impulsion) breaking way
Out at his wound.   ᵃ Limnisius near the shore
Destroy'd Tyroglyphus.   Which frighted sore
The soul of ᵇCalaminth, seeing coming on,   325
For wreak, ᶜ Pternoglyphus; who got him gone
With large leaps to the lake, his target thrown
Into the waters.   ᵈ Hydrocharis slew
King ᵉ Pternophagus, at whose throat he threw
A huge stone, strook it high, and beat his brain   330
Out at his nostrils.   Earth blush'd with the stain
His blood made on her bosom.   For next prise,
Lichopinax to death did sacrifice
ᶠ Borborocœtes' faultless faculties;
His lance enforced it; darkness closed his eyes.   335
On which when ᵍ Prassophagus cast his look,
ʰ Cnissodioctes by the heels he took,
Dragg'd him to fen from off his native ground,
Then seized his throat, and soused him till he drown'd.
    But now Psicharpax wreaks his fellows' deaths,   340
And in the bosom of ⁱ Pelusius sheaths,
In centre of his liver, his bright lance.
He fell before the author of the chance;
His soul to hell fled.   Which ᵏ Pelobates
Taking sad note of, wreakfully did seize   345
His hand's gripe full of mud, and all besmear'd

---

³²³ ᵃ *Paludis incola.*   Lake-liver. C.
³²⁵ ᵇ *Qui in calaminthâ, herbâ palustri, habitat.* C.
³²⁶ ᶜ Bacon-eater. C.   ³²⁸ ᵈ *Qui aquis delectatur.* C.
³²⁹ ᵉ Collup-devourer.   C.   Another of Chapman's false quantities.   ³³⁴ ᶠ Mud-sleeper. C.
³³⁶ ᵍ Leek or scallion lover. C.   A similar error.
³³⁷ ʰ Kitchin-smell haunter, or hunter. C.
³⁴¹ ⁱ Fenstalk. C.   ³⁴⁴ ᵏ *Qui per lutum it.* C.

His forehead with it so, that scarce appear'd
The light to him. Which certainly incensed
His fiery spleen; who with his wreak dispensed
No point of time, but rear'd with his strong hand   350
A stone so massy it oppress'd the land,
And hurl'd it at him; when below the knee
It strook his right leg so impetuously
It piecemeal brake it; he the dust did seize,
Upwards everted. But ᵃ Craugasides   355
Revenged his death, and at his enemy
Discharged a dart that did his point imply
In his mid-belly. All the sharp-pil'd spear
Got after in, and did before it bear
His universal entrails to the earth,   360
Soon as his swoln hand gave his jav'lin birth.
  ᵇ Sitophagus, beholding the sad sight,
Set on the shore, went halting from the fight,
Vex'd with his wounds extremely; and, to make
Way from extreme fate, leap'd into the lake.   365
  Troxartes strook, in th' instep's upper part,
Physignathus; who (privy to the smart
His wound imparted) with his utmost haste
Leap'd to the lake, and fled. Troxartes cast
His eye upon the foe that fell before,   370
And, seeing him half-lived, long'd again to gore
His gutless bosom; and, to kill him quite,
Ran fiercely at him. Which ᶜ Prassæus' sight
Took instant note of, and the first in fight
Thrust desp'rate way through, casting his keen lance
Off at Troxartes; whose shield turn'd th' advance   376

355 ᵃ Vociferator. C.   362 ᵇ Eat-corn. C.
373 ᶜ Scallion-devourer. C.

The sharp head made, and check'd the mortal chance.
  Amongst the Mice fought an egregious
Young springall, and a close-encount'ring Mouse,
Pure ªArtepibulus's dear descent;   380
A prince that Mars himself show'd where he went.
(Call'd ᵇMeridarpax,) of so huge a might,
That only he still domineer'd in fight
Of all the Mouse-host. He advancing close
Up to the lake, past all the rest arose   385
In glorious object, and made vaunt that he
Came to depopulate all the progeny
Of Frogs, affected with the lance of war.
And certainly he had put on as far
As he advanced his vaunt, he was endu'd   390
With so unmatch'd a force and fortitude,
Had not the Father both of Gods and men
Instantly known it, and the Frogs, even then
Given up to ruin, rescued with remorse.
Who, his head moving, thus began discourse: 395
  "No mean amaze affects me, to behold
Prince Meridarpax rage so uncontroll'd,
In thirst of Frog-blood, all along the lake.
Come therefore still, and all addression make,
Despatching Pallas, with tumultuous Mars,   400
Down to the field, to make him leave the wars,
How potently soever he be said
Where he attempts once to uphold his head."
  Mars answer'd: "O Jove, neither She nor I,
With both our aids, can keep depopulacy   405

---

[380] ª Bread-betrayer. C. (Artepibŭlus.)
[382] ᵇ Scrap, or broken-meat-eater. C.
[402] Κρατερός, *validus seu potens in retinendo.* C.

From off the Frogs! And therefore arm we all,
Even thy lance letting brandish to his call
From off the field, that from the field withdrew
The Titanois, the Titanois that slew,
Though most exempt from match of all earth's Seeds,
So great and so inaccessible deeds
It hath proclaim'd to men; bound hand and foot
The vast Enceladus; and rac'd by th' root
The race of upland Giants." This speech past,
Saturnius a smoking lightning cast
Amongst the armies, thund'ring then so sore,
That with a rapting circumflex he bore
All huge heaven over. But the terrible ire
Of his dart, sent abroad, all wrapt in fire,
(Which certainly his very finger was)
Amazed both Mice and Frogs. Yet soon let pass
Was all this by the Mice, who much the more
Burn'd in desire t' exterminate the store
Of all those lance-loved soldiers. Which had been,
If from Olympus Jove's eye had not seen
The Frogs with pity, and with instant speed
Sent them assistants. Who, ere any heed
Was given to their approach, came crawling on
With anvils on their backs, that, beat upon
Never so much, are never wearied yet;
Crook-paw'd, and wrested on with foul cloven feet,
Tongues in their mouths, brick-back'd, all over bone,

⁴¹⁴ *Upland* is constantly used in Chapman for rough, rude; up-land i. e. from the country, as distinguished from the civilization of the town.
⁴²⁹ Νωτάκμονες. *Incudes ferentes*, or anvil-backed. Ἄκμων. *Incus, dicta per syncopen quasi nullis ictibus fatigetur.* C.
⁴³² Ψαλιδοοστμος. *Forcipem in ore habens.* C.

Broad shoulder'd, whence a ruddy yellow shone,
Distorted, and small-thigh'd; had eyes that saw
Out at their bosoms; twice four feet did draw   435
About their bodies; strong-neck'd, whence did rise
Two heads; nor could to any hand be prise;
They call them lobsters; that ate from the Mice
Their tails, their feet, and hands, and wrested all
Their lances from them, so that cold appall   440
The wretches put in rout, past all return.
And now the Fount of Light forbore to burn
Above the earth; when, which men's laws commend,
Our battle in one day took absolute end.

THE END OF HOMER'S BATTLE OF FROGS AND MICE.

ALL THE HYMNS OF HOMER.

A HYMN TO APOLLO.

 WILL remember and express the praise
Of heaven's **Far-darter, the fair King of
days,**
Whom even **the** Gods themselves fear
when he goes
Through Jove's high house; and **when his** goodly **bows**
He goes to bend, all from their thrones arise,   5
And cluster near, t' admire his faculties.
Only Latona stirs not from her seat
Close by **the Thund'rer,** till her Son's retreat
From his **dread archery;** but then she goes,
Slackens his string, **and** shuts his quiver **close,**   10
And (having taken **to her** hand his bow,
From off his able shoulders) doth bestow
Upon a pin of gold the glorious tiller,
The pin of gold fix'd in his father's pillar.
Then doth She to his **throne his** state uphold,   15
Where his great **Father,** in a cup of gold,

¹³ *Tiller*—bow.

A HYMN TO APOLLO.

Serves him with nectar, and shows all the grace
Of his great son. Then th' other Gods take place;
His gracious mother glorying to bear
So great an archer, and a son so clear.   20
   All hail, O blest Latona! to bring forth
An issue of such all-out-shining worth,
Royal Apollo, and the Queen that loves
The hurls of darts. She in th' Ortygian groves,
And he in cliffy Delos, leaning on   25
The lofty Oros, and being built upon
By Cynthus' prominent, that his head rears
Close to the palm that Inops' fluent cheers.
   How shall I praise thee, far being worthiest praise,
O Phœbus? To whose worth the law of lays   30
In all kinds is ascrib'd, if feeding flocks
By continent or isle. All eminent'st rocks
Did sing for joy, hill-tops, and floods in song
Did break their billows, as they flow'd along
To serve the sea; the shores, the seas, and all   35
Did sing as soon as from the lap did fall
Of blest Latona thee the joy of man.
Her child-bed made the mountain Cynthian
In rocky Delos, the sea-circled isle,
On whose all sides the black seas brake their pile, 40
And overflow'd for joy, so frank a gale
The singing winds did on their waves exhale.
   Here born, all mortals live in thy commands,
Whoever Crete holds, Athens, or the strands
Of th' isle Ægina, or the famous land   45
For ships (Eubœa), or Eresia,
Or Peparethus bord'ring on the sea,

[23] Viz. Diana.

Ægas, or Athos that doth Thrace divide
And Macedon ; or Pelion, with the pride
Of his high forehead ; or the Samian isle, 50
That likewise lies near Thrace ; or Scyrus' soil ;
Ida's **steep** tops ; or all that Phocis fill ;
Or Autocanes, with the heaven-high hill ;
Or populous Imber ; Lemnos without ports ;
Or Lesbos, fit for the divine resorts ; 55
And sacred soil of blest Æolion ;
Or Chios that exceeds comparison
For fruitfulness ; with all the isles that lie
Embrac'd with seas ; Mimas, with rocks so high ;
Or lofty-crown'd Corycius ; or the bright 60
Charos ; or Æsagæus' dazzling height ;
Or watery Samos ; Mycale, that bears
Her brows even with the circles **of the** spheres ;
Miletus ; Cous, that the city **is**
Of voice-divided-choice humanities ; 65
High Cnidus ; Carpathus, still strook with wind ;
Naxos, and Paros ; and the rocky-min'd
Rugged Rhenæa. Yet through all these parts
Latona, great-grown with the King of darts,
Travell'd , and tried if any would become 70
To her dear birth an hospitable home.
All which extremely trembled, shook with **fear**,
Nor durst endure so high a birth to **bear**
In their free states, though, for it, they became
Never so fruitful ; till the reverend Dame 75
Ascended Delos, and her soil did seize
With these wing'd words : "O Delos ! Wouldst thou please
To be my son Apollo's native seat,

⁵³ Autocanes.

A HYMN TO APOLLO.

And build a wealthy fane to one so great,
No one shall blame or question thy kind deed. 80
Nor think I, thou dost sheep or oxen feed
In any such store, or in vines exceed,
Nor bring'st forth such innumerable plants,
Which often make the rich inhabitants
Careless of Deity. If thou then shouldst rear 85
A fane to Phœbus, all men would confer
Whole hecatombs of beeves for sacrifice,
Still thronging hither; and to thee would rise
Ever unmeasur'd odours, shouldst thou long
Nourish thy King thus; and from foreign wrong 90
The Gods would guard thee; which thine own address
Can never compass for thy barrenness."

She said, and Delos joy'd, replying thus:
"Most happy sister of Saturnius!
I gladly would with all means entertain 95
The King your son, being now despised of men,
But should be honour'd with the greatest then.
Yet this I fear, nor will conceal from thee:
Your son, some say, will author misery
In many kinds, as being to sustain 100
A mighty empire over Gods and men,
Upon the holy-gift-giver the Earth.
And bitterly I fear that, when his birth
Gives him the sight of my so barren soil,
He will contemn, and give me up to spoil, 105
Enforce the sea to me, that ever will
Oppress my heart with many a wat'ry hill.
And therefore let him choose some other land,
Where he shall please, to build at his command
Temple and grove, set thick with many a tree. 110

For wretched polypuses breed in me
Retiring chambers, and black sea-calves den
In my poor soil, for penury of men.
And yet, O Goddess, wouldst thou please to swear
The Gods' great oath to me, before thou **bear**   115
Thy blessed son here, that thou wilt erect
A fane to him, to render the effect
Of men's demands to them before they fall,
Then will thy son's renown be general,
Men will **his name** in such variety call,   120
And I shall **then** be glad his birth to bear."
This said, the Gods' great oath she thus did swear:
"Know this, O Earth! broad heaven's inferior sphere,
And of black Styx the most infernal lake,
(Which **is** the gravest **oath the Gods** can take)   125
That here shall ever rise to Phœbus' name
An odorous fane and altar; and thy fame
Honour, past all isles else, shall see him employ'd."
Her oath thus took and ended, Delos joy'd
In mighty measure that she should become   130
To far-shot Phœbus' birth the famous home.

   Latona then nine days and nights did fall
In hopeless labour; at whose birth were all
Heaven's most supreme **and** worthy Goddesses,
Dione, Rhæa, and th' Exploratress   135
Themis, and Amphitrite that **will be**
Pursu'd with sighs still; every Deity,
Except the snowy-wristed wife of Jove,
Who held her moods aloft, and would not move;
Only Lucina (to whose virtue vows   140
Each childbirth patient) heard not of her throes,

            [112] *Den*—i. e. make dens.

But sat, by Juno's counsel, on the brows
Of broad Olympus, wrapp'd in clouds of gold.
Whom Jove's proud wife in envy did withhold,
Because bright-lock'd Latona was to bear   145
A son so faultless and in force so clear.
The rest Thaumantia sent before, to bring
Lucina to release the envied king,
Assuring her, that they would straight confer
A carcanet, nine cubits long, on her,   150
All woven with wires of gold. But charg'd her, then,
To call apart from th' ivory-wristed Queen
The childbirth-guiding Goddess, for just fear
Lest, her charge utter'd in Saturnia's ear,
She, after, might dissuade her from descent.   155
When wind-swift-footed Iris knew th' intent
Of th' other Goddesses, away she went,
And instantly she pass'd the infinite space
'Twixt earth and heaven; when, coming to the place
Where dwelt th' Immortals, straight without the gate
She gat Lucina, and did all relate   161
The Goddesses commanded, and inclin'd
To all that they demanded her dear mind.
And on their way they went, like those two doves
That, walking highways, every shadow moves   165
Up from the earth, forc'd with their natural fear.
When ent'ring Delos, She, that is so dear
To dames in labour, made Latona straight
Prone to delivery, and to wield the weight
Of her dear burthen with a world of ease.   170
When, with her fair hand, she a palm did seize,
And, staying her by it, stuck her tender knees

[147] *Thaumantia*—Iris.

Amidst the soft mead, that did smile beneath
Her sacred labour ; **and the child did** breathe
The air in th' instant. All the Goddesses 175
Brake in kind tears and shrieks for **her** quick ease,
And thee, O archer Phœbus, with waves clear
Wash'd sweetly over, swaddled with sincere
And spotless swathbands ; and made then to flow
About thy breast a mantle, white as snow, 180
Fine, and new made ; and cast a veil of gold
Over thy forehead. Nor yet forth did hold
Thy mother for thy food her golden breast,
But Themis, in supply of it, address'd
Lovely Ambrosia, and drunk off to thee 185
A bowl of nectar, interchangeably
With her immortal fingers serving thine.
And when, O Phœbus, that eternal wine
Thy taste had relish'd, and that food divine,
No golden swathband longer could contain 190
Thy panting bosom ; all that would constrain
Thy soon-eas'd Godhead, every feeble chain
Of earthy child-rites, flew in sunder all.
And then didst thou thus to the Deities call :
"Let there **be given** me my lov'd lute and **bow**, 195
I'll prophesy to men, **and** make them know
Jove's perfect counsels." This said, up did fly
From broad-way'd Earth the unshorn Deity,
Far-shot Apollo. All th' Immortals stood
In steep amaze to see Latona's brood. 200
All Delos, looking on him, all with gold
Was loaden straight, and joy'd to be extoll'd
By great Latona so, that she decreed

[179] *Sincere*—pure, unmixed ; the true Latin sense.

A HYMN TO APOLLO. 25

Her barrenness should bear the fruitful'st seed
Of all the isles and continents of earth, 205
And lov'd her from her heart so for her birth.
For so she flourish'd, as a hill that stood
Crown'd with the flow'r of an abundant wood.
And thou, O Phœbus, bearing in thy hand
Thy silver bow, walk'st over every land, 210
Sometimes ascend'st the rough-hewn rocky hill
Of desolate Cynthus, and sometimes tak'st will
To visit islands, and the plumps of men.
And many a temple, all ways, men ordain
To thy bright Godhead; groves, made dark with trees,
And never shorn, to hide the Deities, 216
All high-lov'd prospects, all the steepest brows
Of far-seen hills, and every flood that flows
Forth to the sea, are dedicate to thee.
But most of all thy mind's alacrity 220
Is rais'd with Delos; since, to fill thy fane,
There flocks so many an Ionian,
With ample gowns that flow down to their feet,
With all their children, and the reverend sweet
Of all their pious wives. And these are they 225
That (mindful of thee) even thy Deity
Render more spritely with their champion fight,
Dances, and songs, perform'd to glorious sight,
Once having publish'd, and proclaim'd their strife.
And these are acted with such exquisite life 230
That one would say, "Now, the Ionian strains

213 *Plumps*—crowds, collection. A common old word.
224 *Sweet*—so spelt in the folio; but the word is doubtless *suite*, attendance, retinue. Todd gives an examhle of *suite* from Sir Philip Sydney.
227 *Champion fight*—πυγμαχίη, boxing.
231 *Strains*—families, descent. See Odyssey, Bk. I. 344.

Are turn'd Immortals, nor know what age means."
His mind would take such pleasure from his eye,
To see them serv'd by all mortality,
Their men so human, women so well grac'd, 235
Their ships so swift, their riches so increas'd,
Since thy observance, who, being all before
Thy opposites, were all despis'd and poor.
And to all these this absolute wonder add,
Whose praise shall render all posterities glad: 240
The Delian virgins are thy handmaids all,
And, since they serv'd Apollo, jointly fall
Before Latona, and Diana too,
In sacred service, and do therefore know
How to make mention of the ancient trims 245
Of men and women, in their well-made hymns,
And soften barbarous nations with their songs,
Being able all to speak the several tongues
Of foreign nations, and to imitate
Their musics there, with art so fortunate 250
That one would say, there every one did speak,
And all their tunes in natural accents break,
Their songs so well compos'd are, and their art
To answer all sounds is of such desert.
But come, Latona, and thou King of flames, 255
With Phœbe, rect'ress of chaste thoughts in dames,
Let me salute ye, and your graces call
Hereafter to my just memorial.
And you, O Delian virgins, do me grace,
When any stranger of our earthly race, 260
Whose restless life affliction hath in chace,
Shall hither come and question you, who is,
To your chaste ears, of choicest faculties

In sacred poesy, and with most right
Is author of your absolut'st delight,
Ye shall yourselves do all the right ye can
To answer for our name :—" The sightless man
Of stony Chios. All whose poems shall
In all last ages stand for capital."
This for your own sakes I desire, for I
Will propagate mine own precedency
As far as earth shall well-built cities bear,
Or human conversation is held dear,
Not with my praise direct, but praises due,
And men shall credit it, because 'tis true.

However, I'll not cease the praise I vow
To far-shot Phœbus with the silver bow,
Whom lovely-hair'd Latona gave the light.
O King! both Lycia is in rule thy right,
Fair Mœony, and the maritimal
Miletus, wish'd to be the seat of all.

But chiefly Delos, girt with billows round,
Thy most respected empire doth resound.
Where thou to Pythus went'st, to answer there,
As soon as thou wert born, the burning ear
Of many a far-come, to hear future deeds,
Clad in divine and odoriferous weeds,
And with thy golden fescue play'dst upon
Thy hollow harp, that sounds to heaven set gone.

Then to Olympus swift as thought he flew,

---

[288] *Fescue*—the lexicographers give the derivation from the Latin *festuca*, a young shoot or stalk. It was generally used for a stick for pointing to the letters in teaching children to read. The word in this sense occurs in Dryden and Swift. Here it seems to be an instrument (the *plectrum*) with which Apollo touched the strings of his harp ; a sense which does not seem to have been noted as occurring elsewhere.

To Jove's high house, and had a retinue
Of Gods t' attend him; and then straight did fall
To study of the harp, and harpsical,
All th' Immortals. To whom every Muse
With ravishing voices did their answers use,   295
Singing th' eternal deeds of Deity,
And from their hands what hells of misery
Poor humans suffer, living desperate quite,
And not an art they have, wit, or deceit,
Can make them manage any act aright,   300
Nor find, with all the soul they can engage,
A salve for death, or remedy for age.

But here the fair-hair'd Graces, the wise Hours,
Harmonia, Hebe, and sweet Venus' pow'rs,
Danc'd, and each other's palm to palm did cling.   305
And with these danc'd not a deformed thing,
No forespoke dwarf, nor downward witherling,
But all with wond'rous goodly forms were deckt,
And mov'd with beauties of unpriz'd aspect.

Dart-dear Diana, even with Phœbus bred,   310
Danc'd likewise there; and Mars a march did tread
With that brave bevy. In whose consort fell
Argicides, th' ingenious sentinel.
Phœbus-Apollo touch'd his lute to them
Sweetly and softly, a most glorious beam   315
Casting about him, as he danc'd and play'd,
And even his feet were all with rays array'd;
His weed and all of a most curious trim
With no less lustre grac'd and circled him.
By these Latona, with a hair that shin'd   320

₂₉₈ *Humans*—mortals.
₃₀₇ *Forespoke*—see Iliad, Bk. XVI. 792; XVII. 32.

Like burnish'd gold, and, with the mighty mind,
Heaven's counsellor, Jove, sat with delightsome eyes,
To see their son new rank'd with Deities.
  How shall I praise thee, then, that art all praise?
Amongst the brides shall I thy Deity raise?   325
Or being in love, when sad thou went'st to woo
The virgin Aza, and didst overthrow
The even-with-Gods, Elation's mighty seed,
That had of goodly horse so brave a breed,
And Phorbas, son of sovereign Triopus,   330
Valiant Leucippus, and Ereutheus,
And Triopus himself with equal fall,
Thou but on foot, and they on horseback all?
  Or shall I sing thee, as thou first didst grace
Earth with thy foot, to find thee forth a place   335
Fit to pronounce thy oracles to men?
First from Olympus thou alightedst then
Into Pieria, passing all the land
Of fruitless Lesbos, chok'd with drifts of sand,
The Magnets likewise, and the Perrhæbes;   340
And to Iolcus variedst thy access,
Cenæus' tops ascending, that their base
Make bright Eubœa, being of ships the grace,
And fix'd thy fair stand in Lelantus' field,
That did not yet thy mind's contentment yield   345
To raise a fane on, and a sacred grove.
Passing Euripus then, thou mad'st remove
Up to Earth's ever-green and holiest hill.
Yet swiftly thence, too, thou transcendedst still
To Mycalessus, and didst touch upon   350
Teumessus, apt to make green couches on,
And flowery field-beds. Then thy progress found

A HYMN TO APOLLO.

Thebes out, whose soil with **only** woods was crown'd.
For yet was sacred **Thebes** no human seat,
And therefore were no paths nor highways beat 355
On her free bosom, that flows now with wheat,
But then she only wore on it a wood.
From hence (even loth to part, because it stood
Fit for thy service) thou putt'st on remove
To green Onchestus, Neptune's glorious grove, 360
Where new-tam'd horse, bred, nourish nerves so rare
That still they **frolic, though** they travell'd are
Never so sore, and **hurry after** them
Most heavy coaches, **but are so extreme**
(In usual travel) fiery and free, 365
That though their coachman ne'er **so masterly**
Governs their courages, **he sometimes must**
Forsake his seat, and give **their spirits their** lust,
When after them their empty coach they draw,
Foaming, and neighing, quite exempt from awe. 370
And if their coachman guide through any grove
Unshorn, and vow'd to any Deity's love,
The lords encoach'd leap out, and all their care
Use **to** allay **their** fires, with speaking fair
Stroking **and trimming them,** and in some queach, 375
Or strength of shade, within their nearest reach,
Reining them up, invoke the deified King
Of that unshorn and everlasting spring,
And leave them then to her preserving hands,
Who is the Fate that there the God commands. 380
And this was first the sacred fashion there.
From hence thou went'st, O thou in shafts past peer,

[375] *Queach*—bushy place. See note **on** Odyssey, Bk. XIX. 610. Hymn to Pan, 12.

And found'st Cephissus with thy all-seeing beams,
Whose flood affects so many silver streams,
And from Lilæus pours so bright a wave.   385
Yet forth thy foot flew, and thy fair eyes gave
The view of Ocale the rich in tow'rs;
Then to Amartus that abounds in flow'rs,
Then to Delphusa putt'st thy progress on,
Whose blessed soil nought harmful breeds upon;   390
And there thy pleasure would a fane adorn,
And nourish woods whose shades should ne'er be shorn.
Where this thou told'st her, standing to her close:
"Delphusa, here I entertain suppose
To build a far-fam'd temple, and ordain   395
An oracle t' inform the minds of men,
Who shall for ever offer to my love
Whole hecatombs; even all the men that move
In rich Peloponnesus, and all those
Of Europe, and the isles the seas enclose,   400
Whom future search of acts and beings brings.
To whom I'll prophesy the truths of things
In that rich temple where my oracle sings."
  This said, the All-bounds-reacher, with his bow,
The fane's divine foundations did foreshow;   405
Ample they were, and did huge length impart,
With a continuate tenour, full of art.
But when Delphusa look'd into his end,
Her heart grew angry, and did thus extend
Itself to Phœbus: "Phœbus, since thy mind   410
A far-fam'd fane hath in itself design'd
To bear an oracle to men in me,
That hecatombs may put in fire to thee,
This let me tell thee, and impose for stay

Upon thy purpose: Th' inarticulate neigh
Of fire-hov'd horse will ever disobey
Thy numerous ear, and mules will for their **drink**
Trouble my sacred springs, and **I should think**
That any of the human race had rather
See here the hurries of rich coaches gather,
And hear the haughty neighs of swift-hov'd horse,
Than in his pleasure's place convert recourse
T' a mighty temple; and his wealth bestow
On pieties, where his sports may freely flow,
Or see huge wealth that he shall never owe.
And, therefore, wouldst thou hear my free advice,—
Though mightier far thou art, and much more wise,
O king, than I, thy pow'r being great'st of all
In Crissa, underneath the bosom's fall
Of steep Parnassus,—let thy mind be given
To set thee up a fane, where never driven
Shall glorious coaches be, nor horses' neighs
Storm near thy well-built altars, but thy praise
Let the fair race of pious humans bring
Into thy fane, that Io-pæans sing.
And **those** gifts only let thy deified mind
Be circularly pleas'd with, being the kind
And fair burnt-offerings that true Deities bind."
With this his mind she altered, though she spake
Not for his good, but her own glory's sake.

    From hence, O Phœbus, first thou mad'st retreat,
And of the Phlegians reached the walled seat,
Inhabited with contumelious men,
Who, slighting Jove, took up their dwellings then
Within a large cave, near Cephissus' lake.

    [425] *Owe*—own. Odyssey, Bk. II. 190.

Hence, swiftly moving, thou all speed didst make
Up to the tops intended, and the ground
Of Crissa, under the-with-snow-still-crown'd
Parnassus, reach'd, whose face affects the West;
Above which hangs a rock, that still seems prest   450
To fall upon it, through whose breast doth run
A rocky cave, near which the King the Sun
Cast to contrive a temple to his mind,
And said, " Now here stands my conceit inclin'd
To build a famous fane, where still shall be   455
An oracle to men, that still to me
Shall offer absolute hecatombs, as well
Those that in rich Peloponnesus dwell
As those of Europe, and the isles that lie
Wall'd with the sea, that all their pains apply   460
T' employ my counsels. To all which will I
True secrets tell, by way of prophecy,
In my rich temple, that shall ever be
An oracle to all posterity."
This said, the fane's form he did straight present,   465
Ample, and of a length of great extent;
In which Trophonius and Agamede,
Who of Erginus were the famous seed,
Impos'd the stony entry, and the heart
Of every God had for their excellent art.   470
  About the temple dwelt of human name
Unnumber'd nations, it acquired such fame,
Being all of stone, built for eternal date.
And near it did a fountain propagate
A fair stream far away; when Jove's bright seed,   475
The King Apollo, with an arrow, freed

[450] *Prest*—ready. Frequently used in the Odyssey.

From his strong string, destroy'd the Dragoness
That wonder nourish'd, being **of such** excess
In size, and horridness of monstrous shape,
That on the forc'd earth she wrought many a rape, 480
Many a spoil made on it, many an **ill**
On crook-haunch'd herds brought, being impurpled still
With blood of all sorts; having undergone
The charge of Juno, with the golden throne,
To nourish Typhon, the abhorr'd affright 485
And bane of mortals, whom into the light
Saturnia brought forth, being incensed with Jove,
Because the **most** renown'd fruit of his love
(Pallas) he got, and shook out of his brain.
For which majestic Juno did complain 490
In this kind to the Bless'd Court of the skies:
"Know all ye sex-distinguish'd Deities,
That Jove, assembler of the cloudy throng,
Begins with me first, and affects with wrong
My right in him, made by himself his wife, 495
That knows and does the honour'd marriage life
All honest offices; and yet hath he
Unduly got, without my company,
Blue-eyed Minerva, who of all the sky
Of blest Immortals is the absolute grace; 500
Where I have brought into the Heavenly Race
A son, both taken in his feet and head,
So ugly, and so far from worth my bed,
That, ravish'd into hand, I took and threw
Down to the vast sea his detested view; 505
Where Nereus' daughter, Thetis, who her way
With silver feet makes, and the fair array
Of her bright sisters, saved, and took to guard.

A HYMN TO APOLLO.

But, would to heaven, another yet were spared
The like grace of his godhead! Crafty mate, 510
What other scape canst thou excogitate?
How could thy heart sustain to get alone
The grey-eyed Goddess? Her conception
Nor bringing forth had any hand of mine,
And yet, know all the Gods, I go for thine 515
To such kind uses. But I'll now employ
My brain to procreate a masculine joy,
That 'mongst th' Immortals may as eminent shine,
With shame affecting nor my bed nor thine.
Nor will I ever touch at thine again, 520
But far fly it and thee; and yet will reign
Amongst th' Immortals ever." This spleen spent
(Still yet left angry) far away she went
From all the Deathless, and yet pray'd to all,
Advanced her hand, and, ere she let it fall, 525
Used these excitements: "Hear me now, O Earth!
Broad Heaven above it, and beneath, your birth,
The deified Titanois, that dwell about
Vast Tartarus, from whence sprung all the rout
Of Men and Deities! Hear me all, I say, 530
With all your forces, and give instant way
T' a son of mine without Jove, who yet may
Nothing inferior prove in force to him,
But past him spring as far in able limb
As he past Saturn." This pronounced, she strook 535
Life-bearing Earth so strongly, that she shook
Beneath her numb'd hand. Which when she beheld,
Her bosom with abundant comforts swell'd,
In hope all should to her desire extend.
From hence the year, that all such proofs gives end,

Grew round; yet all that time the bed of Jove
She never touch'd at, never was her love
Enflam'd to sit near his Dædalian throne,
As she accustomed, to consult upon
Counsels kept dark with many a secret skill,
But kept her vow-frequented temple still,
Pleas'd with her sacrifice; till now, the nights
And days accomplish'd, and the year's whole rights
In all her revolutions being expired,
The hours and all run out that were required
To vent a birth-right, she brought forth a son,
Like Gods or men in no condition,
But a most dreadful and pernicious thing,
Call'd Typhon, who on all the human spring
Conferr'd confusion. Which received to hand
By Juno, instantly she gave command
(Ill to ill adding) that the Dragoness
Should bring it up; who took, and did oppress
With many a misery (to maintain th' excess
Of that inhuman monster) all the race
Of men that were of all the world the grace,
Till the far-working Phœbus at her sent
A fiery arrow, that invoked event
Of death gave to her execrable life.
Before which yet she lay in bitter strife,
With dying pains, grovelling on earth, and drew
Extreme short respirations; for which flew
A shout about the air, whence no man knew,
But came by power divine. And then she lay
Tumbling her trunk, and winding every way

⁵⁴³ *Dædalian*—variegated, πολυδαίδαλον.
⁵⁵⁴ *Spring*—race.

About her nasty nest, quite leaving then
Her murderous life, embrued with deaths of men.
  Then Phœbus gloried, saying: "Thyself now lie
On men-sustaining earth, and putrefy,
Who first of putrefaction was inform'd.   575
Now on thy life have death's cold vapours storm'd,
That storm'dst on men the earth-fed so much death,
In envy of the offspring they made breathe
Their lives out on my altars. Now from thee
Not Typhon shall enforce the misery   580
Of merited death, nor She, whose name implies
Such scathe (Chimæra), but black earth make prise
To putrefaction thy immanities,
And bright Hyperion, that light all eyes shows,
Thine with a night of rottenness shall close."   585
  Thus spake he glorying. And then seiz'd upon
Her horrid heap, with putrefaction,
Hyperion's lovely pow'rs; from whence her name
Took sound of Python, and heaven's Sovereign Flame
Was surnam'd Pythius, since the sharp-eyed Sun   590
Affected so with putrefaction
The hellish monster. And now Phœbus' mind
Gave him to know that falsehood had strook blind
Even his bright eye, because it could not find
The subtle Fountain's fraud; to whom he flew,   595
Enflamed with anger, and in th' instant drew
Close to Delphusa, using this short vow:
  "Delphusa! you must look no longer now
To vent your frauds on me; for well I know
Your situation to be lovely, worth   600
A temple's imposition, it pours forth

  [575] *Informed*—made, formed out of. A common word.

So delicate a stream. But your renown
Shall now no longer shine **here, but** mine own."
This said, he thrust her promontory **down,**
And damm'd her fountain up with mighty stones,   605
A temple giving consecrations
In woods adjoining. And in this fane all
On him, by surname of Delphusius, call,
Because Delphusa's sacred flood and fame
His wrath affected so, and hid in shame.   610
   And **then** thought Phœbus what descent of men
To be his ministers he should retain,
To do in stony Pythos sacrifice.
To which his mind contending, his quick eyes
He cast upon the blue sea, and **beheld**   615
A ship, on whose masts sails that wing'd it swell'd,
In which were men transferr'd, many and good,
That in Minoian Cnossus ate their food,
And were Cretensians; who now are those
That all the sacrificing dues dispose,   620
And all the laws deliver to a word
Of Day's great King, that wears the golden sword,
And oracles (out of his Delphian tree
That shrouds her fair arms in the cavity
Beneath Parnassus' mount) pronounce to men.   625
These now his priests, that lived as merchants then,
In traffics and pecuniary rates,
For sandy Pylos and the Pylian states
Were under sail. But now encounter'd them
Phœbus-Apollo, who into the stream   630
Cast himself headlong, and the strange disguise
Took of a dolphin of a goodly size.
Like which he leap'd into their ship, and lay

A HYMN TO APOLLO.

As an ostent of infinite dismay.
For none with any strife of mind could look 635
Into the omen, all the ship-masts shook,
And silent all sat with the fear they took,
Arm'd not, nor strook they sail, but as before
Went on with full trim, and a foreright blore,
Stiff, and from forth the south, the ship made fly. 640
When first they stripp'd the Malean promont'ry,
Touch'd at Laconia's soil, in which a town
Their ship arrived at, that the sea doth crown,
Called Tenarus, a place of much delight
To men that serve Heaven's Comforter of sight. 645
In which are fed the famous flocks that bear
The wealthy fleeces, on a delicate lair
Being fed and seated. Where the merchants fain
Would have put in, that they might out again
To tell the miracle that chanced to them, 650
And try if it would take the sacred stream,
Rushing far forth, that he again might bear
Those other fishes that abounded there
Delighsome company, or still would stay
Aboard their dry ship. But it fail'd t' obey, 655
And for the rich Peloponnesian shore
Steer'd her free sail; Apollo made the blore
Directly guide it. That obeying still
Reach'd dry Arena, and (what wish doth fill)
Fair Argyphæa, and the populous height 660
Of Thryus, whose stream, siding her, doth wait

---

[639] *Blore*—gale.
[641] *Stripp'd*—passed rapidly.
[645] *Heaven's Comforter of sight*—the Sun; τερψίμβροτου ἠελίοιο.
[655] *It fail'd t' obey*—i. e. the ship would not obey the rudder.

With safe pass on Alphæus, Pylos' sands,
And Pylian dwellers; keeping by the strands
On which th' inhabitants of Crunius dwell,
And Helida set opposite to hell;   665
Chalcis and Dymes reach'd, and happily
Made sail by Pheras; all being overjoy'd
With that frank gale that Jove himself employ'd.
And then amongst the clouds they might descry
The hill, that far-seen Ithaca calls her Eye,   670
Dulichius, Samos, and, with timber graced,
Shady Zacynthus. But when now they past
Peloponnesus all, and then when show'd
The infinite veil of Crissa, that doth shroud
All rich Morea with her liberal breast,   675
So frank a gale there flew **out of** the West
As all the sky discover'd; 'twas so great,
And blew so from the very council seat
Of Jove himself, that quickly it might send
The ship through full seas to her journey's end. 680
    From thence they sail'd, quite opposite, to the East,
• **And to** the region where Light leaves his rest,
The Light himself being sacred pilot there,
And made **the** sea-trod ship arrive them near
The grapeful Crissa, where he rest doth take   685
Close to her port and sands. And then forth brake
The far-shot King, like to a star that strows
His glorious forehead where the mid-day glows,
That all in sparkles did his state attire,
Whose lustre leap'd up to the sphere of fire. 690
He trod where no way oped, and pierced the place
That of his sacred tripods held the grace,

        ⁶⁸⁴ *Arrive*—i. e. cause to arrive.

A HYMN TO APOLLO.

In which he lighted such a fluent flame
As gilt all Crissa; in which every dame,
And dame's fair daughter, cast out vehement cries   695
At those fell fires of Phœbus' prodigies,
That shaking fears through all their fancies threw.
Then, like the mind's swift light, again he flew
Back to the ship, shaped like a youth in height
Of all his graces, shoulders broad and straight,   700
And all his hair in golden curls enwrapp'd;
And to the merchants thus his speech he shap'd:
  "Ho! Strangers! What are you? And from what seat
Sail ye these ways that salt and water sweat?
To traffic justly? Or use vagrant scapes   705
Void of all rule, conferring wrongs and rapes,
Like pirates, on the men ye never saw,
With minds project exempt from list or law?
Why sit ye here so stupefied, nor take
Land while ye may, nor deposition make   710
Of naval arms, when this the fashion is
Of men industrious, who (their faculties
Wearied at sea) leave ship, and use the land
For food, that with their healths and stomachs stand?"
  This said, with bold minds he their breast supplied,
And thus made answer the Cretensian guide: 716
  "Stranger! Because you seem to us no seed
Of any mortal, but celestial breed
For parts and person, joy your steps ensue,
And Gods make good the bliss we think your due.   720
Vouchsafe us true relation, on what land
We here arrive, and what men here command.
We were for well-known parts bound, and from Crete
(Our vaunted country) to the Pylian seat

Vow'd our whole voyage; yet arrive we here, 725
Quite cross to those **wills that our motions steer**,
Wishing to make return some other way,
Some other course desirous to **assay**,
To pay our lost pains. But some God hath fill'd
Our frustrate sails, defeating what we will'd." 730
   Apollo answer'd: "Strangers! Though before
Ye dwelt in woody Cnossus, yet no more
Ye must be made your own reciprocals
To your loved city and fair severals
Of wives and houses, but ye shall have here 735
My wealthy temple, honour'd far and near
Of many a nation; for myself am son
To Jove himself, and of Apollo won
The glorious title, who thus safely through
The sea's vast billows still have held your plough, 740
No ill intending, that will yet ye make
My temple here your own, and honours take
Upon yourselves, all that to me are given.
And more, the counsels of the King of Heaven
Yourselves shall know, and with his will receive 745
Ever **the honours** that all men shall give.
Do as I say then instantly, strike sail,
Take down your tackling, and your vessel hale
Up into land; your goods bring forth, and all
The instruments that into sailing fall; 750
Make on this shore an altar, fire enflame,
And barley white cakes offer to my name;
And then, environing the altar, pray,
And call me (as ye saw me in the **day**
When from the windy seas I brake swift way 755
Into your ship) Delphinius, since I took

A HYMN TO APOLLO.

A dolphin's form then. And to every look
That there shall seek it, that my altar shall
Be made a Delphian memorial
From thence for ever. After this, ascend 760
Your swift black ship and sup, and then intend
Ingenuous offerings to the equal Gods
That in celestial seats make blest abodes.
When, having stay'd your healthful hunger's sting,
Come all with me, and Io-pæans sing 765
All the way's length, till you attain the state
Where I your opulent fane have consecrate."
 To this they gave him passing diligent ear,
And vow'd to his obedience all they were.
 First, striking sail, their tacklings then they losed, 770
And (with their gables stoop'd) their mast imposed
Into the mast-room. Forth themselves then went,
And from the sea into the continent
Drew up their ship; which far up from the sand
They rais'd with ample rafters. Then in hand 775
They took the altar, and inform'd it on
The sea's near shore, imposing thereupon
White cakes of barley, fire made, and did stand
About it round, as Phœbus gave command,
Submitting invocations to his will. 780
Then sacrific'd to all the heavenly hill
Of pow'rful Godheads. After which they eat
Aboard their ship, till with fit food replete
They rose, nor to their temple used delay.
Whom Phœbus usher'd, and touch'd all the way 785

[761] *Intend*—See Odyssey, Bk. III. 648.
[779] *Informed*—*supra*, 575.
[783] *Food*—the folio and Mr. Singer, *foot*.

His heavenly lute with art above admired,
Gracefully leading them. When all were fired
With zeal to him, and follow'd wond'ring all
To Pythos; and upon his name did call
With Io-pæans, such as Cretans use.   790
And in their bosoms did the deified Muse
Voices of honey-harmony infuse.

With never-weary feet their way they went,
And made with all alacrity ascent
Up to Parnassus, and that long'd-for place   795
Where they should live, and be of men the grace.
When, all the way, Apollo show'd them still
Their far-stretch'd valleys, and their two-topp'd hill,
Their famous fane, and all that all could raise
To a supreme height of their joy and praise.   800

And then the Cretan captain thus inquired
Of King Apollo: "Since you have retired,
O sovereign, our sad lives so far from friends
And native soil (because so far extends
Your dear mind's pleasure) tell us how we shall   805
Live in your service? To which question call
Our provident minds, because we see not crown'd
This soil with store of vines, nor doth abound
In wealthy meadows, on which we may live,
As well as on men our attendance give."   810

He smiled, and said: "O men that nothing know,
And so are follow'd with a world of woe,
That needs will succour care and curious moan,
And pour out sighs without cessation,
Were all the riches of the earth your own!   815
Without much business, I will render known

    802 *Retired*—i. e. caused to retire.

A HYMN TO APOLLO.

To your simplicities an easy way
To wealth enough : Let every man purvey
A skeane, or slaught'ring steel, and his right hand,
Bravely bestowing, ever more see mann'd   820
With killing sheep, that to my fane will flow
From all far nations. On all which bestow
Good observation, and all else they give
To me make you your own all, and so live.
For all which watch before my temple well,   825
And all my counsels, above all, conceal.
If any give vain language, or to deeds,
Yea or as far as injury, proceeds,
Know that, at losers' hands, for those that gain,
It is the law of mortals to sustain.   830
Besides, ye shall have princes to obey,
Which still ye must, and (so ye gain) ye may.
All now is said ; give all thy memory's stay."
   And thus to thee, Jove and Latona's son,
Be given all grace of salutation !   835
Both thee and others of th' Immortal State
My song shall memorize to endless date.

   [819] *Skeane*—generally used as a sword. A Celtic word. See NARES.

THE END OF THE HYMN TO APOLLO.

A HYMN TO HERMES.

ERMES, the son of Jove and Maia, sing,
O Muse, th' Arcadian and Cyllenian king,
They rich in flocks, he heaven enriching
   still
In **messages** return'd with all his will.
Whom glorious Maia, the nymph rich in hair,   5
Mixing with Jove in amorous affair,
Brought forth to him, sustaining a retreat
From all th' Immortals of the blessed seat,
And living in the same dark cave, where Jove
Inform'd at midnight the effect of love,   10
Unknown to either man or Deity,
Sweet **sleep once having** seized the jealous eye
Of Juno **deck'd with** wrists of ivory.
But when great **Jove's high mind** was consummate,
The tenth month **had in heaven confined the** date   15
Of Maia's labour, and into the sight
She brought in one birth labours infinite;
For then she bore a son, that all tried ways
Could turn and wind to wish'd events assays,
A fair tongu'd, but false-hearted, counsellor,   20
Rector **of** ox-stealers, and for **all** stealths bore

¹⁰ *Inform'd*—Hymn to Apollo, **575.**

A HYMN TO HERMES.

A varied finger; speeder of night's spies,
And guide of all her dream's obscurities;
Guard of door-guardians; and was born to be,
Amongst th' Immortals, that wing'd Deity   25
That in an instant should do acts would ask
The powers of others an eternal task.
Born in the morn, he form'd his lute at noon,
At night stole all the oxen of the Sun;
And all this in his birth's first day was done,   30
Which was the fourth of the increasing moon.
Because celestial limbs sustain'd his strains,
His sacred swath-bands must not be his chains,
So, starting up, to Phœbus' herd he stept,
Found straight the high-roof'd cave where they were kept,
And th' entry passing, he th' invention found   36
Of making lutes; and did in wealth abound
By that invention, since he first of all
Was author of that engine musical,
By this means moved to the ingenious work: 40
Near the cave's inmost overture did lurk
A tortoise, tasting th' odoriferous grass,
Leisurely moving; and this object was
The motive to Jove's son (who could convert
To profitablest uses all desert   45
That nature had in any work convey'd)
To form the lute; when, smiling, thus he said:
"Thou mov'st in me a note of excellent use,
Which thy ill form shall never so seduce
T' avert the good to be inform'd by it,   50
In pliant force, of my form-forging wit."
    Then the slow tortoise, wrought on by his mind,

[41] *Overture*—hidden recess.

He thus saluted: "**All joy to the** kind
Instinct of nature in thee, **born to be**
The spiriter of dances, company 55
For feasts, and following banquets, graced and blest
For bearing light to all the interest
Claim'd in this instrument! **From whence** shall spring
Play fair and sweet, to which may Graces sing.
A pretty painted coat thou putt'st on here, 60
O Tortoise, while thy ill-bred vital sphere
Confines thy fashion; but, surprised by me,
I'll bear thee home, where thou shalt ever **be**
A profit to me; and yet nothing more
Will I contemn thee in my merited store. 65
Goods with good parts got worth and honour gave,
Left goods and honours every **fool may have,**
And since thou first shall give me means to live,
I'll love thee ever. Virtuous qualities give
To live at home with them enough content, 70
Where those that want such inward ornament
Fly out for outward, their life made their load.
'Tis best to be at home, harm lurks abroad.
And certainly **thy** virtue shall be known,
'Gainst great-ill-causing incantation 75
To serve as **for a** lance or amulet.
And where, in comfort of thy vital heat,
Thou now breath'st but a sound confus'd for song,
Expos'd by nature, after death, more strong
Thou shalt in sounds of art be, and command 80
Song infinite sweeter." Thus with either hand
He took it up, and instantly took flight
Back to his cave with that his home delight.
Where (giving to the mountain tortoise **vents**

[54] A Chapmannic periphrasis for killing the tortoise.

A HYMN TO HERMES.

Of life and motion) with fit instruments 85
Forged of bright steel he straight inform'd a lute,
Put neck and frets to it, of which a suit
He made of splitted quills, in equal space
Impos'd upon the neck, and did embrace
Both back and bosom. At whose height (as gins 90
T' extend and ease the string) he put in pins.
Seven strings of several tunes he then applied,
Made of the entrails of a sheep well-dried,
And throughly twisted. Next he did provide
A case for all, made of an ox's hide, 95
Out of his counsels to preserve as well
As to create. And all this action fell
Into an instant consequence. His word
And work had individual accord,
All being as swiftly to perfection brought 100
As any worldly man's most ravish'd thought,
Whose mind care cuts in an infinity
Of varied parts or passions instantly,
Or as the frequent twinklings of an eye.

And thus his house-delight given absolute end, 105
He touch'd it, and did every string extend
(With an exploratory spirit assay'd)
To all the parts that could on it be play'd.
It sounded dreadfully; to which he sung,
As if from thence the first and true force sprung 110
That fashions virtue. God in him did sing.
His play was likewise an unspeakable thing,
Yet, but as an extemporal assay,
Of what show it would make being the first way,
It tried his hand; or a tumultuous noise, 115
Such as at feasts the first-flower'd spirits of boys

Pour out in mutual contumelies still,
As little squaring with his curious will,
Or was as wanton and untaught a store.
Of Jove, and Maia that rich shoes still wore,   120
He sung; who suffer'd ill reports before,
And foul stains under her fair titles bore.
But Hermes sung her nation, and her name
Did iterate ever; all her high-flown fame
Of being Jove's mistress; celebrating all   125
Her train of servants, and collateral
Sumpture of houses; all her tripods there,
And caldrons huge, increasing every year.
All which she knew, yet felt her knowledge stung
With her fame's loss, which (found) she more wish'd sung.
But now he in his sacred cradle laid   131
His lute so absolute, and straight convey'd
Himself up to a watch-tow'r forth his house,
Rich, and divinely odoriferous,
A lofty wile at work in his conceit,   135
Thirsting the practice of his empire's height.
And where impostors rule (since sable night
Must serve their deeds) he did his deeds their right.
For now the never-resting Sun was turn'd
For th' under earth, and in the ocean burn'd   140
His coach and coursers; when th' ingenious spy
Pieria's shady hill had in his eye,
Where the immortal oxen of the Gods
In air's flood solaced their select abodes,
And earth's sweet green flow'r, that was never shorn,
Fed ever down. And these the witty-born,   146
Argicides, set serious spy upon,
Severing from all the rest, and setting gone

A HYMN TO HERMES.

Full fifty of the violent bellowers.
Which driving through the sands, he did reverse   150
(His birth's-craft straight rememb'ring) all their hoves,
And then transpos'd in opposite removes,
The fore behind set, the behind before,
T' employ the eyes of such as should explore.
And he himself, as sly-pac'd, cast away   155
His sandals on the sea sands ; past display
And unexcogitable thoughts in act
Putting, to shun of his stol'n steps the tract,
Mixing both tamrisk and like-tamrisk sprays
In a most rare confusion, to raise   160
His footsteps up from earth. Of which sprays he
(His armful gathering fresh from off the tree)
Made for his sandals ties, both leaves and ties
Holding together ; and then fear'd no eyes
That could affect his feet's discoveries.   165
    The tamrisk boughs he gather'd, making way
Back from Pieria, but as to convey
Provision in them for his journey fit,
It being long and, therefore, needing it.
    An old man, now at labour near the field   170
Of green Onchestus, knew the verdant yield
Of his fair armful; whom th' ingenious son
Of Maia, therefore, salutation
Did thus begin to : "Ho, old man ! that now
Art crooked grown with making plants to grow,   175
Thy nerves will far be spent, when these boughs shall
To these their leaves confer me fruit and all.
But see not thou whatever thou dost see,
Nor hear though hear, but all as touching me
Conceal, since nought it can endamage thee."   180

A HYMN TO HERMES.

This, and no more, **he said, and** on drave still
His broad-brow'd oxen. **Many** a shady hill,
And many an echoing valley, **many** a field
Pleasant **and** wishful, **did** his passage yield
Their safe transcension. But now the divine   185
And black-brow'd Night, his mistress, did decline
Exceeding swiftly; Day's most early light
Fast hasting to her first point, to excite
Worldlings **to work**; and in her watch-tow'r shone
King Pallas-Megamedes' seed (the Moon);   190
When through th' Alphæan flood Jove's powerful son
Phœbus-Apollo's ample-foreheaded herd
(Whose necks the lab'ring yoke had never sphered)
Drave swiftly on; and then into a stall
(Hilly, yet pass'd to through an humble vale   195
And hollow dells, in a most lovely mead)
He gather'd all, and them divinely fed
With odorous cypress, and the ravishing **tree**
That makes his eaters lose the memory
Of name and country. Then he brought withal   200
Much wood, whose sight into his search let fall
The art of making fire; which thus he tried:
He took a branch of laurel, amplified
Past others both in beauty and in size,
Yet lay next hand, rubb'd it, and straight did rise 205
A warm fume from it; steel being that did raise
(As agent) the attenuated bays
To that hot vapour. So that Hermes found
Both fire first, and of it the seed close bound
In other substances; and then the seed   210
He multiplied, of sere-wood making feed

¹⁹⁸ The lotus.

The apt heat of it, in a pile combined
Laid in a low pit, that in flames straight shined,
And cast a sparkling crack up to the sky,
All the dry parts so fervent were, and high   215
In their combustion. And how long the force
Of glorious Vulcan kept the fire in course,
So long was he in dragging from their stall
Two of the crook-haunch'd herd, that roar'd withal,
And raged for fear, t' approach the sacred fire,   220
To which did all his dreadful pow'rs aspire.
When, blust'ring forth their breath, he on the soil
Cast both at length, though with a world of toil,
For long he was in getting them to ground
After their through-thrust and most mortal wound.   225
But work to work he join'd, the flesh and cut,
Cover'd with fat, and, on treen broches put,
In pieces roasted; but in th' intestines
The black blood, and the honorary chines,
Together with the carcases, lay there,   230
Cast on the cold earth, as no Deities' cheer;
The hides upon a rugged rock he spread.
And thus were these now all in pieces shred,
And undistinguish'd from earth's common herd,
Though born for long date, and to heaven endear'd,   235
And now must ever live in dead event.
But Hermes, here hence having his content,
Cared for no more, but drew to places even
The fat-works, that, of force, must have for heaven
Their capital ends, though stol'n, and therefore were 240
In twelve parts cut, for twelve choice Deities' cheer,
By this devotion. To all which he gave

    ²²⁷ *Treen broches*—branches of trees.

A HYMN TO HERMES.

Their several honours, and did wish to have
His equal part thereof, as free and well
As th' other Deities; but the fatty smell   245
Afflicted him, though he Immortal were,
Playing mortal parts, and being like mortals here.
Yet his proud mind nothing the more obey'd
For being a God himself, and his own aid
Having to cause his due, and though in heart   250
He highly wish'd it; but the weaker part
Subdued the stronger, and went on in ill.
Even heavenly pow'r had rather have his will
Than have his right; and will's the worst of all,
When but in least sort it is criminal,   255
One taint being author of a number still.
And thus, resolved to leave his hallow'd hill,
First both the fat parts and the fleshy all
Taking away, at the steep-entried stall
He laid all, all the feet and heads entire,   260
And all the sere-wood, making clear with fire.
And now, he leaving there then all things done,
And finish'd in their fit perfection,
The coals put out, and their black ashes thrown
From all discovery by the lovely light   265
The cheerful moon cast, shining all the night,
He straight assumed a novel voice's note,
And in the whirl-pit-eating flood afloat
He set his sandals. When now, once again
The that-morn-born Cyllenius did attain   270
His home's divine height; all the far-stretch'd way
No one bless'd God encount'ring his assay,
Nor mortal man; nor any dog durst spend
His born-to-bark mouth at him; till in th' end

A HYMN TO HERMES.

He reach'd his cave, and at the gate went in
Crooked, and wrapt into a fold so thin
That no eye could discover his repair,
But as a darkness of th' autumnal air.
When, going on fore-right, he straight arrived
At his rich fane ; his soft feet quite deprived
Of all least noise of one that trod the earth,
They trod so swift to reach his room of birth.
Where, in his swath-bands he his shoulders wrapt,
And (like an infant, newly having scap't
The teeming straits) as in the palms he lay
Of his loved nurse.   Yet instantly would play
(Freeing his right hand) with his bearing cloth
About his knees wrapt, and straight (loosing both
His right and left hand) with his left he caught
His most-loved lute.   His mother yet was taught
His wanton wiles, nor could a God's wit lie
Hid from a Goddess, who did therefore try
His answer thus : " Why, thou made-all-of-sleight,
And whence arriv'st thou in this rest of night ?
Improvident inpudent !   In my conceit
Thou rather shouldst be getting forth thy gate,
With all flight fit for thy endanger'd state,
(In merit of th' inevitable bands
To be impos'd by vex'd Latona's hands,
Justly incens'd for her Apollo's harms)
Than lie thus wrapt, as ready for her arms,
To take thee up and kiss thee.   Would to heaven,
In cross of that high grace, thou hadst been given
Up to perdition, ere poor mortals bear
Those black banes, that thy Father Thunderer
Hath planted thee of purpose to confer

On them and Deities!" He returned reply
"As master of the feats of policy,
Mother, why aim you thus amiss at me,
As if I were a son that infancy   310
Could keep from all the skill that age can teach,
Or had in cheating but a childish reach,
And of a mother's mandates fear'd the breach?
I mount that art at first, that will be best
When all times consummate their cunningest,   315
Able to counsel now myself and thee,
In all things best, to all eternity.
We cannot live like Gods here without gifts,
No, nor without corruption and shifts,
And, much less, without eating; as we must   320
In keeping thy rules, and in being just,
Of which we cannot undergo the loads.
'Tis better here to imitate the Gods,
And wine or wench out all time's periods,
To that end growing rich in ready heaps,   325
Stored with revenues, being in corn-field reaps
Of infinite acres, than to live enclosed
In caves, to all earth's sweetest air exposed.
I as much honour hold as Phœbus does;
And if my Father please not to dispose   330
Possessions to me, I myself will see
If I can force them in; for I can be
Prince of all thieves. And, if Latona's son
Make after my stealth indignation,
I'll have a scape as well as he a search,   335
And overtake him with a greater lurch;
For I can post to Pythos, and break through

[336] *Lurch*—deceit, falsehood.

A HYMN TO HERMES.

His huge house there, where harbours wealth enough,
Most precious tripods, caldrons, steel, and gold,
Garments rich wrought, and full of liberal fold.   340
All which will I at pleasure own, and thou
Shalt see all, wilt thou but thy sight bestow."

Thus changed great words the Goat-hide-wearer's son,
And Maia of majestic fashion.

And now the air-begot Aurora rose   345
From out the Ocean great-in-ebbs-and-flows,
When, at the never-shorn pure-and-fair grove
(Onchestus) consecrated to the love
Of round-and-long-neck'd Neptune, Phœbus found
A man whom heavy years had press'd half round,   350
And yet at work in plashing of a fence
About a vineyard, that had residence
Hard by the highway; whom Latona's son
Made it not strange, but first did question,
And first saluted: "Ho you! aged sire,   355
That here are hewing from the vine the briar,
For certain oxen I come here t' inquire
Out of Pieria; females all, and rear'd
All with horns wreath'd, unlike the common herd;
A coal-black bull fed by them all alone;   360
And all observ'd, for preservation,
Through all their foody and delicious fen
With four fierce mastiffs, like one-minded men.
These left their dogs and bull (which I admire)
And, when was near set day's eternal fire,   365

---

[343] *Goat-hide-wearer*—Jupiter.
[351] *Plashing*—to *plash* a fence is still used for half-cutting down the saplings and loftier branches of a hedge, and entwining them horizontally.
[364] *Which I admire*—which I am astonished at.

From their fierce guardians, from their delicate fare,
Made clear departure. To me then declare,
O old man, long since born, if thy grave ray
Hath any man seen making stealthful way
With all those oxen." Th' old man made reply: 370
"'Tis hard, O friend, to render readily
Account of all that may invade mine eye,
For many a traveller this highway treads,
Some in much ills search, some in noble threads,
Leading their lives out; but I this young day,   375
Even from her first point, have made good display
Of all men passing this abundant hill
Planted with vines, and no such stealthful ill
Her light hath shown me; but last evening, late,
I saw a thing that show'd of childish state   380
To my old lights, and seem'd as he pursued
A herd of oxen with brave heads endued,
Yet but an infant, and retain'd a rod;
Who wearily both this and that way trod,
His head still backwards turn'd." This th' old man spake;
Which he well thought upon, and swiftly brake   385
Into his pursuit with abundant wing,
That strook but one plain, ere he knew the thing
That was the thief to be th' impostor born;
Whom Jove yet with his son's name did adorn.   390
In study and with ardour then the King
(Jove's dazzling son) placed his exploring wing
On sacred Pylos, for his forced herd,
His ample shoulders in a cloud enspher'd
Of fiery crimson. Straight the steps he found   395
Of his stol'n herd, and said: "Strange sights confound

₃₆₈ *Ray*—vision, eye.

My apprehensive powers, for here I see
The tracks of oxen, but aversively
Converted towards the Pierian hills,
As treading to their mead of daffodils : 400
But nor mine eye men's feet nor women's draws,
Nor hoary wolves', nor bears', nor lions', paws,
Nor thick-neck'd bulls, they show. But he that does
These monstrous deeds, with never so swift shoes
Hath pass'd from that hour hither, but from hence 405
His foul course may meet fouler consequence."
With this took Phœbus wing; and Hermes still,
For all his threats, secure lay in his hill
Wall'd with a wood; and more, a rock, beside,
Where a retreat ran, deeply multiplied 410
In blinding shadows, and where th' endless Bride
Bore to Saturnius his ingenious son ;
An odour, worth a heart's desire, being thrown
Along the heaven-sweet hill, on whose herb fed
Rich flocks of sheep, that bow not where they tread 415
Their horny pasterns. There the Light of men
(Jove's son, Apollo) straight descended then
The marble pavement, in that gloomy den.
On whom when Jove and Maia's son set eye,
Wroth for his oxen, on then, instantly, 420
His odorous swath-bands flew ; in which as close
Th' impostor lay, as in the cool repose
Of cast-on ashes hearths of burning coals
Lie in the woods hid, under the controls
Of skilful colliers ; even so close did lie 425
Inscrutable Hermes in Apollo's eye,
Contracting his great Godhead to a small

[411] *Endless*—immortal, νύμφη ἀμβροσίη.

And infant likeness, feet, hands, head, and all.
And as a hunter hath been often view'd,
From chase retired, with both his hands embrued   434
In his game's blood, and doth for water call
To cleanse his hands, and to provoke withal
Delightsome sleep, new-wash'd and laid to rest;
So now lay Hermes in the close-compress'd
Chace of his oxen, his new-found-out lute   435
Beneath his arm held, as if no pursuit
But that prise, and the virtue of his play,
His heart affected.   But to Phœbus lay
His close heart open; and he likewise knew
The brave hill-nymph there, and her dear son, new-
Born, and as well wrapt in his wiles as weeds.   441
All the close shrouds too, for his rapinous deeds,
In all the cave he knew; and with his key
He open'd three of them, in which there lay
Silver and gold-heaps, nectar infinite store,   445
And dear ambrosia; and of weeds she wore,
Pure white and purple, a rich wardrobe shined,
Fit for the bless'd states of Pow'rs so divined.
All which discover'd, thus to Mercury
He offer'd conference: "Infant! You that lie   450
Wrapt so in swath-bands, instantly unfold
In what conceal'd retreats of yours you hold
My oxen stol'n by you; or straight we shall
Jar, as beseems not Pow'rs Celestial.
For I will take and hurl thee to the deeps   455
Of dismal Tartarus, where ill Death keeps
His gloomy and inextricable fates,
And to no eye that light illuminates

<small>435 *Chace*—enclosure for cattle, like the Latin *saltus*.</small>

A HYMN TO HERMES.

Mother nor Father shall return thee free,
But under earth shall sorrow fetter thee, 460
And few repute thee their superior."
  On him replied craft's subtlest Counsellor :
" What cruel speech hath passed Latona's care !
Seeks he his stol'n wild-cows where Deities are ?
I have nor seen nor heard, nor can report 465
From others' mouths one word of their resort
To any stranger. Nor will I, to gain
A base reward, a false relation feign.
Nor would I, could I tell. Resemble I
An ox-thief, or a man ? Especially 470
A man of such a courage, such a force
As to that labour goes, that violent course ?
No infant's work is that. My pow'rs aspire
To sleep, and quenching of my hunger's fire
With mother's milk, and, 'gainst cold shades, to arm
With cradle-cloths my shoulders, and baths warm, 476
That no man may conceive the war you threat
Can spring in cause from my so peaceful heat.
And, even amongst th' Immortals it would bear
Event of absolute miracle, to hear 480
A new-born infant's forces should transcend
The limits of his doors ; much less contend
With untam'd oxen. This speech nothing seems
To savour the decorum of the beams
Cast round about the air Apollo breaks, 485
Where his divine mind her intention speaks.
I brake but yesterday the blessed womb,
My feet are tender, and the common tomb
Of men (the Earth) lies sharp beneath their tread.
But, if you please, even by my Father's head 490

A HYMN TO HERMES.

I'll take the great **oath, that nor** I protest
Myself to author on your **interest**
Any such usurpation, nor have I
Seen any other that feloniously
Hath forced your oxen. Strange thing! What are those
Oxen of yours? Or what are oxen? Knows   495
My rude mind, think you? My ears only touch
At their renown, and hear that there are such."

   This speech he pass'd; and, ever as he **spake,**
Beams from the hair about his eyelids brake,   500
His eyebrows **up and down** cast, and his eye
Every way look'd **askance and** carelessly,
And he into a lofty **whistling fell,**
As if he idle thought Apollo's spell.

   Apollo, gently smiling, **made reply:**   505
"O thou impostor, whose thoughts ever lie
In labour with deceit! For **certain, I**
Retain opinion, that thou (even **thus soon)**
Hast ransack'd many a house, and not in one
Night's-work alone, nor in **one** country neither,   510
Hast **been** besieging house and man together,
Rigging and rifling always, and no noise
Made with **thy soft feet,** where it all destroys.
Soft, therefore, **well, and** tender, thou may'st call
The feet that thy **stealths** go and fly withal,   515
For many a field-bred herdsman (unheard still)
Hast thou made drown the caverns of **the hill,**
Where his retreats lie, with his helpless **tears,**
When any flesh-stealth thy desire endears,
And thou encount'rest either flocks of sheep,   520
Or herds of oxen! Up **then!** Do not sleep

⁵¹² *Rigging*—tricking.

Thy last nap in thy cradle, but come down,
Companion of black night, and, for this crown
Of thy young rapines, bear from all the state
And style of Prince Thief, into endless date." 525
    This said, he took the infant in his arms,
And with him the remembrance of his harms,
This presage utt'ring, lifting him aloft:
" Be evermore the miserably-soft
Slave of the belly, pursuivant of all, 530
And author of all mischiefs capital."
    He scorn'd his prophecy, so he sneezed in's face
Most forcibly; which hearing, his embrace
He loathed and hurl'd him 'gainst the ground; yet still
Took seat before him, though, with all the ill 535
He bore by him, he would have left full fain
That hewer of his heart so into twain.
Yet salv'd all thus: " Come, you so-swaddled thing!
Issue of Maia, and the Thunder's King!
Be confident, I shall hereafter find 540
My broad-brow'd oxen, my prophetic mind
So far from blaming this thy course, that I
Foresee thee in it to posterity
The guide of all men, always, to their ends."
This spoken, Hermes from the earth ascends, 545
Starting aloft, and as in study went,
Wrapping himself in his integument,
And thus ask'd Phœbus: " Whither force you me,
Far-shot, and far most powerful Deity?
I know, for all your feigning, you're still wroth 550
About your oxen, and suspect my troth.
O Jupiter! I wish the general race
Of all earth's oxen rooted from her face.

I steal your oxen! I again profess
That neither I have stol'n them, nor can guess   555
Who else should steal them. What strange beasts are
    these
Your so-loved oxen? I must say, to please
Your humour thus far, that even my few hours
Have heard their fame. But be the sentence yours
Of the debate betwixt us, or to Jove   560
(For more indifferency) the cause remove."

  Thus when the solitude-affecting God,
And the Latonian seed, had laid abroad
All things betwixt them; though not yet agreed,
Yet, might I speak, Apollo did proceed   565
Nothing unjustly, to charge Mercury
With stealing of the cows he does deny.
But his profession was, with filed speech,
And craft's fair compliments, to overreach
All, and even Phœbus. Who because he knew   570
His trade of subtlety, he still at view
Hunted his foe through all the sandy way
Up to Olympus. Nor would let him stray
From out his sight, but kept behind him still.

  And now they reach'd the odorif'rous hill   575
Of high Olympus, to their father Jove,
To arbitrate the cause in which they strove.
Where, before both, talents of justice were
Propos'd for him whom Jove should sentence clear,
In cause of their contention. And now   580
About Olympus, ever crown'd with snow,
The rumour of their controversy flew.
All the Incorruptible, to their view,

    ⁵⁶⁸ *Filed speech*—see Odyssey, Bk. VI. **219.**

A HYMN TO HERMES.

On Heaven's steep mountain made return'd repair.
Hermes, and He that light hurls through the air,   585
Before the Thund'rer's knees stood ; who begun
To question thus far his illustrious Son :
" Phœbus ! To what end bring'st thou captive here
Him in whom my mind puts delights so dear?
This new-born infant, that the place supplies   590
Of Herald yet to all the Deities?
This serious business, you may witness, draws
The Deities' whole Court to discuss the cause."
  Phœbus replied : " And not unworthy is
The cause of all the Court of Deities,   595
For, you shall hear, it comprehends the weight
Of devastation, and the very height
Of spoil and rapine, even of Deities' rights.
Yet you, as if myself loved such delights,
Use words that wound my heart. I bring you here   600
An infant, that, even now, admits no peer
In rapes and robb'ries. Finding out his place,
After my measure of an infinite space,
In the Cyllenian mountain, such a one
In all the art of opprobration,   605
As not in all the Deities I have seen,
Nor in th' oblivion-mark'd whole race of men.
In night he drave my oxen from their leas,
Along the lofty roar-resounding seas,
From out the road-way quite ; the steps of them   610
So quite transpos'd, as would amaze the beam
Of any mind's eye, being so infinite much
Involv'd in doubt, as show'd a deified touch
Went to the work's performance ; all the way,
Through which my cross-hoved cows he did convey,   615

E

A HYMN TO HERMES.

Had dust so darkly-hard to search, and he
So past all measure wrapt in subtilty.
For, nor with feet, nor hands, he form'd **his steps,**
In passing through the dry way's sandy heaps,
But used another counsel to keep hid   620
His monstrous tracts, that show'd as one had slid
On oak or other boughs, that swept **out still**
The footsteps of his oxen, and did fill
Their prints up ever, to the daffodill
(Or dainty-feeding meadow) as they trod,   625
Driven by this cautelous and infant God.

A mortal man, yet, saw him driving on
His prey to Pylos. **Which when he** had done,
And got his pass sign'd, **with a** sacred fire,
In peace, and freely (though **to** his desire, 630
Not to the Gods, he offer'd part of these
My ravish'd oxen) he retires, **and** lies,
Like to the gloomy night, in his dim den,
All hid in darkness; and in **clouts** again
Wrapp'd him so closely, that the sharp-seen eye 635
Of your own eagle could not see him lie.
For with his hands the air he rarified
(This way, **and** that moved) till bright gleams did glide
About his being, that, if any eye
Should dare **the** darkness, light appos'd so nigh 640
Might blind **it** quite with her antipathy.
Which wile he wove, in curious care t' illude
Th' extreme of any eye that could intrude.
On which relying, he outrageously
(When I accus'd him) trebled his reply: 645
'I did not see, I did not hear, **nor** I

₆₂₆ *Cautelous*—artful. A common word.
₆₄₅ *Trebled*—whined, spoke in a whining tone.

A HYMN TO HERMES.

Will tell at all, that any other stole
Your broad-brow'd beeves. Which an impostor's soul
Would soon have done, and any author fain
Of purpose only a reward to gain.' 650
And thus he colour'd truth in every lie."
  This said, Apollo sat; and Mercury
The Gods' Commander pleased with this reply:
"Father! I'll tell thee truth (for I am true,
And far from art to lie): He did pursue 655
Even to my cave his oxen this self day,
The sun new-raising his illustrious ray;
But brought with him none of the Bliss-endued,
Nor any ocular witness, to conclude
His bare assertion; but his own command 660
Laid on with strong and necessary hand,
To show his oxen; using threats to cast
My poor and infant powers into the vast
Of ghastly Tartarus; because he bears
Of strength-sustaining youth the flaming years, 66
And I but yesterday produced to light.
By which it fell into his own free sight,
That I in no similitude appear'd
Of power to be the forcer of a herd.
And credit me, O Father, since the grace 670
Of that name, in your style, you please to place,
I drave not home his oxen, no, nor prest
Past mine own threshold; for 'tis manifest,
I reverence with my soul the Sun, and all
The knowing dwellers in this heavenly Hall, 675
Love you, observe the least; and 'tis most clear
In your own knowledge, that my merits bear
No least guilt of his blame. To all which I

A HYMN TO HERMES.

Dare add heaven's great oath, boldly swearing by
All these so well-built entries of the Blest.   680
And therefore when I saw myself so prest
With his reproaches, I confess I burn'd
In my pure gall, and harsh reply return'd.
Add your aid to your younger then, and free
The scruple fixt in Phœbus' jealousy."   685

  This said he wink'd upon his Sire ; and still
His swathbands held beneath his arm ; no will
Discern'd in him to hide, but have them shown.
  Jove laugh'd aloud at his ingenious Son,
Quitting himself with art, so likely wrought,   690
As show'd in his heart not a rapinous thought ;
Commanding both to bear atoned minds
And seek out th' oxen ; in which search he binds
Hermes to play the guide, and show the Sun
(All grudge exil'd) the shrowd to which he won   695
His fair-eyed oxen ; then his forehead bow'd
For sign it must be so ; and Hermes show'd
His free obedience ; so soon he inclined
To his persuasion and command his mind.
  Now, then, Jove's jarring Sons no longer stood,   700
But sandy Pylos and th' Alphæan flood
Reach'd instantly, and made as quick a fall
On those rich-feeding fields and lofty stall
Where Phœbus' oxen Hermes safely kept,
Driven in by night. When suddenly he stept   705
Up to the stony cave, and into light
Drave forth the oxen. Phœbus at first sight
Knew them the same, and saw apart dispread

    695 *Shrowd*—den, caves underground. The crypt of a church sometimes so called.

Upon a high-rais'd rock the hides new flead
Of th' oxen sacrific'd. Then Phœbus said :   710
"O thou in crafty counsels undisplaid !
How couldst thou cut the throats, and cast to earth
Two such huge oxen, being so young a birth,
And a mere infant? I admire thy force,
And will, behind thy back. But this swift course   715
Of growing into strength thou hadst not need
Continue any long date, O thou Seed
Of honour'd Maia!" Hermes (to show how
He did those deeds) did forthwith cut and bow
Strong osiers in soft folds, and strappled straight   720
One of his hugest oxen, all his weight
Lay'ng prostrate on the earth at Phœbus' feet,
All his four cloven hoves eas'ly made to greet
Each other upwards, all together brought.
In all which bands yet all the beast's powers wrought
To rise, and stand; when all the herd about   725
The mighty Hermes rush'd in, to help out
Their fellow from his fetters. Phœbus' view
Of all this up to admiration drew
Even his high forces; and stern looks he threw   730
At Hermes for his herd's wrong, and the place
To which he had retir'd them, being in grace
And fruitful riches of it so entire ;
All which set all his force on envious fire.
All whose heat flew out of his eyes in flames,   735
Which fain he would have hid, to hide the shames
Of his ill-govern'd passions. But with ease
Hermes could calm them, and his humours please
Still at his pleasure, were he ne'er so great
In force and fortitude, and high in heat.   740

In all which he his lute took, and assay'd
A song upon him, and so strangely play'd,
That from his hand a ravishing horror flew.
Which Phœbus into laughter turn'd, and grew
Pleasant past measure; tunes so artful clear   745
Strook even his heart-strings, and his mind made hear.
His lute so powerful was in forcing love,
As his hand rul'd it, that from him it **drove**
All fear of Phœbus; yet he gave him still
The upper hand; and, to advance his skill   750
To utmost miracle, he play'd sometimes
Single awhile; in which, **when** all the climes
Of rapture he had reach'd, to make the Sun
Admire enough, O then his voice would run
Such points upon his play, and did so move,   755
They took Apollo prisoner **to** his love.
And now the deathless Gods and deathful Earth
He sung, beginning at their either's birth
To full extent of all their empery.
And, first, the honour to Mnemosyne,   760
The Muses' mother, of all Goddess states
He gave; even forced to't by the equal fates.
And then (as it did in priority fall
Of age and birth) he celebrated all.
And with such elegance and order sung   765
(His lute still touch'd, to stick more off his tongue)
That Phœbus' heart with infinite love he eat.
Who, therefore, thus did his deserts entreat:

"Master of sacrifice! Chief soul of feast!
Patient of all pains! Artizan so blest,   770
That all things thou canst do **in** any one!
Worth fifty oxen **is th'** invention

A HYMN TO HERMES.

Of this one lute. We both shall now, I hope,
In firm peace work to all our wishes' scope.
Inform me (thou that every way canst wind,
And turn to act, all wishes of thy mind)
Together with thy birth came all thy skill?
Or did some God, or God-like man, instill
This heavenly song to thee? Methinks I hear
A new voice, such as never yet came near
The breast of any, either man or God,
Till in thee it had prime and period.
What art, what Muse that med'cine can produce
For cares most cureless, what inveterate use
Or practice of a virtue so profuse
(Which three do all the contribution keep
That Joy or Love confers, or pleasing Sleep,)
Taught thee the sovereign facture of them all?
I of the Muses am the capital
Consort, or follower; and to these belong
The grace of dance, all worthy ways of song,
And ever-flourishing verse, the delicate set
And sound of instruments. But never yet
Did anything so much affect my mind
With joy and care to compass, as this kind
Of song and play, that for the spritely feast
Of flourishing assemblies are the best
And aptest works that ever worth gave act.
My powers with admiration stand distract,
To hear with what a hand to make in love
Thou rul'st thy lute. And (though thy yong'st hours move
At full art in old councils) here I vow
(Even by this cornel dart I use to throw)
To thee, and to thy mother, I'll make thee

Amongst the Gods of glorious degree, 805
Guide of men's ways and theirs ; and **will impart**
To thee the mighty imperatory art,
Bestow rich gifts on thee, and in the end
Never deceive thee." Hermes (as a friend
That wrought on all advantage, and made gain 810
His capital object) thus did entertain
Phœbus Apollo : " Do thy dignities,
Far-working God and circularly wise,
Demand my virtues? Without envy I
Will teach thee to ascend my faculty. 815
And this day thou shalt reach it ; finding **me,**
In acts and counsels, all ways kind to thee,
As one that all things knows, and first tak'st seat
Amongst th' Immortals, being good and great,
And therefore to Jove's love mak'st free access, 820
Even out of his accomplisht holiness.
Great gifts he likewise gives thee ; who, fame says,
Hast won thy greatness by his will, his ways,
By him know'st all the powers prophetical,
O thou far-worker, and the fates of all ! 825
Yea, and I know thee rich, yet apt to learn,
And even thy wish dost but discern and earn.
And since thy soul so burns to know the way
So play and sing as I do, sing, and play ;
Play, and perfection in thy play employ ; 830
And be thy care, to learn things good, thy joy.
Take thou my lute (my love) and give thou me
The glory of so great a faculty.
This sweet-tuned consort, held but in thy hand,
Sing, and perfection in thy song command. 835
For thou already hast the way to speak

A HYMN TO HERMES.

Fairly and elegantly, and to break
All eloquence into thy utter'd mind.
One gift from heaven found may another find.
Use then securely this thy gift, and go
To feasts and dances that enamour so,
And to that covetous sport of getting glory,
That day nor night will suffer to be sory.
Whoever does but say in verse, sings still;
Which he that can of any other skill
Is capable, so he be taught by art
And wisdom, and can speak at every part
Things pleasing to an understanding mind;
And such a one that seeks this lute shall find.
Him still it teaches eas'ly, though he plays
Soft voluntaries only, and assays
As wanton as the sports of children are,
And (even when he aspires to singular
In all the mast'ries he shall play or sing)
Finds the whole work but an unhappy thing,
He, I say, sure shall of this lute be king.
But he, whoever rudely sets upon
Of this lute's skill th' inquest or question
Never so ardently and angrily,
Without the aptness and ability
Of art, and nature fitting, never shall
Aspire to this, but utter trivial
And idle accents, though sung ne'er so loud,
And never so commended of the crowd.
But thee I know, O eminent Son of Jove,
The fiery learner of whatever Love
Hath sharpen'd thy affections to achieve,
And thee I give this lute. Let us now live

Feeding upon the hill and horse-fed earth
Our never-handled oxen; whose dear birth
Their females, fellow'd with their males, let flow
In store enough hereafter; nor must you
(However cunning-hearted your wits are)
Boil in your gall a grudge too circular."

 Thus gave he him his lute, which he embrac'd,
And gave again a goad, whose bright head cast
Beams like the light forth; leaving to his care
His oxen's keeping. Which, with joyful fare,
He took on him. The lute Apollo took
Into his left hand, and aloft he shook
Delightsome sounds up, to which God did sing.

 Then were the oxen to their endless spring
Turn'd; and Jove's two illustrous Offsprings flew
Up to Olympus where it ever snew,
Delighted with their lute's sound all the way.
Whom Jove much joy'd to see, and endless stay
Gave to their knot of friendship. From which date
Hermes gave Phœbus an eternal state
In his affection, whose sure pledge and sign
His lute was, and the doctrine so divine
Jointly conferr'd on him; which well might be
True symbol of his love's simplicity.
On th' other part, Apollo in his friend
Form'd th' art of wisdom, to the binding end
Of his vow'd friendship; and (for further meed)
Gave him the far-heard fistulary reed.

 For all these forms of friendship, Phœbus yet
Fear'd that both form and substance where not met
In Mercury's intentions; and, in plain,

  [884] *Snew*—past tense of snow; still a provincialism.

A HYMN TO HERMES.

Said (since he saw him born to craft and gain, 900
And that Jove's will had him the honour done
To change at his will the possession
Of others' goods) he fear'd his breach of vows
In stealing both his lute and cunning bows,
And therefore wish'd that what the Gods affect 905
Himself would witness, and to his request
His head bow, swearing by th' impetuous flood
Of Styx that of his whole possessions not a good
He would diminish, but therein maintain
The full content in which his mind did reign. 910
And then did Maia's son his forehead bow,
Making, by all that he desired, his vow
Never to prey more upon anything
In just possession of the far-shot King,
Nor ever to come near a house of his. 915
 Latonian Phœbus bow'd his brow to this,
With his like promise, saying: "Not any one
Of all the Gods, nor any man, that son
Is to Saturnius, is more dear to me,
More trusted, nor more honour'd is than thee. 920
Which yet with greater gifts of Deity
In future I'll confirm, and give thy state
A rod that riches shall accumulate,
Nor leave the bearer thrall to death, or fate,
Or any sickness. All of gold it is, 925
Three-leaved, and full of all felicities.
And this shall be thy guardian, this shall give
The Gods to thee in all the truth they live,
And, finally, shall this the tut'ress be

---

[903] *Goods*—the folio, followed by Mr. Singer, has *Gods*, but it is obviously a misprint; unless we read *other Gods*. It is an interpolation of Chapman's.

Of all the words and works informing me 930
From Jove's high counsels, making known **to thee**
All my instructions. But **to** prophesy,
O best of Jove's beloved, and that high skill
Which to obtain lies burning in thy will,
Nor thee, nor any God, will Fate let learn. 935
Only Jove's mind hath insight to discern
What that importeth; yet am I allow'd
(My **known** faith trusted, and my forehead bow'd,
Our great oath taken, to resolve to none
Of all th' Immortals the restriction 940
Of that deep knowledge) of **it all** the mind.
Since then it sits in such fast bounds confin'd,
O brother, when the golden rod is held
In thy strong hand, seek not to **have** reveal'd
Any sure fate that Jove will have conceal'd. 945
For no man shall, by know'ng, prevent his fate;
And therefore will I hold in my free state
The pow'r to hurt and help what man I will,
Of all the greatest, or least touch'd with ill,
That walk within the circle of mine eye, 950
In all the tribes and sexes it shall try.
Yet, truly, **any man shall** have his will
To reap the fruits **of** my prophetic skill,
Whoever seeks it by the voice or wing
Of birds, born truly such events **to sing**. 955
Nor will I falsely, nor with fallacies,
Infringe the truth on which his faith relies,
But he that truths in chattering plumes would find,
Quite opposite **to** them that prompt my mind,
And learn by natural forgers of vain lies 960
The more-than-ever-certain Deities,

That man shall sea-ways tread that leave no tracts,
And false or no guide find for all his facts.
And yet will I his gifts accept as well
As his to whom the simple truth I tell.
　One other thing to thee I'll yet make known,
Maia's exceedingly renowned son,
And Jove's, and of the Gods' whole session
The most ingenious genius: There dwell
Within a crooked cranny, in a dell
Beneath Parnassus, certain Sisters born,
Call'd Parcæ, whom extreme swift wings adorn,
Their number three, that have upon their heads
White barley-flour still sprinkled, and are maids;
And these are schoolmistresses of things to come,
Without the gift of prophecy. Of whom
(Being but a boy, and keeping oxen near)
I learn'd their skill, though my great Father were
Careless of it, or them. These flying from home
To others' roofs, and fed with honeycomb,
Command all skill, and (being enraged then)
Will freely tell the truths of things to men.
But if they give them not that Gods' sweet meat,
They then are apt to utter their deceit,
And lead men from their way. And these will I
Give thee hereafter, when their scrutiny
And truth thou hast both made and learn'd; and then
Please thyself with them, and the race of men
(Wilt thou know any) with thy skill endear,
Who will, be sure, afford it greedy ear,
And hear it often if it prove sincere.
　Take these, O Maia's son, and in thy care
Be horse and oxen, all such men as are

A HYMN TO HERMES.

Patient of labour, lions, white-tooth'd boars,
Mastiffs, and flocks that feed the flow'ry shores,   995
And every four-foot beast; **all** which shall stand
In awe of thy high imperatory **hand.**
Be thou to Dis, **too,** sole Ambassador,
Who, though **all gifts** and bounties he abhor,
On **thee** he will bestow a wealthy one."   1000
 Thus king Apollo honour'd Maia's son
With all the rites of friendship; all whose **love**
Had imposition from the will **of** Jove.
 And thus with Gods and mortals Hermes lived,
Who truly help'd **but few,** but all deceived   1005
With an undifferencing respect, **and made**
Vain **words and** false persuasions his trade.
His deeds were all associates of the night,
In which his close wrongs cared **for no** man's right.
 So all salutes to Hermes that are due,   1010
Of **whom,** and all Gods, shall my Muse sing true.

THE END OF THE HYMN TO HERMES.

A HYMN TO VENUS.

THE force, O Muse, and functions now unfold
Of Cyprian Venus, grac'd with mines of
  gold;
Who even in Deities lights love's sweet
  desire,
And all Death's kinds of men makes kiss her fire,
All air's wing'd nation, all the belluine,   5
That or the earth feeds, or the seas confine.
To all which appertain the love and care
Of well-crown'd Venus' works. Yet three there are
Whose minds She neither can deceive nor move;
Pallas, the Seed of Ægis-bearing Jove,   10
Who still lives indevirginate, her eyes
Being blue, and sparkling like the freezing skies,
Whom all the gold of Venus never can
Tempt to affect her facts with God or man.
She, loving strife, and Mars's working banes,   15
Pitch'd fields and fights, and famous artizans,
Taught earthy men first all the arts that are,
Chariots, and all the frames vehicular,
Chiefly with brass arm'd, and adorn'd for war.
Where Venus only soft-skinn'd wenches fills   20

[20] *Wenches*—See Odyssey, Bk. IV. 977.

With wanton house-works, and suggests those skills
Still to their studies.   Whom Diana neither,
That bears the golden distaff, and together
Calls horns, and hollows, and the cries of hounds,
And owns the epithet of loving sounds   25
For their sakes, springing from such spritely sports,
Can catch with her kind lures ; but hill resorts
To wild-beasts, slaughters, accents far-off heard
Of harps and dances, and of woods unshear'd
The sacred shades she loves, yet likes as well   30
Cities where good men and their offspring dwell.
The third, whom her kind passions nothing please,
Is virgin Vesta ; whom Saturnides
Made reverend with his counsels, when his Sire,
That adverse counsels agitates, life's fire   35
Had kindled in her, being his last-begot.
Whom Neptune woo'd to knit with him the knot
Of honour'd nuptials, and Apollo too ;
Which with much vehemence she refused to do,
And stern repulses put upon them both,   40
Adding to all her vows the Gods' great oath,
And touching Jove's chin, which must consummate
All vows so bound, that she would hold her state,
And be th' invincible Maid of Deities
Through all her days' dates.   For Saturnides   45
Gave her a fair gift in her nuptials' stead,
To sit in midst of his house, and be fed
With all the free and richest feast of heaven,
In all the temples of the Gods being given
The prize of honour.   Not a mortal man,   50

²⁴ *Hollows*—shouts ; or, as Mr. Singer prints, *halloos*.
⁴² See Iliad, Bk. I. 481.

(That either, of the Pow'rs Olympian
His half-birth having, may be said to be
A mortal of the Gods, or else that he,
Deities' wills doing, is of Deity)
But gives her honour of the amplest kind.   55
Of all these three can Venus not a mind
Deceive, or set on forces to reflect.
Of all Pow'rs else yet, not a sex, nor sect,
Flies Venus; either of the blessed Gods,
Or men confin'd in mortal periods.   60
But even the mind of Jove she doth seduce,
That chides with thunder so her lawless use
In human creatures, and by lot is given
Of all most honour, both in earth and heaven.
And yet even his all-wise and mighty mind   65
She, when she lists, can forge affects to blind,
And mix with mortal dames his Deity,
Conceal'd at all parts from the jealous eye
Of Juno, who was both his sister born,
And made his wife; whom beauty did adorn   70
Past all the bevy of Immortal Dames,
And whose so chiefly-glorified flames
Cross-counsell'd Saturn got, and Rhæa bore,
And Jove's pure counsels (being conqueror)
His wife made of his sister. Ay, and more,   75
Cast such an amorous fire into her mind
As made her (like him) with the mortal kind
Meet in unmeet bed; using utmost haste,
Lest she should know that he lived so unchaste,
Before herself felt that fault in her heart,   80
And gave her tongue too just edge of desert

[71] *Bevy*—See Odyssey, Bk. VI. 115.

To tax his lightness. With this end, beside,
Lest laughter-studying Venus should deride
The Gods more than the Goddesses, and say
That she the Gods commix'd in amorous play 85
With mortal dames, begetting mortal seed
T' **immortal** sires, and not make Goddesses breed
The like with mortal fathers. But, t' acquite
Both Gods and Goddesses of her despite,
Jove took (even in herself) on him her pow'r, 90
And made her with a mortal paramour
Use as deform'd **a** mixture as the rest;
Kindling a kind affection **in** her breast
To God-like-limb'd Anchises, **as** he kept,
On Ida's top-on-top-to-heaven's-pole-heapt, 95
Amongst the many fountains there, his herd.
For, after his brave person had appear'd
To her bright eye, her heart flew all on fire,
And to amaze she burn'd in his desire,
Flew straight to Cyprus, to her odorous fane 100
And altars, that the people Paphian
Advanced to her. Where, soon as enter'd, she
The **shining gates** shut; and the Graces three
Wash'd, **and** with **oils of** everlasting scent
Bathed, as became, her deathless lineament. 105
Then her ambrosian mantle she assum'd,
With rich and odoriferous airs perfum'd.
Which being put on, and all her trims beside
Fair, and with all allurements amplified,
The all-of-gold-made laughter-loving Dame 110
Left odorous Cyprus, and for Troy became

⁹⁵ Ἀκροπόλος. *Altissimum habens verticem, cujus summitas ipsum polum attingit.*—CHAPMAN.

A swift contendress, her pass cutting all
Along the clouds, and made her instant fall
On fountful Ida, that her mother-breasts
Gives to the preyful brood of savage beasts.   115
And through the hill she went the ready way
T' Anchises' oxstall, where did fawn and play
About her blessed feet wolves grisly-gray,
Terrible lions, many a mankind bear,
And lybberds swift, insatiate of red deer.   120
Whose sight so pleas'd, that, ever as she past
Through every beast, a kindly love she cast,
That, in their dens obscured with shadows deep,
Made all, distinguish'd in kind couples, sleep.
   And now she reach'd the rich pavilion   125
Of the heroë, in whom heavens had shown
A fair and goodly composition,
And whom she in his oxstall found, alone,
His oxen feeding in fat pastures by,
He walking up and down, sounds clear and high   130
From his harp striking. Then before him she
Stood like a virgin, that invincibly
Had borne her beauties; yet alluringly
Bearing her person, lest his ravish'd eye
Should chance t' affect him with a stupid fear.   135
Anchises seeing her, all his senses were
With wonder stricken, and high-taken heeds
Both of her form, brave stature, and rich weeds.
For, for a veil, she shin'd in an attire
That cast a radiance past the ray of fire.   140
Beneath which wore she, girt to her, a gown

[119] *Mankind*—masculine, ferocious.
[120] *Lybberds*—leopards.

Wrought all with growing-rose-buds, reaching down
T' her slender smalls, which buskins did divine,
Such as taught Thetis' **silver feet to** shine.
Her soft white neck rich carquenets embraced,
Bright, and with gold in all variety graced,
That to her breasts let down lay there and shone,
As, at her joyful full, the rising Moon.
Her sight show'd miracles.   Anchises' heart
Love took into his hand, and made him part
With these high salutations: "Joy, O Queen!
Whoever of **the Blest thy** beauties been
That light these entries; **or the Deity**
That darts affecteth; **or that gave the Eye**
Of heaven his heat and lustre; **or that moves**
The hearts of all with all-commanding loves;
Or generous Themis; or the blue-eyed Maid;
Or of the Graces any that are laid
With all the Gods in comparable scales,
And whom fame up to immortality calls;
Or any of the Nymphs, that unshorn groves,
Or that **this fair** hill-habitation, loves,
Or valleys flowing with earth's fattest goods,
Or fountains pouring forth eternal floods!
Say, which of **all** thou **art,** that in **some place**
Of circular prospect, for **thine eyes' dear grace,**
I may an altar build, and to thy pow'rs
Make sacred all the year's devoted hours,
With consecrations sweet and opulent.
Assur'd whereof, be thy benign mind bent

---

[143] *Carquenets*—sometimes spelt *carcanets* and *carknets*.

[152] *The Deity,* &c.—Diana; *that gave the eye,* &c.—Latona, mother of Apollo; *that moves the hearts*—Venus; *the blue-eyed Maid*—Minerva.

A HYMN TO VENUS.

To these wish'd blessings of me: Give me parts
Of chief attraction in Trojan hearts;
And, after, give me the refulgency
Of most renown'd and rich posterity;
Long, and free life, and heaven's sweet light as long;
The people's blessings, and a health so strong   170
That no disease it let my life engage,
Till th' utmost limit of a human age."
   To this Jove's Seed this answer gave again:
"Anchises! Happiest of the human strain!   180
I am no Goddess! Why, a thrall to death
Think'st thou like those that immortality breathe?
A woman brought me forth; my father's name
Was Otreüs, if ever his high fame
Thine ears have witness'd, for he govern'd all   185
The Phrygian state, whose every town a wall
Impregnable embrac'd. Your tongue, you hear,
I speak so well, that in my natural sphere
(As I pretend) it must have taken prime.
A woman, likewise, of the Trojan clime   190
Took of me, in her house, the nurse's care
From my dear mother's bosom; and thus are
My words of equal accent with your own.
How here I come, to make the reason known,
Argicides, that bears the golden rod,   195
Transferr'd me forcibly from my abode
Made with the maiden train of Her that joys
In golden shafts, and loves so well the noise
Of hounds and hunters (heaven's pure-living Pow'r)
Where many a nymph and maid of mighty dow'r   200
Chaste sports employ'd, all circled with a crown
               197 Diana.

Of infinite multitude, to see so shown
Our maiden pastimes. Yet, from all the fair
Of this so forceful concourse, up in air
The golden-rod-sustaining Argus'-Guide
Rapt me in sight of all, and made me ride
Along the clouds with him, enforcing me
Through many a labour of mortality,
Through many an unbuilt region, and a rude,
Where savage beasts devour'd preys warm and crude,
And would not let my fears take one foot's tread
On Her by whom are all lives comforted,
But said my maiden state must grace the bed
Of king Anchises, and bring forth to thee
Issue as fair as of divine degree.
Which said, and showing me thy moving grace,
Away flew he up to th' Immortal Race.
And thus came I to thee; Necessity,
With her steel stings, compelling me t' apply
To her high pow'r my will. But you must I
Implore by Jove, and all the reverence due
To your dear parents, who, in bearing you,
Can bear no mean sail, lead me home to them
An untouch'd maid, being brought up in th' extreme
Of much too cold simplicity to know
The fiery cunnings that in Venus glow.
Show me to them then, and thy brothers born,
I shall appear none that parts disadorn,
But such as well may serve a brother's wife,
And show them now, even to my future life,
If such or no my present will extend.
To horse-breed-vary'ng Phrygia likewise send,

[212] The Earth.

T' inform my sire and mother of my state,
That live for me extreme disconsolate;
Who gold enough, and well-woven weeds, will give.   235
All whose rich gifts in my amends receive.
All this perform'd, add celebration then
Of honour'd nuptials, that by God and men
Are held in reverence." All this while she said,
Into his bosom jointly she convey'd   240
The fires of love; when, all-enamour'd, he
In these terms answer'd: "If mortality
Confine thy fortunes, and a woman were
Mother to those attractions that appear
In thy admir'd form, thy great father given   245
High name of Otreüs; and the Spy of heaven
(Immortal Mercury) th' enforceful cause
That made thee lose the prize of that applause
That modesty immaculate virgins gives,
My wife thou shalt be call'd through both our lives.   250
Nor shall the pow'rs of men nor Gods withhold
My fiery resolution to enfold
Thy bosom in mine arms; which here I vow
To firm performance, past delay, and now.
Nor, should Apollo with his silver bow   255
Shoot me to instant death, would I forbear
To do a deed so full of cause so dear.
For with a heaven-sweet woman I will lie,
Though straight I stoop the house of Dis, and die."
  This said, he took her hand, and she took way   260
With him, her bright eyes casting round; whose stay
She stuck upon a bed, that was before
Made for the king, and wealthy coverings wore.
On which bears' hides and big-voic'd lions' lay,

Whose preyful lives the king had made his prey, 265
Hunting th' Idalian hills. This bed when they
Had both ascended, first he took from her
The fiery weed, that was her utmost wear;
Unbutton'd her next rosy robe; and loos'd
The girdle that her slender waist enclos'd; 270
Unlac'd her buskins; all her jewelry
Took from her neck and breasts, and all laid by
Upon a golden-studded chair of state.
Th' amaze of all which being remov'd, even Fate
And council of the equal Gods gave way 275
To this, that with a deathless Goddess lay
A deathful man; since, what his love assum'd,
Not with his conscious knowledge was presum'd.

   Now when the shepherds and the herdsmen, all,
Turn'd from their flow'ry pasture to their stall, 280
With all their oxen, fat and frolic sheep,
Venus into Anchises cast a sleep,
Sweet and profound; while with her own hands now
With her rich weeds she did herself endow;
But so distinguish'd, that he clear might know 285
His happy glories; then (to her desire
Her heavenly person put in trims entire)
She by the bed stood of the well-built stall,
Advanc'd her head to state celestial,
And in her cheeks arose the radiant hue 290
Of rich-crown'd Venus to apparent view.
And then she rous'd him from his rest, and said:
"Up, my Dardanides, forsake thy bed.
What pleasure, late employ'd, lets humour steep
Thy lids in this inexcitable sleep? 295
Wake, and now say, if I appear to thee

A HYMN TO VENUS.

Like her that first thine eyes conceited me."
  This started him from sleep, though deep and dear,
And passing promptly he enjoy'd his ear.
But when his eye saw Venus' neck and eyes,   300
Whose beauties could not bear the counterprise
Of any other, down his own eyes fell,
Which pallid fear did from her view repell,
And made him, with a main respect beside,
Turn his whole person from her state, and hide   305
(With his rich weed appos'd) his royal face,
These wing'd words using: "When, at first, thy grace
Mine eyes gave entertainment, well I knew
Thy state was deified; but thou told'st not true;
And therefore let me pray thee (by thy love   310
Born to thy father, Ægis-bearing Jove)
That thou wilt never let me live to be
An abject, after so divine degree
Taken in fortune, but take ruth on me.
For any man that with a Goddess lies,   315
Of interest in immortalities,
Is never long-liv'd." She replied: "Forbear,
O happiest of mortal men, this fear,
And rest assured, that (not for me, at least)
Thy least ills fear fits; no, nor for the rest   320
Of all the Blessed, for thou art their friend;
And so far from sustaining instant end,
That to thy long-enlarg'd life there shall spring
Amongst the Trojans a dear son, and king,
To whom shall many a son, and son's son, rise   325
In everlasting great posterities;
His name Æneas; therein keeping life,
For ever, in my much-conceited grief,

That I, immortal, fell into the bed
Of one whose blood mortality must shed.   330
But rest thou comforted, and all the race
That Troy shall propagate, in this high grace:
That, past all races else, the Gods stand near
Your glorious nation, for the forms ye bear,
And natures so ingenuous and sincere.   335
For which, the great-in-counsels (Jupiter)
Your gold-lock'd Ganemedes did transfer
(In rapture far from men's depressed fates)
To make him consort with our Deified States,
And scale the tops of the Saturnian skies,   340
He was so mere a marvel in their eyes.
And therefore from a bowl of gold he fills
Red nectar, that the rude distension kills
Of winds that in your human stomach breed.
But then did languor on the liver feed   345
Of Tros, his father, that was king of Troy,
And ever did his memory employ
With loss of his dear beauty so bereaven,
Though with a sacred whirlwind rapt to heaven.
But Jove, in pity of him, saw him given   350
Good compensation, sending by Heaven's Spy
White-swift-hov'd horse, that Immortality
Had made firm-spirited; and had, beside,
Hermes to see his ambassy supplied
With this vow'd bounty (using all at large   355
That his unalter'd counsels gave in charge)
That he himself should immortality breathe,
Expert of age and woe as well as death.

₃₄₇ ἄληστος. *Cujus memoria erit perpetua.*—CHAPMAN.
₃₅₈ *Expert*—in the classical sense, *free from, unaccompanied by.*

A HYMN TO VENUS.

"This ambassy express'd, he mourn'd no more,
But up with all his inmost mind he bore,
Joying that he, upon his swift-hov'd horse,
Should be sustain'd in an eternal course.
"So did the golden-throned Aurora raise,
Into her lap, another that the praise
Of an immortal fashion had in fame,
And of your nation bore the noble name,
(His title Tithon) who, not pleased with her,
As she his lovely person did transfer,
To satisfy him, she bade ask of Jove
The gift of an Immortal for her love.
Jove gave, and bound it with his bowed brow,
Performing to the utmost point his vow.
Fool that she was, that would her love engage,
And not as long ask from the bane of age
The sweet exception, and youth's endless flow'r!
Of which as long as both the grace and pow'r
His person entertain'd, she loved the man,
And (at the fluents of the ocean
Near Earth's extreme bounds) dwelt with him; but when
(According to the course of aged men)
On his fair head, and honourable beard,
His first grey hairs to her light eyes appear'd,
She left his bed, yet gave him still for food
The Gods' ambrosia, and attire as good.
Till even the hate of age came on so fast
That not a lineament of his was grac'd
With pow'r of motion, nor did still sustain,
Much less, the vigour had t' advance a vein,
The virtue lost in each exhausted limb,

A HYMN TO VENUS.

That at his wish before would answer him;
All pow'rs so quite **decay'd, that when he** spake
His voice no perceptible accent **brake.**
Her counsel then thought best to strive no more,
But lay him **in his** bed and lock his door.
Such **an** Immortal would not I wish **thee,**
T' extend all days so to eternity.
But if, as now, thou couldst perform thy **course**
In grace of form, and all corporeal force,
To an eternal date, thou then should'st bear
My husband's worthy name, and not a tear
Should I need rain, for thy deserts declin'd,
From my all-clouded bitterness of mind.
But now the stern storm of relentless age
Will quickly circle thee, **that waits t'** engage
All men alike, even loathsomeness, and bane
Attending with it, every human wane,
Which even the Gods hate. Such a penance lies
Impos'd on flesh and blood's infirmities!
Which **I** myself must taste in great degree,
And date as endless, for consorting thee.
All the Immortals **with** my opprobry
Are full by this time; on their hearts so lie
(Even to the sting of fear) my cunnings us'd,
And wiving conversations infus'd
Into the bosoms of the best of them
With women, that the frail and mortal stream
Doth daily ravish. All this long since done.
Which now no more, but with effusion
Of tears, I must in heaven so much as name,
I have so forfeited in this my fame,
And am impos'd pain of so great a kind

A HYMN TO VENUS.

For so much erring from a Goddess' mind.
For I have put beneath my girdle here
A son, whose sire the human mortal sphere
Gives circumscription. But, when first the light 425
His eyes shall comfort, Nymphs that haunt the height
Of hills, and breasts have of most deep receipt,
Shall be his nurses; who inhabit now
A hill of so vast and divine a brow,
As man nor God can come at their retreats; 430
Who live long lives, and eat immortal meats,
And with Immortals in the exercise
Of comely dances dare contend, and rise
Into high question which deserves the prize.
The light Sileni mix in love with these, 435
And, of all Spies the Prince, Argicides;
In well-trimm'd caves their secret meetings made.
And with the lives of these doth life invade
Or odorous fir-trees, or high-foreheaded oaks,
Together taking their begetting strokes, 440
And have their lives and deaths of equal dates,
Trees bearing lovely and delightsome states,
Whom Earth first feeds, that men initiates.
On her high hills she doth their states sustain,
And they their own heights raise as high again. 445
Their growths together made, Nymphs call their groves
Vow'd to th' Immortals services and loves;
Which men's steels therefore touch not, but let grow.
But when wise Fates times for their fadings know,
The fair trees still before the fair Nymphs die, 450
The bark about them grown corrupt and dry,
And all their boughts fall'n yield to Earth her right;
And then the Nymphs' lives leave the lovely night.

A HYMN TO VENUS.

"And these Nymphs in their caves shall nurse my son,
Whom (when in him youth's first grace is begun) 455
The Nymphs, his nurses, shall present to thee,
And show thee what a birth thou hast by me.
And, sure as now I tell thee all these things,
When Earth hath cloth'd her plants in five fair springs,
Myself will make return to this retreat, 460
And bring that flow'r of thy enamour'd heat;
Whom when thou then seest, joy shall fire thine eyes,
He shall so well present the Deities.
And then into thine own care take thy son
From his calm seat to windy Ilion, 465
Where, if strict question be upon the past,
Asking what mother bore beneath her waist
So dear a son, answer, as I afford
Fit admonition, nor forget a word:
They say a Nymph, call'd Calucopides, 470
That is with others an inhabitress
On this thy wood-crown'd hill, acknowledges
That she his life gave. But, if thou declare
The secret's truth, and art so mad to dare
(In glory of thy fortunes) to approve 475
That rich-crown'd Venus mix'd with thee in love,
Jove, fired with my aspersion so dispread,
Will with a wreakful lightning dart thee dead.
"All now is told thee, comprehend it all.
Be master of thyself, and do not call 480
My name in question; but with reverence vow
To Deities' angers all the awe ye owe."
This said, She reach'd heaven, where airs ever flow.

⁴⁷⁵ *Glory*—boast.

And so, O Goddess, ever honour'd be,
In thy so odorous Cyprian empery! 485
My Muse, affecting first thy fame to raise,
Shall make transcension now to other's praise.

THE END OF THE FIRST HYMN TO VENUS.

TO THE SAME.

THE reverend, rich-crown'd, and fair Queen
    I sing,
Venus, that owes in fate the fortressing
Of all maritimal Cyprus; where the force
Of gentle-breathing Zephyr steer'd her course
Along the waves of the resounding sea, 5
While, yet unborn, in that soft foam she lay
That brought her forth; whom those fair Hours that bear
The golden bridles joyfully stood near,
Took up into their arms, and put on her
Weeds of a never-corruptible wear. 10
On her immortal head a crown they plac'd,
Elaborate, and with all the beauties grac'd
That gold could give it; of a weight so great,
That, to impose and take off, it had set
Three handles on it, made, for endless hold, 15
Of shining brass, and all adorn'd with gold.
Her soft neck all with carquenets was grac'd,
That stoop'd, and both her silver breasts embrac'd,
Which even the Hours themselves wear in resort
To Deities' dances, and her Father's court. 20

² *Owes*—owns.

Grac'd at all parts, they brought **to heaven** her graces;
Whose first sight seen, **all** fell into embraces,
Hugg'd her white hands, saluted, wishing all
To wear her maiden flow'r in festival
Of sacred Hymen, and to lead her **home**; 25
All, to all admiration, overcome
With Cytherea with the violet crown.

 So to the Black-brow'd Sweet-spoke **all renown**!
Prepare my song, and give me, in the **end**,
The victory to whose palm all contend! 30
So shall my Muse for ever honour thee,
And, for thy sake, **thy fair posterity**.

BACCHUS, **OR THE PIRATES**.

OF Dionysus, noble Semele's Son,
 I now intend to render mention,
 As on a prominent shore his person shone,
Like **to a youth** whose flow'r was newly blown,
Bright azure **tresses play'd** about his head, 5
And **on his bright broad** shoulders was dispread
A purple mantle. Strait he was descried
By certain manly pirates, that applied
Their utmost speed to prise him, being aboard
A well-built bark, about whose broad sides roar'd 10
The wine-black Tyrrhene billows; death as black
Brought them upon him in their future wrack.
For, soon as they had purchas'd but his view,
Mutual signs past them, and ashore they flew,

BACCHUS, OR THE PIRATES.

Took him, and brought him instantly aboard,   15
Soothing their hopes to have obtain'd a hoard
Of riches with him; and a Jove-kept king
To such a flow'r must needs be natural spring.
And therefore straight strong fetters they must fetch,
To make him sure. But no such strength would stretch
To his constrain'd pow'rs. Far flew all their bands   21
From any least force done his feet or hands.
But he sat casting smiles from his black eyes
At all their worst. At which discoveries
Made by the master, he did thus dehort   25
All his associates: "Wretches! Of what sort
Hold ye the person ye assay to bind?
Nay, which of all the Pow'r fully-divin'd
Esteem ye him, whose worth yields so much weight
That not our well-built bark will bear his freight?   30
Or Jove himself he is, or He that bears
The silver bow, or Neptune. Nor appears
In him the least resemblance of a man,
But of a strain at least Olympian.
Come! Make we quick dismission of his state,   35
And on the black-soil'd earth exonerate
Our sinking vessel of his deified load,
Nor dare the touch of an intangible God,
Lest winds outrageous, and of wrackful scathe,
And smoking tempests, blow his fiery wrath."   40
This well-spoke master the tall captain gave
Hateful and horrible language; call'd him slave,
And bade him mark the prosp'rous gale that blew,

---

[28] *Pow'r fully-divin'd*—Mr. Singer has wrongly altered this to *pow'rfully-divined;* but Chapman says *fully-divin'd Pow'r*, i. e. Godhead.

[41] i. e. the tall captain replied to the master.

And how their vessel with her mainsail flew;
Bade all take arms, and said, their works requir'd   45
The cares of men, and not of an inspir'd
Pure zealous master; his firm hopes being fir'd
With this opinion, that they should arrive
In Ægypt straight, or Cyprus, or where live
Men whose brave breaths above the north wind blow;
Yea, and perhaps beyond their region too.   51
And that he made no doubt but in the end
To make his prisoner tell him every friend
Of all his offspring, brothers, wealth, and all;
Since that prise, certain, must some God let fall.   55

   This said, the mast and mainsail up he drew,
And in the mainsail's midst a frank gale blew;
When all his ship took arms to brave their prise.
But straight strange works appear'd to all their eyes:
First, sweet wine through their swift-black bark did flow,
Of which the odours did a little blow   61
Their fiery spirits, making th' air so fine
That they in flood were there as well as wine.
A mere immortal-making savour rose,
Which on the air the Deity did impose.   65
The seamen see'ng all, admiration seiz'd;
Yet instantly their wonders were increas'd,
For on the topsail there ran, here and there,
A vine that grapes did in abundance bear,
And in an instant was the ship's mainmast   70
With an obscure-green ivy's arms embrac'd,
That flourish'd straight, and were with berries grac'd;
Of which did garlands circle every brow
Of all the pirates, and no one knew how.

      ⁶⁴ *Mere*—See Odyssey, Bk. VIII. 115.

Which when they saw, they made the master steer
Out to the shore; whom Bacchus made forbear,
With showing more wonders. On the hatches He
Appear'd a terrible lion, horribly
Roaring; and in the mid-deck a male bear,
Made with a huge mane; making all, for fear,
Crowd to the stern, about the master there,
Whose mind he still kept dauntless and sincere,
But on the captain rush'd and ramp'd, with force
So rude and sudden, that his main recourse
Was to the main-sea straight: and after him
Leapt all his mates, as trusting to their swim
To fly foul death; but so found what they fled,
Being all to dolphins metamorphosed.
The master he took ruth of, sav'd, and made
The blessed'st man that ever tried his trade,
These few words giving him: "Be confident,
Thou God-inspired pilot, in the bent
Of my affection, ready to requite
Thy late-to-me-intended benefit.
I am the roaring God of spritely wine,
Whom Semele (that did even Jove incline
To amorous mixture, and was Cadmus' care)
Made issue to the mighty Thunderer."
  And thus, all excellence of grace to thee,
Son of sweet-count'nance-carry'ng Semele.
I must not thee forget in least degree,
But pray thy spirit to render so my song
Sweet, and all ways in order'd fury strong.

TO MARS.

MARS, most-strong, gold-helm'd, **making**
    chariots crack ;
    Never without a shield cast on thy back ;
Mind-master, town-guard, with darts never driven ;
Strong-handed, all arms, fort, and fence of heaven ;
Father **of** victory with fair strokes given ;   5
Joint surrogate **of** justice, lest she fall
In unjust strifes a tyrant ; general
Only of just men justly ; that dost **bear**
Fortitude's sceptre ; to heaven's fiery sphere
Giver of circular motion, between   10
That and the Pleiads that still wand'ring been,
Where thy still-vehemently-flaming horse
About the third heaven make their fiery course ;
Helper **of** mortals ; hear !—As thy fires give
The fair **and** present boldnesses that strive   15
In youth **for** honour, being the sweet-beam'd light
That darts **into their lives,** from all their height,
The fortitudes **and fortunes** found in fight ;
So would I likewise **wish to have the** pow'r
To keep off from my head thy bitter **hour,**   20
And that false fire, cast from my soul's low **kind,**
Stoop to the fit rule of my highest mind,
Controlling that so eager sting **of** wrath
That stirs me on still to that horrid scathe
Of war, that God still sends to wreak his spleen   25
(Even by whole tribes) of proud injurious men.
    But O thou Ever-Blessed ! give me still

Presence of mind to put in act my will,
Varied, as fits, to all occasion;
And to live free, unforc'd, unwrought upon, 30
Beneath those laws of peace that never are
Affected with pollutions popular
Of unjust hurt, or loss to any one;
And to bear safe the burthen undergone
Of foes inflexive, and inhuman hates, 35
Secure from violent and harmful fates.

TO DIANA.

DIANA praise, Muse, that in darts delights,
Lives still a maid, and had nutritial rights
With her born-brother, the far-shooting Sun.
That doth her all-of-gold-made chariot run
In chase of game, from Meles that abounds 5
In black-brow'd bulrushes, and, where her hounds
She first uncouples, joining there her horse,
Through Smyrna carried in most fiery course
To grape-rich Claros; where (in his rich home,
And constant expectation She will come) 10
Sits Phœbus, that the silver bow doth bear,
To meet with Phœbe, that doth darts transfer
As far as He his shafts. As far then be
Thy chaste fame shot, O Queen of archery!
Sacring my song to every Deity. 15

[15] *Sacring*—consecrating. The reader will remember the *sacring-bell*.

TO VENUS.

TO Cyprian Venus still my verses vow,
Who gifts as sweet as honey doth bestow
On all mortality; that ever smiles,
And rules a face that all foes reconciles;
Ever sustaining in her hand a flow'r
That all desire keeps ever in her pow'r.

Hail, then, O **Queen** of well-built Salamine,
And all the state that **Cyprus** doth confine,
Inform my song with that celestial fire
That in thy beauties kindles all desire.
So shall my Muse for ever honour thee,
And any other thou commend'st **to me.**

TO PALLAS.

ALLAS Minerva only I begin
To give my song; that makes **war's** terrible
din,
Is patroness of cities, and with Mars
Marshall'd in all the care and cure of wars,
And in everted cities, fights, and cries.
But never doth herself set down **or rise**
Before a city, but at both times She
All injur'd people sets on foot and free.
Give, with thy war's force, fortune then to me,
And, with thy wisdom's force, felicity.

TO JUNO.

SATURNIA, and her throne of gold, I sing,
That was of Rhea the eternal spring,
And empress of a beauty never yet
Equall'd in height of tincture. Of the great
Saturnius (breaking air in awful noise) 5
The far-fam'd wife and sister; whom in joys
Of high Olympus all the Blessed love,
And honour equal with unequall'd Jove.

TO CERES.

THE rich-hair'd Ceres I assay to sing;
A Goddess, in whose grace the natural spring
Of serious majesty itself is seen;
And of the wedded, yet in grace still green,
Proserpina, her daughter, that displays 5
A beauty casting every way her rays.
    All honour to thee, Goddess! Keep this town;
And take thou chief charge of my son's renown!

TO THE MOTHER OF THE GODS.

MOTHER of all, both Gods and men, commend,
O Muse, whose fair form did from Jove
    descend;
That doth with cymbal sounds delight her life,
And tremulous divisions of the fife;

Love's dreadful lions' roars, and wolves' hoarse howls, 5
Sylvan retreats, and hills, whose hollow knolls
Raise repercussive sounds about her ears.
And so may honour ever crown thy years
With all-else Goddesses, and ever be
Exalted in the Muses' harmony! 10

TO LION-HEARTED HERCULES.

ALCIDES, forcefullest of all the brood
　　Of men enforc'd with need of earthy food,
　　My Muse shall memorise; the son of Jove,
Whom, in fair-seated Thebes (commix'd in love
With great heaven's sable-cloud-assembling State) 5
Alcmena bore to him; and who, in date
Of days forepast, through all the sea was sent,
And Earth's inenarrable continent,
To acts that king Eurystheus had decreed;
Did many a petulant and imperious deed 10
Himself, and therefore suffer'd many a toil;
Yet now inhabits the illustrious soil
Of white Olympus, and delights his life
With still-young Hebe, his well-ankled wife.
　　Hail, King, and Son of Jove! Vouchsafe thou me 15
Virtue, and, her effect, felicity!

TO ÆSCULAPIUS.

WITH Æsculapius, the physician,
That cur'd all sickness, and was Phœbus' son,
My Muse makes entry; to whose life gave
    yield
Divine Coronis in the Dotian field,
(King Phlegius' daughter) who much joy on men   5
Conferr'd, in dear case of their irksome pain.
For which, my salutation, worthy king,
And vows to thee paid, ever when I sing!

TO CASTOR AND POLLUX.

CASTOR and Pollux, the Tyndarides,
Sweet Muse illustrate; that their essences
Fetch from the high forms of Olympian Jove,
And were the fair fruits of bright Leda's love,
Which she produc'd beneath the sacred shade   5
Of steep Taygetus, being subdu'd, and made
To serve th' affections of the Thunderer.
And so all grace to you, whom all aver
(For skill in horses, and their manage given)
To be the bravest horsemen under heaven!   10

    ⁶ *Taÿgetus.*—It is hardly necessary to remind the reader that Chapman's quantity is wrong, as is often the case.

TO MERCURY.

HERMES I honour, the Cyllenian Spy,
King of Cyllenia, and of Arcady
With flocks abounding ; and the Messenger
Of all th' Immortals, that doth still infer
Profits of infinite value to their store ;   5
Whom to Saturnius bashful Maia bore,
Daughter of **Atlas, and did** therefore fly
Of all th' Immortals the society,
To that dark cave, where, in the dead of night,
Jove join'd with **her** in love's divine delight,   10
When golden sleep shut Juno's jealous eye,
Whose arms had wrists as **white as** ivory,
From whom, and all, both men **and** Gods beside,
The fair-hair'd nymph her scape kept undescried.
  Joy to the Jove-got then, and Maia's care,   15
'Twixt men and Gods the general Messenger,
Giver of good grace, gladness, and the flood
Of all that men or Gods account their good !

[14] *Scape.*—See Iliad, II. 312.

TO PAN.

ING, Muse, this chief of Hermes' love-got joys,
Goat-footed, two-horn'd, amorous of noise,
That through the fair greens, all adorn'd
with trees,

Together goes with Nymphs, whose nimble knees
Can every dance foot, that affect to scale
The most inaccessible tops of all
Uprightest rocks, and ever use to call
On Pan, the bright-hair'd God of pastoral;
Who yet is lean and loveless, and doth owe
By lot all loftiest mountains crown'd with snow;
All tops of hills, and cliffy highnesses,
All sylvan copses, and the fortresses
Of thorniest queaches, here and there doth rove,
And sometimes, by allurement of his love,
Will wade the wat'ry softnesses. Sometimes
(In quite oppos'd *capriccios*) he climbs
The hardest rocks, and highest, every way
Running their ridges. Often will convey
Himself up to a watch-tow'r's top, where sheep
Have their observance. Oft through hills as steep
His goats he runs upon, and never rests.
Then turns he head, and flys on savage beasts,
Mad of their slaughters; so most sharp an eye
Setting upon them, as his beams let fly
Through all their thickest tapistries. And then
(When Hesp'rus calls to fold the flocks of men)
From the green clossets of his loftiest reeds
He rushes forth, and joy with song he feeds.
When, under shadow of their motions set,
He plays a verse forth so profoundly sweet,
As not the bird that in the flow'ry spring,
Amidst the leaves set, makes the thickets ring

[2] *Owe*—own.
[13] *Queaches*—thickets. See Odyssey, Bk. xix. 610.
[25] *Tapistries*—i. e. hiding-places, where they *tapish* or hide.
[27] *Clossets*—closes. The word should be noted.

Of her sour sorrows, **sweeten'd** with her song,
Runs her divisions varied **so** and strong.
And then the **sweet-voic'd** Nymphs that crown his
    mountains 35
(Flock'd round about the deep-black-water'd fountains)
Fall in with their contention of song.
To which the echoes all the hills along
Their repercussions add. Then here and **there**
(Plac'd **in** the midst) the God the guide doth bear 40
Of all their dances, winding in and out,
A lynce's hide, besprinkled round about
With blood, cast **on** his shoulders. **And thus He,**
With well-made songs, maintains th' alacrity
Of his free mind, in silken meadows crown'd 45
With hyacinths and saffrons, that abound
In sweet-breath'd odours, **that th'** unnumber'd grass
(Besides their scents) give as through all they pass.
And these, in all their pleasures, ever raise
The blessed Gods' and long Olympus' praise : 50
Like zealous Hermes, who of all I said
Most profits up to all the Gods convey'd.
Who, likewise, came into th' Arcadian state,
(That's rich in fountains, and all celebrate
For nurse of flocks,) where He had vow'd **a grove** 55
(Surnam'd Cyllenius) to his Godhead's love.
Yet even himself (although **a** God he **were)**
Clad in a squalid sheepskin, govern'd there
A mortal's sheep. For soft love ent'ring him
Conform'd his state to his conceited trim, 60
And made him long, in an extreme degree,
T' enjoy the fair-hair'd virgin Dryope.
Which ere **he** could, she made him consummate

VULCAN.

The flourishing rite of Hymen's honour'd state ;
And brought him such a piece of progeny
As show'd, at first sight, monstrous to the eye,
Goat-footed, two-horn'd, full of noise even then,
And (opposite quite to other children)
Told, in sweet laughter, he ought death no tear.
Yet straight his mother start, and fled, in fear,
The sight of so unsatisfying a thing,
In whose face put forth such a bristled spring.
Yet the most useful Mercury embrac'd,
And took into his arms, his homely-fac'd,
Beyond all measure joyful with his sight ;
And up to heaven with him made instant flight,
Wrapp'd in the warm skin of a mountain hare,
Set him by Jove, and made most merry fare
To all the Deities else with his son's sight ;
Which most of all fill'd Bacchus with delight ;
And Pan they call'd him, since he brought to all
Of mirth so-rare and full a festival.

And thus all honour to the shepherds' King,
For sacrifice to thee my Muse shall sing !

⁶⁹ *Ought*—owed.   ⁷⁰ *Start*—the past tense.

TO VULCAN.

PRAISE Vulcan, now Muse ; whom fame gives
the prize
For depth and fracture of all forge-devise ;
Who, with the sky-ey'd Pallas, first did give
Men rules of buildings, that before did live

In caves and dens, and hills, like savage beasts, 5
But now, by art-fam'd **Vulcan's** interests
In all their civil industries, **ways** clear
Through th' all-things-bringing-to-their-ends (the year)
They work out **to** their ages' ends, at ease
Lodg'd **in safe** roofs from Winter's utmost prease. 10
   But, **Vulcan,** stand propitious to me,
Virtue safe granting, and felicity!

TO PHŒBUS.

   PHŒBUS! Even the swan from forth
     her wings,
Jumping her proyning-bank, thee sweetly
     sings,
By bright Peneus' whirl-pit-making streams.
Thee, that thy lute mak'st sound so to thy beams,
Thee, first **and** last, the sweet-voic'd singer still 5
Sings, **for** thy song's all-songs-transcending skill.
   Thy pleasure, then, shall my song still supply,
And so salutes thee King of Poesy.

    ² *Proyning bank*—where she preens or proins herself.

TO **NEPTUNE.**

NEPTUNE, the mighty marine God, I sing,
   Earth's mover, and the fruitless ocean's King
   That Helicon and th' Ægean deeps dost hold.
O thou Earth-shaker! Thy command two-fold

The Gods have sorted; making thee of horses
The awful tamer, and of naval forces
The sure preserver. Hail, O Saturn's birth!
Whose graceful green hair circles all the earth.
Bear a benign mind; and thy helpful hand
Lend all submitted to thy dread command.

TO JOVE.

JOVE now I sing, the greatest and the best
   Of all these Pow'rs that are with Deity blest,
   That far-off doth his dreadful voice diffuse,
And, being King of all, doth all conduce
To all their ends. Who (shut from all Gods else
With Themis, that the laws of all things tells)
Their fit composures to their times doth call,
Weds them together, and preserves this all.
  Grace then, O far-heard Jove, the grace thou'st given,
Most Glorious, and most Great of Earth and Heaven!

TO VESTA.

VESTA, that as a servant oversees
   King Phœbus' hallow'd house, in all degrees
   Of guide about it, on the sacred shore
Of heavenly Pythos, and hast evermore
Rich balms distilling from thy odorous hair,
Grace this house with thy housewifely repair!

Enter, and bring a mind that most may move,
Conferring even, the great in counsels, Jove,
And let my verse taste of **your** either's love.

TO THE MUSES AND APOLLO.

THE Muses, Jove, and Phœbus, now I sing,
    For from the far-off-shooting Phœbus spring
    All poets and musicians, and from Jove
Th' ascents of kings. The man the **Muses love**,
Felicity blesses; elocution's choice   5
In syrup lay'ng of sweetest breath his voice.
  Hail, Seed of Jove, my song your honours give,
And so in mine shall yours and others' live.

TO BACCHUS.

IVY-crown'd Bacchus iterate in thy praises,
    O Muse; whose voice all loftiest echoes raises,
    And he with all th' illustrious **Seed** of Jove
Is join'd in honour, being the fruit of love
To him, and Semele the-great-in-graces;   5
And from the King his father's kind embraces
By fair-hair'd Nymphs was taken to the dales
Of Nyssa, and with curious festivals
Given his fair grought, far from his father's view,
In caves from whence eternal odours flew,   10
And in high number of the Deities plac'd.

        9 Grought—growth.

TO DIANA.

Yet when the many-hymn-given God had past
His Nurse's cares, in ivies and in bays
All over thicketed, his varied ways
To sylvan coverts evermore He took,   15
With all his Nurses, whose shrill voices shook
Thickets, in which could no foot's entry fall,
And he himself made captain of them all.
  And so, O grape-abounding Bacchus, be
Ever saluted by my Muse and me!   20
Give us to spend with spirit our hours out here,
And every hour extend to many a year.

TO DIANA.

DIANA, that the golden spindle moves,
  And lofty sounds as well as Bacchus loves,
  A bashful virgin, and of fearful hearts
The death-affecter with delighted darts,
By sire and mother Phœbus' sister born,   5
Whose thigh the golden falchion doth adorn,
I sing; who likewise over hills of shade
And promontories that vast winds invade,
Amorous of hunting, bends her all-gold bow,
And sigh-begetting arrows doth bestow   10
In fates so dreadful that the hill-tops quake,
And bristled woods their leafy foreheads shake,
Horrors invade earth, and [the] fishy seas
Impassion'd furies; nothing can appease
The dying brays of beasts. And her delight   15
In so much death affects so with affright

Even all inanimate natures; for, while she
Her sports applies, their general progeny
She all ways turns upon to all their banes.
Yet when her fiery pleasures find their wanes, 20
Her yielding bow unbent, to th' ample house,
Seated in Delphos, rich and populous,
Of her dear brother, her retreats advance.
Where th' instauration of delightsome dance
Amongst the Muses and the Graces she 25
Gives form; in which herself the regency
(Her unbent bow hung up, and casting on
A gracious robe) assumes, and first sets gone
The dances' entry; to which all send forth
Their heavenly voices, and advance the worth 30
Of her fair-ankled mother, since to light
She children brought the far most exquisite
In counsels and performances of all
The Goddesses that grace the heavenly hall.
 Hail then, Latona's fair-hair'd Seed, and Jove's! 35
My song shall ever call to mind your loves.

TO PALLAS.

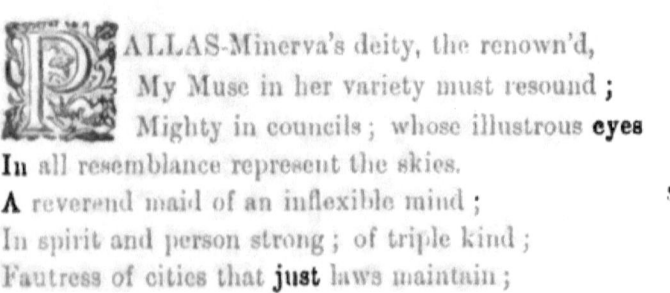ALLAS-Minerva's deity, the renown'd,
 My Muse in her variety must resound;
 Mighty in councils; whose illustrous eyes
In all resemblance represent the skies.
A reverend maid of an inflexible mind; 5
In spirit and person strong; of triple kind;
Fautress of cities that just laws maintain;

Of Jove, the-great-in-councils, very brain
Took prime existence, his unbounded brows
Could not contain her, such impetuous throes
Her birth gave way to, that abroad she flew,
And stood, in gold arm'd, in her Father's view,
Shaking her sharp lance. All Olympus shook
So terribly beneath her, that it took
Up in amazes all the Deities there.
All earth resounded with vociferous fear.
The sea was put up all in purple waves,
And settled suddenly her rudest raves.
Hyperion's radiant son his swift-hov'd steeds
A mighty time stay'd, till her arming weeds,
As glorious as the Gods', the blue-ey'd Maid
Took from her deathless shoulders; but then stay'd
All these distempers, and heaven's counsellor, Jove,
Rejoic'd that all things else his stay could move.
   So I salute thee still; and still in praise
Thy fame, and others', shall my memory raise.

TO VESTA AND MERCURY.

ESTA I sing, who, in bequest of fate,
   Art sorted out an everlasting state
   In all th' Immortals' high-built roofs, and all
Those of earth-dwelling men, as general
And ancient honours given thee for thy gift
Of free-liv'd chastity, and precious thrift.
Nor can there amongst mortals banquets be,
In which, both first and last, they give not thee

116   TO EARTH.

Their endless gratitudes in pour'd-out wine,
As gracious sacrifice to thy divine   10
And useful virtues; being invok'd by all,
Before the least taste of their festival
In wine or food affect their appetites.
And **Thou, that** of th' adorn'd-with-all-delights
Art the **most** useful angel, born a God   15
Of Jove and Maia, of heaven's golden rod
The sole sustainer, and hast pow'r to **bless**
With all good **all men**, great Argicides,
Inhabit all good houses, see'ng no wants
Of mutual minds' **love in th' inhabitants,**   20
Join in kind blessing with the bashful maid
And all-lov'd virgin, Vesta; **either's aid**
Combin'd in every hospitable house;
Both being best seen in all the gracious
House-works of mortals. Jointly follow then,   25
Even from their youths, the minds **of** dames and men.
    Hail then, old Daughter of the oldest God,
And thou Great Bearer of Heaven's golden rod!
Yet **not to** you alone my vows belong,
Others as well claim th' homage of my song.   30

     [15] *Angel*—messenger, ἄγγελος.

TO EARTH, THE MOTHER OF ALL.

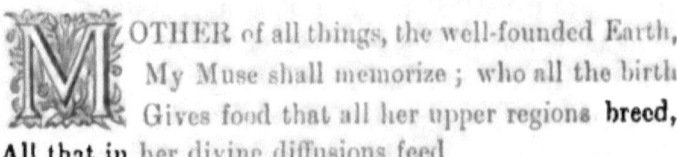

MOTHER of all things, the well-founded Earth,
    My Muse shall memorize; who all the birth
    Gives food that all her upper regions **breed,**
All that in her divine diffusions feed

In under continents, all those that live
In all the seas, and all the air doth give
Wing'd expeditions, of thy bounties eat;
Fair children, and fair fruits, thy labour's sweat,
O great in reverence; and referr'd to thee,
For life and death is all the pedigree
Of mortal humans. Happy then is he
Whom the innate propensions of thy mind
Stand bent to honour. He shall all things find
In all abundance; all his pastures yield
Herds in all plenties; all his roofs are fill'd
With rich possessions; he, in all the sway
Of laws best order'd, cuts out his own way
In cities shining with delicious dames,
And takes his choice of all those striving flames;
High happiness and riches, like his train,
Follow his fortunes, with delights that reign
In all their princes; glory invests his sons;
His daughters, with their crown'd selections
Of all the city, frolic through the meads,
And every one her call'd-for dances treads
Along the soft-flow'r of the claver-grass.
All this, with all those, ever comes to pass,
That thy love blesses, Goddess full of grace,
And treasurous Angel t' all the human race.

   Hail, then, Great Mother of the Deified Kind,
Wife to the cope of stars! Sustain a mind
Propitious to me for my praise, and give
(Answering my mind) my vows fit means to live.

---

[26] *Claver-grass.*—Mr. Singer has printed *clover.* I retain the old orthography, though Halliwell says it is only a North-country provincialism for *clover.*

TO THE SUN.

THE radiant Sun's divine renown diffuse,
Jove's daughter, great Calliope, my Muse
Whom ox-ey'd Euryphaëssa gave birth
To the bright Seed of starry Heaven and Earth.
For the far-fam'd Hyperion took to wife 5
His sister Euryphaëssa, that life
Of his high race gave to these lovely three :
Aurora, with the rosy-wrists ; and She
That owns th' enamouring tresses, the bright Moon ;
Together with the never-wearied Sun, 10
Who (his horse mounting) gives both mortals light
And all th' Immortals. Even to horror, bright
A blaze burns from his golden burgonet,
Which to behold exceeds the sharpest set
Of any eye's intention, beams so clear 15
It all ways pours abroad. The glorious cheer
Of his far-shining face up to his crown
Casts circular radiance, that comes streaming down
About his temples, his bright cheeks, and all,
Retaining the refulgence of their fall. 20
About his bosom flows so fine a weed
As doth the thinness of the wind exceed
In rich context ; beneath whose deep folds fly
His masculine horses round about the sky,
Till in this hemisphere he renders stay 25
T' his gold-yok'd coach and coursers ; and his way,

---

[13] *Burgonet*—generally spelt *burganet*, a species of helmet.

Let down by heaven, the heavenly coachman makes
Down to the ocean, where his rest he takes.
  My salutations then, fair King, receive,
And in propitious returns relieve   30
My life with mind-fit means; and then from thee,
And all the race of complete Deity,
My song shall celebrate those half-god States,
That yet sad death's condition circulates,
And whose brave acts the Gods show men that they   35
As brave may aim at, since they can but die.

TO THE MOON.

THE Moon, now, Muses, teach me to resound,
   Whose wide wings measure such a world of
      ground;
Jove's daughter, deck'd with the mellifluous tongue,
And seen in all the sacred art of song.
Whose deathless brows when she from heaven displays,
All earth she wraps up in her orient rays.   6
A heaven of ornament in earth is rais'd
When her beams rise. The subtle air is sais'd
Of delicate splendour from her crown of gold.
And when her silver bosom is extoll'd,   10
Wash'd in the ocean, in day's equall'd noon
Is midnight seated; but when she puts on
Her far-off-sprinkling-lustre evening weeds,
(The month in two cut; her high-breasted steeds

---

⁸ *Sais'd*—seised, put in possession.

Man'd all with curl'd **flames,** put in coach and **all,** 15
Her huge orb fill'd,) **her** whole **trims then exhale**
Unspeakable splendours from the glorious sky.
And out of that state mortal men imply
Many predictions. **And** with her then,
In love mix'd, lay the King of Gods and men; 20
By whom made fruitful, she Pandea bore,
And added her state to th' Immortal Store.
Hail, Queen, **and** Goddess, th' ivory-wristed **Moon**
Divine, prompt, fair-hair'd! With thy grace begun,
My Muse shall forth, and celebrate the praise 25
Of men whose states the Deities did raise
To semi-deities; whose **deeds t' endless date**
Muse-lov'd and sweet-sung poets celebrate.

TO CASTOR AND POLLUX.

JOVE'S fair Sons, father'd by th' Oebalian king,
Muses well-worth-all men's beholdings, sing!
The dear birth that bright-ankl'd Leda bore;
Horse-taming **Castor,** and, the conqueror
Of tooth-tongu'd **Momus,** Pollux; whom beneath 5
Steep-brow'd Taygetus she gave half-god breath,
In love mix'd with the black-clouds King **of** Heaven;
Who, both of men and ships, being tempest driven,
When Winter's wrathful empire is in force
Upon th' implacable seas, preserve the course. 10
For when the gusts begin, if near the shore,
The seamen leave their ship, and, evermore
Bearing two milk-white lambs aboard, they now

Kill them ashore, and to Jove's issue vow,
When though their ship, in height of all the roar
The winds and waves confound, can live no more
In all their hopes, then suddenly appear
Jove's saving Sons, who both their bodies bear
'Twixt yellow wings down from the sparkling pole,
Who straight the rage of those rude winds control,
And all the high-waves couch into the breast
Of th' hoary seas. All which sweet signs of rest
To seamen's labours their glad souls conceive,
And end to all their irksome grievance give.
  So, once more, to the swift-horse-riding race
Of royal Tyndarus, eternal grace!

TO MEN OF HOSPITALITY.

REVERENCE a man with use propitious
That hospitable rites wants; and a house
(You of this city with the seat of state
To ox-ey'd Juno vow'd) yet situate
Near Pluto's region. At the extreme base
Of whose so high-hair'd city, from the race
Of blue-wav'd Hebrus lovely fluent, grac'd
With Jove's begetting, you divine cups taste.

CERTAIN EPIGRAMS AND OTHER POEMS OF HOMER.

TO CUMA.

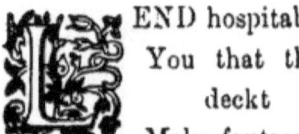END hospitable rites and house-respect,
  You that the virgin with the fair eyes
    deckt
  Make fautress of your stately-seated town,
At foot of Sardes, with the high-hair'd crown,
Inhabiting rich Cuma; where ye taste
Of Hermus' heavenly fluent, all embrac'd
By curl'd-head whirlpits; and whose waters move
From the divine seed of immortal Jove.

IN HIS RETURN TO CUMA.

WIFTLY my feet sustain me to the town,
  Where men inhabit whom due honours
    crown,
Whose minds with free-given faculties are mov'd,
And whose grave counsels best of best approv'd.

UPON THE SEPULCHRE OF MIDUS,

CUT IN BRASS, IN THE FIGURE OF A VIRGIN.

A MAID of brass I am, infixed here
T' eternize honest Midus' sepulchre ;
And while the stream her fluent seed receives,
And steep trees curl their verdant brows with leaves,
While Phœbus rais'd above the earth gives sight, 5
And th' humorous Moon takes lustre from his light,
While floods bear waves, and seas shall wash the shore,
At this his sepulchre, whom all deplore,
I'll constantly abide ; all passers by
Informing, " Here doth honest Midus lie." 10

⁶ *Humorous*—moist.

CUMA.

REFUSING HIS OFFER TO ETERNIZE THEIR STATE, THOUGH BROUGHT THITHER BY THE MUSES.

TO what fate hath Father Jove given o'er
My friendless life, born ever to be poor!
While in my infant state he pleas'd to save me,
Milk on my reverend mother's knees he gave me,
In delicate and curious nursery ; 5
Æolian Smyrna, seated near the sea,
(Of glorious empire, and whose bright sides
Sacred Meletus' silver current glides,)

Being native sent to me. Which, in the force
Of far-past time, the breakers of wild horse,   10
Phriconia's noble nation, girt with tow'rs;
Whose youth in fight put on with fiery pow'rs.
From hence, the Muse-maids, Jove's illustrous Seed,
Impelling me, I made impetuous speed,
And went with them **to** Cuma, with intent   15
T' eternize all the sacred continent
And state of Cuma. They, in proud ascent
From off their bench, refus'd with usage **fierce**
The sacred voice **which I aver** is verse.
Their follies, yet, **and madness borne by me,**   20
Shall by some pow'r **be** thought **on** futurely,
To wreak of him whoever, **whose** tongue sought
With false impair my fall. **What** fate God brought
Upon my birth I'll bear with any pain,
But undeserv'd defame unfelt sustain.   25
Nor feels my person (dear to me though poor)
Any great lust to linger any more
In Cuma's holy highways; but my mind
(No thought impair'd, for cares of any kind
Borne in my body) rather vows to try   30
The influence of any other sky,
And spirits of people bred **in any land**
Of ne'er so slender and obscure command.

AN ASSAY OF HIS BEGUN ILIADS.

ILION, and all the brave-horse-breeding soil,
Dardania, I sing; that many a toil
Impos'd upon the mighty Grecian pow'rs,
Who were of Mars the manly servitours.

TO THESTOR'S SON,*

INQUISITIVE OF HOMER ABOUT THE CAUSES OF THINGS.

THESTORIDES! of all the skills unknown
To errant mortals, there remains not one
Of more inscrutable affair to find
Than is the true state of a human mind.

TO NEPTUNE.

HEAR, pow'rful Neptune, that shak'st earth
in ire,
King of the great green, where dance all
the quire

---

* Homer intimated, in this his answer to Thestorides, a will to have him learn the knowledge of himself, before he inquired so curiously the causes of other things. And from hence had the great peripatetic, Themistius, his most grave epiphoneme, *Anima quæ seipsum ignorat, quid sciret ipsa de aliis?* And, therefore, according to Aristotle, advises all philosophical students to begin with that study.—CHAPMAN.

Of fair-hair'd Helicon; give **prosperous** gales,
And good pass, **to** these guiders of our sails,
Their voyage rend'ring happily directed,
And their return with no ill fate affected.
Grant likewise at rough Mimas' lowest roots,
Whose strength **up to** her tops prærupt rocks shoots,
My passage safe arrival; and that I
My bashful disposition may apply
To pious men, and wreak myself upon
The man **whose** verbal circumvention
In me did wrong **t'** hospitious Jove's whole **state**,
And th' hospitable table **violate**.

TO THE CITY ERYTHRÆA.

WORSHIPFUL Earth, Giver of all things
        good!
    Giver of even felicity; whose flood
The mind all-over steeps in honeydew;
That to some men dost infinite kindness shew,
To others that despise thee art a shrew,
And **giv'st them** gamester's galls; who, once their main
Lost with **an** ill chance, **fare** like abjects slain.

TO MARINERS.

YE wave-trod watermen, as ill as she
    That all the earth in infelicity
    Of rapine plunges; who upon your fare
As sterv'd-like-ravenous as cormorants are;

The lives ye lead, but in the worst degree,
Not to be envied more than misery;
Take shame, and fear the indignation
Of Him that thunders from the highest throne,
Hospitious Jove, who, at the back, prepares
Pains of abhorr'd effect of him that dares
The pieties break of his hospitious squares.

THE PINE.

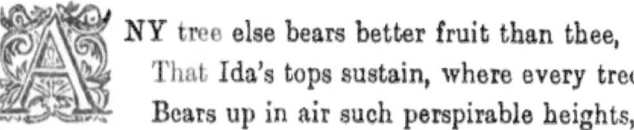NY tree else bears better fruit than thee,
That Ida's tops sustain, where every tree
Bears up in air such perspirable heights,
And in which caves and sinuous receipts
Creep in such great abundance. For about
Thy roots, that ever all thy fruits put out,
As nourish'd by them, equal with thy fruits,
Pour Mars's iron-mines their accurs'd pursuits.
So that when any earth-encroaching man,
Of all the martial brood Cebrenian,
Plead need of iron, they are certain still
About thy roots to satiate every will.

TO GLAUCUS,

WHO WAS SO MISERABLY SPARING THAT HE FEARED ALL MEN'S ACCESS TO HIM.

LAUCUS! though **wise** enough, yet one
    word more
      Let my advice add to thy wisdom's store,
For 'twill be better **so**: Before thy door
Give still thy mastiffs meat, that will be sure
To lie there, therefore, still, and not endure   5
(With waylaid ears) the softest foot can fall,
But men and beasts make fly thee **and** thy **stall**.

AGAINST THE SAMIAN MINISTRESS,
OR NUN.

EAR me, O Goddess, that invoke thine ear,
    Thou that dost feed and form the youthful
      year,
And grant that this dame may the loves refuse,
And beds, of young men, and affect to **use**
Humans whose temples hoary **hairs** distain,   5
Whose pow'rs are passing coy, whose wills would fain.

WRITTEN ON THE COUNCIL CHAMBER.

F men, sons are the crowns of cities' towr's;
 Of pastures, horse are the most beauteous
   flow'rs;
Of seas, ships are the grace; and money still
With trains and titles doth the family fill.
But royal counsellors, in council set,   5
Are ornaments past all, as clearly great
As houses are that shining fires enfold,
Superior far to houses nak'd and cold.

THE FURNACE CALLED IN TO SING
BY POTTERS.

F ye deal freely, O my fiery friends,
  As ye assure, I'll sing, and serve your ends.
  Pallas, vouchsafe thou here invok'd access,
Impose thy hand upon this Forge, and bless
All cups these artists earn so, that they may   5
Look black still with their depth, and every way
Give all their vessels a most sacred sale.
Make all well-burn'd; and estimation call
Up to their prices. Let them market well,
And in all highways in abundance sell.   10

Till riches to their utmost wish arise,
And, as thou mak'st them rich, so make me wise.
  But if ye now turn all to impudence,
And think to pay with lies my patience,
Then will I summon 'gainst your Furnace all   15
Hell's harmfull'st spirits; Maragus I'll call,
Sabactes, Asbett, and Omadamus,
Who ills against your art innumerous
Excogitates, supplies, and multiplies.
Come, Pallas, then, and all command to rise,   20
Infesting forge and house with fire, till all
Tumble together, and to ashes fall,
These potters selves dissolv'd in tears as small.
And as a horse-cheek chides his foaming bit,
So let this Forge murmur in fire and flit,   25
And all this stuff to ashy ruins run.
And thou, O Circe, daughter of the Sun,
Great-many-poison-mixer, come, and pour
Thy cruell'st poisons on this Potters' floor,
Shivering their vessels; and themselves affect   30
With all the mischiefs possible to direct
'Gainst all their beings, urg'd by all thy fiends.
Let Chiron likewise come; and all those friends
(The Centaurs) that Alcides' fingers fled,
And all the rest too that his hand strook dead,   35
(Their ghosts excited) come, and macerate
These earthen men; and yet with further fate
Affect their Furnace; all their tear-burst eyes
Seeing and mourning for their miseries,
While I look on, and laugh their blasted art   40
And them to ruin. Lastly, if apart

Any lies lurking, and sees yet, his face
Into a coal let th' angry fire embrace,
That all may learn by them, in all their lust,
To dare deeds great, to see them great and just.   45

EIRESIONE, OR, THE OLIVE BRANCH.

HE turrets of a man of infinite might,
    Of infinite action, substance infinite,
    We make access to; whose whole being rebounds
From earth to heaven, and nought but bliss resounds.
Give entry then, ye doors; more riches yet   5
Shall enter with me; all the Graces met
In joy of their fruition, perfect peace
Confirming all; all crown'd with such increase,
That every empty vessel in your house
May stand replete with all things precious;   10
Elaborate Ceres may your larders fill
With all dear delicates, and serve in still;
May for your son a wife make wish'd approach
Into your tow'rs, and rapt in in her coach
With strong-kneed mules; may yet her state prove staid,
With honour'd housewiferies; her fair hand laid   16
To artful loomworks; and her nak'd feet tread
The gum of amber to a golden bead.
  But I'll return; return, and yet not press
Your bounties now assay'd with oft access,   20
Once a year only, as the swallow prates
Before the wealthy Spring's wide open gates.

132 EPIGRAMS.

Meantime **I stand at** yours, **nor** purpose stay
More time t' entreat. Give, **or not give, away**
My feet shall bear me, that did never come
With any thought to make **your** house my home.

25

TO CERTAIN FISHER BOYS

PLEASING HIM WITH INGENIOUS RIDDLES.

YET **from the** bloods even of your self-like sires
Are you descended, that could make **ye** heirs
To no huge hoards of **coin,** nor leave ye able
To feed flocks of innumerable **rabble.**

THE END OF ALL THE ENDLESS WORKS OF HOMER.

THE *work that I was born to do is done!*
Glory to Him that the conclusion
Makes the beginning of my life; and never
Let me be said to live, till I live ever.
  Where's the outliving of my fortunes then,   5
Ye errant vapours of Fame's Lernean fen,
That, like possess'd storms, blast all not in herd
With your abhorr'd heads; who, because cashier'd
By men for monsters, think men monsters all,
That are not of your pied Hood and your Hall,   10
When you are nothing but the scum of things,
And must be cast off; drones, that have no stings;
Nor any more soul than a stone hath wings?
  Avaunt, ye hags! Your hates and scandals are
The crowns and comforts of a good man's care;   15
By whose impartial perpendicular,
All is extuberance, and excretion all,
That you your ornaments and glories call.
Your wry mouths censure right! Your blister'd tongues,
That lick but itches! And whose ulcerous lungs   20
Come up at all things permanent and sound!
O you, like flies in dregs, in humours drown'd!
Your loves, like atoms, lost in gloomy air,
I would not retrieve with a wither'd hair.

Hate, and cast still your stings then, for your kisses 25
Betray but truth, and your applauds are hisses.
  To see our supercilious wizards frown,
Their facts fall'n like fogs, and coming down,
Stinking the sun out, makes me shine the more;
And like a check'd flood bear above the shore, 30
That their profane opinions fain would set
To what they see not, know not, nor can let.
Yet then our learn'd men with their torrents come,
Roaring from their forc'd hills, all crown'd with foam,
That one not taught like them, should learn to know 35
Their Greek roots, and from thence the groves that grow.
Casting such rich shades from great HOMER'S wings,
That first and last command the Muses' springs.
Though he's best scholar, that, through pains and vows
Made his own master only, all things knows. 40
Nor pleads my poor skill form, or learned place,
But dauntless labour, constant prayer, and grace.
And what's all their skill, but vast varied reading?
As if broad-beaten highways had the leading
To Truth's abstract, and narrow path, and pit: 45
Found in no walk of any worldly wit.
And without Truth, all's only sleight of hand,
Or our law-learning in a foreign land,
Embroidery spent on cobwebs, braggart show
Of men that all things learn, and nothing know. 50
For ostentation humble Truth still flies,
And all confederate fashionists defies.
And as some sharp-brow'd doctor, English born,
In much learn'd Latin idioms can adorn
A verse with rare attractions, yet become 55
His English Muse like an Arachnean loom,

Wrought spite of Pallas, and therein bewrays
More tongue than truth, begs, and adopts his bays;
So Ostentation, be he never so
Larded with labour to suborn his show, 60
Shall sooth within him but a bastard soul,
No more heaven heiring than, Earth's son, the mole.
But as in dead calms emptiest smokes arise,
Uncheck'd and free, up straight into the skies;
So drowsy Peace, that in her humour sleeps 65
All she affects, let such rise while she sleeps.
Many, and most men, have of wealth least store,
But none the gracious shame that fits the poor.
So most learn'd men enough are ignorant,
But few the grace have to confess their want, 70
Till lives and learnings come concomitant.
Far from men's knowledges their lives'-acts flow;
Vainglorious acts then vain prove all they know.
As night the life-inclining stars best shows,
So lives obscure the starriest souls disclose. 75

   For me, let just men judge by what I show
In acts expos'd how much I err or know;
And let not envy make all worse than nought,
With her mere headstrong and quite brainless thought,
Others, for doing nothing, giving all, 80
And bounding all worth in her bursten gall.

   GOD *and my dear* REDEEMER *rescue me*
From men's immane and mad impiety,
And by my life and soul (sole known to Them)
Make me of palm, or yew, an anadem. 85
And so my sole GOD, *the* THRICE-SACRED TRINE,
Bear all th' ascription of all me and mine.

Supplico tibi, Domine, Pater, **et Dux rationis** nostræ, ut nostræ nobilitatis recordemur **quâ** Tu nos ornasti; et ut Tu nobis præstó sis, ut iis **qui per** sese moventur; ut et à corporis contagio, brutorumque affectuum, repurgemur, eosque superemus, atque regamus, et, sicut decet, **pro** instrumentis iis utamur. Deinde, ut nobis ad-**jumento** sis, ad accuratam rationis nostræ correctionem, et conjunctionem cum iis qui verè sunt per lucem veritatis. Et tertiùm, Salvatori supplex oro, ut ab oculis animorum nostrorum, caliginem prorsus abstergas, ut norimus bene qui Deus, aut mortalis, habendus. *Amen.*

Sine honore vicam, nulloque numero ero.

FINIS.

THE GEORGICS OF HESIOD.

THE
GEORGICKS
OF
HESIOD,

By GEORGE CHAPMAN ;

TRANSLATED ELABORATELY

out of the Greek :

Containing Doctrine of Hufbandrie, Moralitie,
and Pietie; with a perpetuall Calendar of Good
and Bad Daies; Not fuperftitious, but neceffarie
(as farre as naturall Caufes compell) for all
*Men to obferue, and difference in fol-
lowing their affaires.*

Nec caret vmbra Deo.

LONDON,
Printed by *H. L.* for *Miles Partrich*, and are to be folde
at his Shop neare Saint *Dunftans* Church in
Fleet ftreet. 1618.

TO THE MOST NOBLE COMBINER OF LEARNING
AND HONOUR,

SIR FRANCIS BACON, KNIGHT,

LORD HIGH CHANCELLOR OF ENGLAND, ETC.

NCIENT wisdom being so worthily eternised by the now-renewed instance of it in your Lordship; and this ancient Author, one of the most authentic for all wisdom crowned with justice and piety; to what sea owe these poor streams their tribute, but to your Lordship's ocean? The rather, since others of the like antiquity, in my Translation of Homer, teach these their way, and add comfort to their courses, by having received right cheerful countenance and approbation from your Lordship's most grave and honoured predecessor.

All judgments of this season (savouring anything the truth) preferring, to the wisdom of all other nations, these most wise, learned, and circularly-spoken Grecians. According to that of the poet:—

> *Graiis ingenium, Graiis dedit ore rotundo*
> *Musa loqui.*

And why may not this Roman elogy of the *Graians* extend in praiseful intention (by way of prophetic poesy) to *Graies-Inne* wits and orators? Or if the allusion (or petition of the principle) beg with too broad a licence in the general, yet serious truth, for the particular, may most worthily apply it to your Lordship's truly Greek inspiration, and absolutely Attic elocution. Whose all-acknowledged faculty hath banished flattery therein even from the Court; much more from my country and more-than-upland simplicity. Nor were those Greeks so circular in their elegant utterance, but their inward judgments and learnings were as round and solid; their solidity proved in their eternity; and their eternity propagated by love of all virtue and integrity;—that love being the only parent and argument of all truth, in any wisdom or learning, without which all is sophisticate and adulterate, howsoever painted and splinted with degrees and languages. Your Lordship's "*Advancement of Learning*," then, well showing your love to it, and in it, being true, to all true goodness, your learning, strengthening that love, must needs be solid and eternal. This ἴστωρ φώς,* therefore, expressed in this Author, is used here as if prophesied by him then, now to take life in your Lordship, whose life is chief soul and essence to all knowledge and virtue; so few there are that live now combining honour and learning. This time resembling the terrible time whereof this poet prophesied; to which he desired he might not live, since not a Grace would then smile on any pious or worthy; all greatness much more gracing impostors

---

* Vir verè (seu clarè) sciens; aut illustris Judex, vel procul videns Arbiter, quia eos acutos visu, seu gnaros esse oporteat rei de quâ agitur. CHAPMAN.

than men truly desertful. The worse depraving the better; and that so frontlessly, that shame and justice should fly the earth for them. To shame which ignorant barbarism now emboldened, let your Lordship's learned humanity prove nothing the less gracious to Virtue for the community of Vice's graces; but shine much the more clear on her for those clouds that eclipse her; no lustre being so sun-like as that which passeth above all clouds unseen, over fields, turrets, and temples, and breaks out, in free beams, on some humblest cottage. In whose like Jove himself hath been feasted; and wherein your Lordship may find more honour than in the fretted roofs of the mighty. To which honour, oftentimes, nothing more conduceth than noble acceptance of most humble presentments. On this nobility in your Lordship my prostrate humility relying, I rest ever submitted, in all simple and hearty vows,

Your Honour's most truly,
And freely devoted,
GEORGE CHAPMAN.

OF HESIODUS.

ESIODUS, surnamed Ascræus, was one, as of the most ancient Greek poets, so one of the purest and pressest writers. He lived in the latter time of Homer, and was surnamed Ascræus, of Ascra, a town in Helicon; in which was built a temple sacred to the Muses; whose priest Hesiodus was consecrate; whom Virgil, among so many writers of Georgics, only imitated, professing it in this:

Ascræumque cano Romana per oppida carmen, Ἔργα καὶ Ἡμέραι. Nor is there any doubt (saith Mel.) *quin idem Virgilius initio Georgicorum hanc inscriptionem expresserit hoc versu:* 'Quid facit lætas segetes, quo sidere terram,' &c. His authority was such amongst the ancients, that his verses were commonly learned as *axioms* or *oracles*, all teaching good life and humanity; which though never so profitable for men's now readings, yet had they rather (saith Isocrates) consume their times still in their own follies, than be any time conversant in these precepts of wisdom; of which (with Homer) he was first father, whose interpreters were all the succeeding philosophers—not Aristotle himself excepted:—who before Thales, Solon, Pittacus, Socrates, Plato, &c. writ of life, of manners, of God, of nature, of the stars, and general state of the universe. Nor are his writings the less worthy, that Poesy informed them, but of so much the more dignity and eternity. Not Thales, nor Anaxagoras, (as Aristotle ingenuously confesseth,) having profited the world so much, with all their writings, as Homer's one Ulysses or Nestor. And sooner shall all the atoms of Epicurus sustain division; the fire of Heraclitus be utterly quenched; the water that Thales extols so much be exhausted; the spirit of Anaximenes vanish; the discord of Empedocles be reconciled, and all dissolved to nothing; before by their most celebrated faculties they do the world so much profit, for all human instruction, as this one work of Hesiodus! Here being no dwelling on any one subject but of all human affairs instructively concluded.

TO MY WORTHY FRIEND MR. GEORGE CHAPMAN, AND HIS TRANSLATED HESIOD.

HAPMAN, we find, by thy past-prized fraught,
What wealth thou dost upon this land confer,
Th' old Grecian prophets hither that has brought,
Of their full words the true interpreter;
And by thy travell strongly hast exprest   5
The large dimensions of the English tongue,
Delivering them so well, the first and best
That to the world in numbers ever sung.
Thou hast unlock'd the treasury wherein
All art and knowledge have so long been hidden;   10
Which, till the graceful Muses did begin
Here to inhabit, was to us forbidden.
 In blest Elysium, (in a place most fit)
Under that tree due to the Delphian God,
Musæus and that Iliad Singer sit,   15
And near to them that noble Hesiod,
Smoothing their rugged foreheads; and do smile,
After so many hundred years, to see
Their Poems read in this far western isle,

Translated from their ancient Greek by thee; [20]
Each his good Genius whispering in his ear,
That with so lucky and auspicious fate
Did still attend them whilst they living were,
And gave their verses such a lasting date.
    Where, slightly passing by the Thespian spring, [25]
Many long after did but only sup;
Nature, then fruitful, forth these men did bring,
To fetch deep roses from Jove's plenteous cup.
    In thy free labours, friend, then rest content,
Fear not Detraction, neither fawn on Praise; [30]
When idle Censure all her force hath spent,
Knowledge can crown herself with her own bays.
Their lines that have so many lives outworn,
Clearly expounded, shall base Envy scorn.

MICHAEL DRAYTON.

TO MY WORTHY AND HONOURED FRIEND
MR. GEORGE CHAPMAN,
ON HIS TRANSLATION OF HESIOD'S WORKS AND DAYS.

WHOSE work could this be, CHAPMAN, to refine
Old HESIOD's ore, and give it us, but thine,
Who had'st before wrought in rich
HOMER's mine?

What treasure hast thou brought us! and what store
Still, still, dost thou arrive with at our shore,　　　5
To make thy honour and our wealth the more!

If all the vulgar tongues that speak this day
Were ask'd of thy discoveries, they must say,
To the Greek coast thine only knew the way.

Such passage hast thou found, such returns made,　　10
As, now of all men, it is called thy trade;
And who make thither else rob, or invade!

BEN JONSON

THE GEORGICS OF HESIOD.

BY GEORGE CHAPMAN.

THE FIRST BOOK.[a]

USES! that, out of your Pierian state,
All worth in sacred numbers celebrate,
Use[b] here your faculties so much renown'd,
To sing your Sire;[c] and him in hymns[d]
  resound
By whom all humans, that to death are bound,   5
Are bound together; both the great in fame,[e]
And men whose poor fates fit them with no name,[f]
Noble,[g] and base;[h] great Jove's will orders all;
For he with ease extols, with ease lets fall;

[a] To approve my difference from the vulgar and verbal exposition, and other amplifications fit and necessary for the true rendering and illustration of my author, I am enforced to annex some words of the original to my other annotations.
3 [b] Δεῦτε, *huc agite.*
4 [c] Jove.
4 [d] Ὑμνείουσαι, *hymnis decantantes.*
6 [e] Φατός, *de quo magna fama est.*
7 [f] Ἄφατος, *non dicendus, incelebris.*
8 [g] Ῥητός, *honoratus, nobilis.*
8 [h] Ἄρρητος, *ignobilis, ad nullam functionem seu dignitatem assumptus.*

Eas'ly diminisheth the most in grace,   10
And lifts the most obscure to loftiest place;
Eas'ly sets straight¹ the quite shrunk up together,ᵏ
And makes the most elated¹ beauty wither;
And **this** is Jove, that breaks his voice so high
In horrid sounds, and dwells above the sky.   15

  Hear, then, O Jove, that dost both see and hear,
And, for thy justice' sake, be orderer
To these just precepts,ᵐ that in prophecyⁿ
I use, to teach my brother piety.

  Not one Contention on the earth there reigns   20
To raise men's fortunes and peculiar gains,
But two. The one the **knowing man** approves;
The otherº hate should force from human loves,
Since it derives our reasonable kind,
In twoᵖ parts parting man's united mind;   25
And is so harmful, for pernicious War
It feeds, and bites at every Civil Jar;
Which no manᑫ loves, but strong Necessity
Doth this Contention, as his plague, imply
By Heaven's hid counsels. Th' other Strife black Night
Begat before; which Jove, that in the light   31

  ¹² ¹ Ἰθύς, *rectus, erectus, non tortuosus.* Metaph.
  ¹² ᵏ Σκολιὸς, *tortuosus, incurvus.*
  ¹³ ¹ Ἀγήνορα κάρφει, *superbum, seu florentem, facit ut deflorescat.*
  ¹⁸ ᵐ Δίκῃ δ' ἰθύνε θέμιστας, *judicia vel vera præcepta de moribus, seu pietate.*
  ¹⁸ ⁿ Μυθέομαι, *vaticinor.*
  ²³ º Ἐπιμωμητὸς, *reprehensione, et derisione, dignus.*
  ²⁵ ᵖ Ἄνδιχα, *duas partes.*
  ²⁸ ᑫ Οὔτις. He says no man loves this war *per se*, but *per accidens;* because men cannot discern from things truly worthy of their loves those that falsely pretend worth and retain none; which he ascribes to some secret counsel of Jove, that, for plague to their impieties, strikes blind their understandings.

Of all the stars dwells, and, though thron'd aloft,
Of each man weighs yet both the work and thought,
Put in the roots of earth; from whose womb grow
Men's needful means to pay the debt they owe   35
To life and living. And this Strife is far
More fit for men, and much the sprightlier;
For he in whose hands^r lives no love of art,
Nor virtuous industry, yet plucks up heart,
And falls to work for living. Any one,   40
Never so stupid and so base a drone,
Seeing a rich man haste to sow, and plant,
And guide his house well, feels with shame his want,
And labours like him. And this Strife is good.
When Strife for riches warms and fires the blood,   45
The neighbour doth the neighbour emulate,^s
The potter doth the potter's profit hate,
The smith the smith with spleen inveterate,^t
Beggar maligns the beggar for good done,
And the musician the musician.   50
    This Strife, O Perses, see remember'd still;
But fly Contention that insults on th' ill^u
Of other men, and from thy work doth draw
To be a well-seen man in works of law.
Nor to those courts afford affected ear;   55
For he that hath not, for the entire year,

³⁸ ^r'Απάλαμνος, *cujus manibus nulla ars, nulla sedulitas, inest.*
  ⁴⁶ ^s Ζηλοῖ. He shows artizans' emulations for *riches*, and approves that kind of contention. Notwithstanding Plato in *Lysias*, Aristotle in the 5. of his *Pol.* and 2. of his *Rhetor.* and Galen, refer this strife to the first harmful discord, yet Plutarch takes our author's part, and ascribes it to the virtuous contention.
  ⁴⁸ ^t Κοτέω, *æstuo irâ quam diu pressi in pectore.*
  ⁵² ^u"Ερις κακόχαρτος, *alienis insultans calamitatibus contentio;* which he calls their going to law.

Enough laid up beforehand, little need
Hath to take care those factious courts to feed
With what earth bears, and Ceres doth bestow.
With which when thou are satiate, nor dost know   60
What to do with it, then to these wars go
For others' goods; but see no more spent so
Of thine hereafter. Let ourselves decide,
With dooms direct, all differences implied
In our affairs; and, what is ratified   65
By Jove's will to be ours, account our own;
For that thrives ever best. Our discord, grown
For what did from our father's bounty fall,
We ended lately, and shared freely all;   69
When thou much more than thine hadst ravish'd home,
With which thou mad'st proud,ˣ and didst overcome,
With partial affection to thy cause,
Those gift-devouring kings that sway our laws,
Who would have still retain'd us in their powers,
And given by their dooms what was freely ours.   75
  O fools, that all things into judgment call,
Yet know not how muchʸ half is more than all!
Nor how the mean life is the firmest still,
Nor of the mallow and the daffodill

---

⁷¹ ˣ Μέγα κυδαίνων, *valde gloriosos reddens.* Βασιλῆας δωροφάγους, *reges donivoros.*

⁷⁷ ʸ Πλέον ἥμισυ παντός, *dimidium plus* **toto.** He commends the mean, and reproves those kings or judges that are too indulgent to their covetous and glorious appetites, from the frugal and competent life declining *ad πλεονεξίαν*, i. e. *ad plus habendi aviditatem inexhaustam.* Showing how ignorant they are; that the virtue of justice and mediocrity is to be preferred to injustice and insatiate avarice. By ἥμισυ he understands *medium inter lucrum et damnum*, which mean is more profitable and notable than παντός, i. e. *toto quo et sua pars retinetur, et alterius ad se pertrahitur.*

How great a good the little meals contain. 80
But God hath hid from men the healthful mean;
For otherwise a man might heap, and play,
Enough to serve the whole year in a day,
And straight his draught-tree hang up in the smoke,
Nor more his labouring mules nor oxen yoke. 85
    But Jove man's knowledge of his best bereav'd,
Conceiving anger, since he was deceiv'd
By that same wisdom-wresting[z] Japhet's son;
For which all ill all earth did overrun.
For Jove close keeping in a hollow cave 90
His holy fire, to serve the use of man,
Prometheus stole it, by his human sleight,
From him that hath of all heaven's wit the height;
For which He angry, thus to him began
The Cloud-assembler: "Thou most crafty man, 95
That joy'st to steal my fire, deceiving me,
Shalt feel that joy the greater grief to thee,
And therein plague thy universal race;
To whom I'll give a pleasing ill, in place
Of that good fire, and all shall be so vain 100
To place their pleasure in embracing pain."
    Thus spake and laugh'd of Gods and Men the Sire,
And straight enjoin'd the famous God of Fire

---

[88] [z] 'Αγκυλομήτης, he calls Prometheus, i. e. *qui obliqua agitat consilia;* who wrests that wisdom, which God hath given him to use to his glory, to his own ends; which is cause to all the miseries men suffer, and of all their impious actions that deserve them. Jove's Fire signifies Truth, which Prometheus stealing, figures learned men's over-subtle abuse of divine knowledge, wresting it in false expositions to their own objects, thereby to inspire and puff up their own profane earth, intending their corporeal parts, and the irreligious delights of them. But, for the mythology of this, read my Lord Chancellor's book, *De Sapientiâ Veterum,* cap. 26, being infinitely better.

To mingle, instantly, with water earth;
The voice and vigour of **a human** birth[a]   105
Imposing in it, and so fair a **face**
As match'd th' Immortal Goddesses in grace,
Her form presenting a most lovely maid.
Then on Minerva his command he laid
To make her work, and wield the witty loom.   110
And, for her beauty, such as might become
The golden Venus, he commanded her
Upon her brows **and** countenance to confer
Her own bewitchings; stuffing all her breast
With wild[b] desires incapable of rest,   115
And cares that feed to all satiety
All human lineaments.   The crafty Spy
And Messenger of Godheads, Mercury,
He charg'd t' inform her with a dogged[c] mind,
And thievish manners.   All as he design'd   120
Was put in act.   A creature straight had frame
Like to a virgin, mild and full of shame;
Which Jove's suggestion made the Both-foot-lame
Form so deceitfully, and all of earth
To forge the living matter of her birth.   125
Grey-eyed Minerva put her girdle on,
And show'd how loose parts, well composed, shone.
The deified Graces, and the **Dame**[d] **that sets**
Sweet words in chief form, golden carquenets
Embrac'd her neck withal.   The fair-hair'd Hours   130

105 a Jove's creation of a woman.
115 b Καὶ πόθον. An unwearied and wanton desire to exceed others, or an insatiate longing to be loved of all. Γυιοκόρος, membra ad satietatem usque depascens. Μελεδώνας, cares, or meditations of voluptuous satisfactions.
119 c Κύνεόν τε νόον, caninam mentem, vel impudentem, καὶ ἐπίκλοπον ἦθος, furaces mores.
128 d Πειθώ, or Suada, Goddess of persuasion, **or** eloquence.

Her gracious temples crown'd with fresh spring-flowers.
But of all these, employ'd in several place,
Pallas gave order° the impulsive grace.
Her bosom Hermes, the great God of spies,
With subtle fashions fill'd, fair words, and lies; 135
Jove prompting still. But all the voice ͟ f she us'd
The vocal herald of the Gods infus'd,
And call'd her name Pandora, since on her
The Gods did all their several gifts confer;
Who made her such, in every moving strain, 140
To be the bane of curious-minded men.

    Her harmful and inevitable frame
At all parts perfect, Jove dismiss'd the Dame
To Epimetheus, in his herald's guide,
With all the God's plagues in a box beside. 145
Nor Epimetheus kept one word in store
Of what Prometheus had advised before,
Which was: That Jove should fasten on his hand
No gift at all, but be his while withstand,
And back return it, lest with instant ill 150
To mortal men he all the world did fill.
But he first took the gift, and after griev'd.ᵍ

    [133] e 'Εφήρμοσε, *impetu inspirabat*, gave special force to all her attractions; which he says Pallas did, to show that to all beauty wisdom and discreet behaviour give the chief excitement.
    [136] f Φωνήν. Her voice the vocal or high-spoken herald of the gods imposed; all fair women affecting to be furthest heard, as well as most seen.
    [152] g 'Ενόησε. When he had received and tried the ill, he knew it was ill, and grieved; but then was so infected with affection to it, that he could not reform nor refine it. For man's corporeal part, which is figured in Epimetheus, signifying the inconsiderate and headlong force of affection, not obeying his reasonable part or soul, nor using foresight fit for the prevention of ill, which is figured in Prometheus, he is deceived with a false shadow of pleasure; for the substantial

For first the families of mortals liv'd
Without and free from ill ; **harsh labour** then,
Nor sickness, hasting **timeless** age on men,   155
Their hard and wretched tasks impos'd on them
For many **years** ; but now a violent stream
Of all afflictions in an instant came,
And quench'd life's light that shin'd before in **flame.**
For when the woman[h] the unwieldy lid   160
Had once discover'd, all the miseries hid
In that curs'd cabinet dispers'd and flew
About the **world** ; joys pined, and sorrows grew.
Hope only rested in the box's brim,
And took not wing from thence. Jove **prompted him**
That ow'd the cabinet **to** clap it close   165
Before she parted ; but unnumber'd **woes**
Besides encount'red men in all their ways ;
Full **were** all shores of them, and full all seas.

and true delight, fit to be embraced, which, found by **Event**
(the schoolmaster of fools), he repents too late. And, therefore, Horace truly, *nocet empta dolore voluptas.*

[160] [h] Ἀλλὰ γυνὴ, of this came the proverb, γυναικῶν ὄγεθρος, the plague of women ; and by the woman is understood Appetite, or Effeminate Affection, and customary or fashionable indulgence to the blood, not only in womanish affections, but in the general fashions of men's judgments and actions, both δημαγωγική, *id est, populariter,* or *gratiâ et authoritate quâ quis valet apud populum ;* and ψυχαγωγική, *id est, vi ducendi et flectendi animum,* intending illusively, by this same *docta ignorantia,* of which many learned leaders of the mind are guilty ; and συρφερώδης, *id est,* the common source or sink of the vulgar, prevailing past the nobility and piety of humanity and religion, by which all sincere discipline is dissolved or corrupted, and so that discipline taken away (*tanquam opercula Pandoræ*), both the human body's and mind's dissolution, instantly (as out of the cave of Æolus) let the winds or forces of corruption violently break, *qua data porta, ruunt, et terras turbine perflant.* All which notwithstanding, no course or custom is so desperate in infection, but some hope is left to escape their punishment in every man, according to Ovid, *vivere spe vidi, qui moriturus erat*

Diseases, day and night, with natural wings   170
And silent entries stole on men their stings;
The great in counsels, Jove, their voices reft,
That not the truest might avoid their theft,
Nor any 'scape the ill, in any kind,
Resolv'd at first in his almighty mind.   175

  And, wert thou willing, I would add to this
A second cause of men's calamities,
Sing all before, and since, nor will be long,
But short, and knowing; and t' observe my song,
Be thy conceit and mind's retention strong.   180

  When first both Gods and Men had one time's birth,
The Gods of diverse-languag'd men on Earth
A Golden[i] world produc'd, that did sustain
Old Saturn's rule when he in heaven did reign;
And then liv'd men, like Gods,[k] in pleasure here,   185
Indued with minds secure; from toils, griefs, clear;
Nor noisome age made any crooked; there
Their feet went ever naked as their hands;
Their cates were blessed, serving their commands,
With ceaseless plenties; all days sacred made   190
To feasts, that surfeits never could invade.
Thus liv'd they long, and died as seis'd with sleep;
All good things serv'd them; fruits did ever keep
Their free fields crown'd, that all abundance bore;

  [183] [i] Χρύσεον. Not only this description of Ages (as the critics observe) is imitated by all the Latin poets, but all the rest of this author; and chiefly by Virgil himself. His sentence and invention made so common, that their community will darken the rarity of them in their original. And this was called the Golden Age (according to Plato) for the virtuous excellency of men's natural dispositions and manners.

  [185] [k] "Ὥστε θεοί, sed ut dii vivebant homines. The poet, says Melancthon, could not but have some light of our parents' lives in Paradise.

All which all equal shared, **and** none wish'd more.   195
And, when the Earth had hid them, Jove's will was,
The good should into heavenly natures pass;
Yet still held state on earth, and guardians[1] were
Of all best mortals still surviving there,
Observ'd works just and unjust, clad in air,   200
And, gliding undiscover'd everywhere,
Gave riches where they pleased; and so were reft
Nothing **of all** the royal rule they left.

   The Second Age, that next succeeded this,
Was far the worse; which heaven-hous'd Deities   205
Of Silver-fashion'd; not like that of Gold
In disposition, nor so **wisely** soul'd.
For children then liv'd in their mothers' cares
(All that time growing still) **a** hundred years;
And were such great fools at that age, that they   210
Could not themselves dispose a family.
And when they youths grew, having reached the date
That rear'd their forces up to man's estate,
They **liv'd** small space, and spent it all in **pain,**

---

[1] 198 Φύλακες ἀνθρώπων, *custodes hominum*; from hence the opinion springeth that every man hath his good angel; which sort of spirits, however discredited now to attend and direct men, Plutarch, in his Commentaries *De Oraculorum Defectu*, defends to retain assured being, in this sort; as if a man should take away the interjected air betwixt the earth and the moon, that man must likewise dissolve all the coherence and actual unity of the universe, leaving *vacuum in medio*, and necessary bond of it all; so they that admit no *Genii* leave betwixt God and men no reasonable mean for commerce, the interpretative and administering faculty, as Plato calls it, betwixt them utterly destroying, and withdrawing consequently all their reciprocal and necessary uses; as the witches of Thessaly are said to pluck the moon out of her sphere. But these men being good, turned only good *Genii*; the next Age, men, being bad, turned in their next being bad *Genii*, of which after was held a man's good and bad *Genius*.

Caused by their follies; not of power t' abstain 215
From doing one another injury.
Nor would they worship any Deity,
Nor on the holy altars of the Blest
Any appropriate sacrifice addrest,
As fits the fashion of all human birth. 220
For which Jove, angry, hid them straight in earth,
Since to the blessed Deities of heaven
They gave not those respects they should have given.
But when the Earth had hid these like the rest,
They then were call'd the subterrestial blest,^m 225
And in bliss second, having honours then
Fit for the infernal spirits of powerful men,
    Then form'd our Father Jove a Third Descent,
Whose Age was Brazen; clearly different
From that of Silver. All the mortals there 230
Of wild ash fashion'd, stubborn and austere;
Whose minds the harmful facts of Mars affected,
And petulant injury. All meats rejected
Of natural fruits and herbs. And these were they
That first began that table cruelty 235
Of slaught'ring beasts; and therefore grew they fierce,
And not to be endur'd in their commerce.
Their ruthless minds in adamant were cut,

---

[225] m ‛Υποχθόνιοι μάκαρες, *subterranei beati mortales vocantur.* Out of their long lives and little knowledges, in neglect of religion, subject to painful and bitter death; where the former good men sweetly slept him out. But for the powers of their bodies, being fashioned of the world's yet fresh and vigorous matter, their spirits that informed their bodies are supposed secondly powerful; and that is intended in their recourse to earthly men, such as themselves were, furthering their affections and ambitions to ill, for which they had honour of those men, and of them were accounted blest, as the former good *Genii* were so, indeed, for exciting men to goodness.

Their strengths were dismal, **and** their shoulders **put**
Inaccessible hands out over all ;   240
Their brawny limbs arm'd with a brazen **wall**.
Their houses all were brazen, all of brass
Their working instruments, for black iron was
As yet unknown.   And these (their own lives ending,
The vast and cold-sad house of hell descending)   245
No grace had in their ends ;ⁿ but though they were
Never so powerful, and enforcing fear,
Black death reduc'd their greatness in their spight
T" a little room,° and stopp'd their cheerful light.

   When these left life, a Fourth Kind Jove gave birth
Upon the many-a-creature-nourishing earth ;   254
More just, and better than this race before—
Divine heröes, that the surnames bore
Of semigods ;ᵖ yet these impetuous fight
And bloody war bereft of life and light.   255
Some, in Cadmæan earth, contentious

   ²⁴⁸ ⁿ Νώνυμνοι.   These he intends were such rude **and** powerful men, as not only refused, like the second sort, to do honour to the Deities, but directly rebelled against them, and affected here **in** earth celestial empery ; for which the Celestials let **them** see that they need none but themselves to take down their affectations ; and for their so huge conceit of themselves had never any least honour of others, which many great men of this Iron Age need not be ignorant, therefore, is the event of such great ones ; and, howsoever they laugh in their sleeves at any other being than this, they may take notice by their wisers, that, even according to reason, both, there are other beings, and differences of those beings, both **in honours** and miseries.
   ²⁴⁹ ° Εἰλέω, in arctum cogo, seu in angustum redigo.
   ²⁵⁴ ᵖ Ἡμίθεοι, semidei.   Intending Hercules, Jason, and others of these Argonauts whose ship was νηὸς Ἀργὼ πασιμέλουσα, navis omnibus curo, because it held the care of all men in those that were in her ; intending of all the virtuous men that **were** then of name who were called semigods for their godlike virtues.

GEORGICS OF HESIOD. 161

To prise the infinite wealth of Œdipus,
Before seven-ported P Thebes; some shipp'd upon
The ruthless waves, and led to Ilion,
For fair-hair'd Helen's love; where, likewise, they   260
In bounds of death confin'd the beams of day.

    To these yet Jove gave second life, and seat
At ends of all the earth; in a retreat
From human feet, where souls secure they bear,
Amids the Blessed Islands,q situate near   265
The gulfy-whirl-pit-eating ocean flood,
Happy heroes living; for whose food
The plenty-bearing Tellus, thrice a year,
Delicious fruits and fragrant herbs doth bear.

    O that I might not live now, to partake   270
The Age that must the Fifth succession make,
But either die before, or else were born
When all that Age is into ashes worn!
For that which next springs, in supply of this,
Will all of Ironr produce his families;   275
Whose bloods shall be so banefully corrupt
They shalt not let them sleep, but interrupt
With toils and miseries all their rests and fares,
The Gods such grave and soul-dissecting cares
Shall steep their bosoms in. And yet some good   280

---

   258 p'Επταπύλῳ. He calls this seven-ported Thebes, to distinguish it from that of Egypt, that had 100 ports, besides that Hyppoplace in Cilicia.

   265 q'Ἐν μακάρων νήσοισι, *in beatorum insulis;* of which Fortunate Islands, vide Hom. Odyss. 8.

   275 r Γένος ἐστὶ σιδήρεον, *cujus genus est ferreum.* This Fifth Age he only prophesied of, almost three thousand years since; which falling out in this age especially true shows how divine a truth inspired him; and whether it be lawful or not, with Plato and all the formerly learned, to give these worthiest poets the commendation of divine.

L

Will God mix with their bad; for when the blood
Faints in their nourishment, and leaves their hair
A little gray, Jove's hand will stop the air
'Twixt them and life, and take them straight away.
'Twixt men and women shall be such foul play   285
In their begetting pleasures, and their race
Spring from such false seed, that the son's stol'n face
Shall nought be like the sire's, the sire no more
Seen in his issue. No friend, as before,
Shall like his friend be; nor no brother rest   290
Kind like his brother; no guest like a guest
Of former times; no child use like a child
His aged parents, but with manners wild
Revile and shame them; their impiety
Shall never fear that *God's all-seeing eye*   295
Is fixt upon them, but shall quite despise
Repayment of their education's price,
ᵃ Bear their law in their hands, and when they get
Their father's free-given goods, account them debt.
City shall city ransack; not a grace   300
To any pious man shall show her face,
Nor to a just or good man. All, much more,
Shall grace a beastly and injurious bore.
No right shall seize on any hand of theirs,
Nor any shame make blush their black affairs.   305
The worse shall worse the better with bad words,
And swear him out of all his right affords.
Ill-lung'd,ᵇ ill-liver'd, ill-complexion'd Spight

---

²⁹⁸ ᵃ Χειροδίκαι, *quibus jus est in manibus;* all this Ovid
translates: *Nec hospes ab hospite tutus, non socer à genero;
fratrum quoque gratia rara est.*
²⁹⁹ [*Bore*—boor.]
³⁰⁸ ᵇ Δυσκέλαδος, *male seu graviter sonans;* κακόχαρτος, *malis*

Shall consort all the miserable plight
Of men then living.   Justice then, and Shame,   310
Clad in pure white (as if they never came
In touch of those societies) shall fly
Up to the Gods' immortal family,
From broad-way'd earth ; and leave grave griefs to men,
That (desp'rate of amends) must bear all then.   315

But now to kings a fable I'll obtrude,
Though clear they savor all it can include :
The hawk ⁿ once having trust up in his seres
The sweet-tun'd nightingale, and to the spheres
His prey transferring, with his talons she   320
Pinch'd too extremely, and incessantly
Crying for anguish, this imperious speech
He gave the poor bird : " Why complain'st thou wretch ?
One holds thee now that is thy mightier far ;
Go as he guides, though ne'er so singular   325
Thou art a singer ; it lies now in me
To make thee sup me, or to set thee free.
Fool that thou art, whoever will contend
With one whose faculties his own transcend
Both fails of conquest, and is likewise sure   330
Besides his wrong he shall bad words endure."
Thus spake the swift and broad-wing'd bird of prey.
But hear ˣ thou justice, and hate injury.

gaudens, vel quo mali gaudent et delectantur, vel alienis insultans calamitatibus ; στυγερώπης, inviso aspectu, et torvis oculis cernens ; all epithets of ξῆγος.

³¹⁸ ⁿ"Ιρηξ, *accipiter.* The manners of the mighty towards the mean are figured in this fiction by the nightingale understanding learned and virtuous men. The following verse, ἄφρων, *imprudens,* &c. follows the most Sacred Letter, *non esse reluctandum potentioribus.*

³³³ ˣ Ὦ Πέρση. He speaks to his brother and returns to his first proposition ; of the fit contention to which he per-

Wrong touches near a miserable man ;
For (though most patient) yet he hardly can 335
Forbear just words, and feel injurious deeds.
Unjust loads vex ; he hardly bears that bleeds.
And yet hath Wrong to Right a better way,
For in the end will Justice win the day.
Till which who bears sees then amends arise ; 340
The fool ⁷ first suffers, and is after wise.
But crooked ² Justice jointly hooks with it
Injurious Perjury ; and that unfit
Outrage brib'd judges use, that makes them draw
The way their gifts go, ever cuts out law 345
By crooked measures. Equal Justice then,
All clad in air, th' ill minds of bribed men
Comes after mourning, mourns the city's ill,
Which, where she is expelled, she brings in still.
But those that with impartial dooms extend 350
As well to strangers as their household friend
The law's pure truth, and will in no point stray
From forth the straight tract of the equal way,
With such the city all things noble nourish,

suaded him before ; and though shame and injustice are fled in others, yet he wisheth him to love and embrace them. The elegant description immediately before being truly philosophical, and is handled at large by Plato in Protagoras.

³⁴¹ ⁷ Παθὼν νήπιος, *passus vero stultus sapit*, which was since usurped proverbially ; signifying that wisdom to be folly that we learn but of our own first suffered afflictions, which yet I think far exceeds any wisdom that was never taught nor confirmed by first feeling infortunes and calamities.

³⁴² ² Σκολιῇσι δίκῃσιν, properly signifies *curvis vel tortuosis judiciis*, which, he says, ravish together with them perjury. Alluding to crooked things, or things wrapt together like brambles, that catch and keep with them whatsoever touches them. Our proverb, to overtake with a crooked measure, not ridiculously applied to this grave metaphor; σκολιοὶ δίκαι, not signifying in this place what four critics teach, *vid. lites iniquas*, but *judicia iniqua seu tortuosa*.

With such the people in their profits flourish;   355
Sweet Peace along the land goes, nor to them
All-seeing Jove will destinate th' extreme
Of baneful war. No hunger ever comes,
No ill, where judges use impartial dooms.
But goods well got maintain still neighbour feasts; 360
The fields flow there with lawful interests;
On hills the high oak acorns bears; in dales
Th' industrious bee her honey sweet exhales,
And full-fell'd sheep are shorn with festivals;
There women bring forth children like their sire,   365
And all, in all kinds, find their own entire;
Nor ever plow they up the barren seas,
Their own fat fields yield store enough to please.
But whom rude Injury delights, and acts
That misery and tyranny contracts,   370
Sharp-sighted Jove for such predestines pain;
And oftentimes[a] the whole land doth sustain,
For one man's wickedness, that thriving in
Inequal dooms, still makes him sentence him.
For where such men bear privileg'd office still,   375

[372] a Πολλάκι. Oftentimes for one ill man a whole city suffers; which sentence, in near the same words, is used in Ecclesiastes, *Sæpe universa civitas mali viri pœnam luit.* And as before he recounts the blessings that accompany good kings or judges, so here he remembers the plagues that pursue the bad, enforcing in both, as I may say, the ebbing or flowing of every commonwealth by them. For law being soul to every such politic body, and judges, as if essence to that soul, in giving it form and being, according to their sentence and expositions of it, the body politic of force must fare well or ill, as it is governed well or ill; no otherwise than as the body of a man suffers good or ill by his soul's good or bad information and discipline. These threats used here, saith Melancthon, as in divers others places of this divine poet, he questionless gathered out of the doctrine of Moses and the Prophets, with whom the like comminations are everywhere frequent.

There Jove pours down whole deluges of ill;
Famine and Pestilence together **go**;
The people perish; women barren grow;
Whole houses vanish there sometimes in peace;
And sometimes armies, rais'd to shield th' increase   380
The Gods late gave them, even those Gods destroy,
Their rampires ruin, and let Rapine joy
The goods Injustice gather'd; or, elsewhere,
Jove **sinks** their ships, and leaves their ventures there.
Weigh, then, ᵇyourselves this justice, O ye kings;   385
For howsoever oft unequal things
Obtain their pass, they pass not so the eyes
Of all the all-discerning Deities;
For close and conversant their **virtues be**
With men; and, how they grate each other, see,   390
With wrested judgments; yielding no cares due
To those sure wreaks with which the Gods pursue
Unequal judges. Though on earth there are
Innumerable Gods that minister
Beneath great Jove, that keep men, clad in air,   395
Corrupt dooms noting, and each false affair,
And, gliding through the earth, are everywhere.
Justice is seed to Jove, in all fame dear,
And reverend to the **Gods** inhabiting **Heaven**,
And still a Virgin; whom when men ill given   400
Hurt, and abhorring from the right shall wrong,
She, for redress, to Jove her sire complains

³⁸⁵ ᵇ Καὶ αὑτοί. He would have judges enter into consideration themselves of the dangers in injustice, which presently after he reduces into three arguments. The first, οἱ αὑτῷ, *sibi ipsi*, which sentence to admiration agrees to that of the Scripture, *Incidit in foveam quam fecit;* the second for fear of further punishment from God; the third he makes out of the natural indignity and absurdity of the thing.

Of the unjust mind every man sustains,
And prays the people may repay the pains
Their kings have forfeited in their offences,   405
Depraving justice, and the genuine senses
Of laws corrupted in their sentences.
Observing this, ye gift-devouring kings,
Correct your sentences; and to their springs
Remember ever to reduce those streams   410
Whose crooked courses every man condemns.
Whoever forgeth for another ill,
With it himself is overtaken still.
In ill men run on that they most abhor;
Ill counsel worst is to the councellor.   415
For Jove's eye all things seeing, and knowing all,
Even these things, if he will, of force must fall
Within his sight and knowledge; nor to him
Can these brib'd dooms in cities shine so dim
But he discerns them, and will pay them pain;   420
Else would not I live justly amongst men,
Nor to my justice frame my childeren,
If to be just is ever to be ill,
And that the unjust finds most justice still,
And Jove gave each man in the end his will.   425
But he that loves the lightning (I conceive)
To these things thus will no conclusion give.
However, Perses,[c] put these in thy heart,

[c] *Ὦ Πέρση. He persuades his brother to the love of justice by argument taken from the true nature of man, that, by virtue of his divine soul, naturally loves it; because God infused into that divine beam of his being immortal a love to that that preserved immortality without that immortal destruction affected in injustice. Fishes, beasts, and fowls, endued naturally with no such love to justice, but allowed by God to do like themselves and devour one another; which that men should do as well as they, is most inhuman and full

And to the equity of things convert
Thy mind's whole forces, all thought striking **dead**
To that foul Rapine that hath now such head.
For in our manhoods Jove hath justice clos'd,
And **as a law upon** our souls impos'd.
Fish, **fowl, and** savage beasts, (whose law is pow'r)
Jove lets each other mutually devour,
Because they lack the equity he gives
To **govern men,** as far best for their lives;
And **therefore men** should follow it with strives.
For he that knows the justice of **a cause,**
And will in public ministry of laws
Give sentence to his knowledge, be he sure
God will enrich **him.** But who dares abjure
His conscious knowledge, and belie the law,
Past cure will that wound in his conscience draw,
And for his radiance now his race shall be
The deeper plung'd in all obscurity.
The just man's state shall in his seed exceed,
And, after him, breed honours as they breed.

But why men's ills prevail so much with them,
I, that the good know, will uncloud the beam
In whose light lies the reason. With much ease
To Vice, and her love, men may make **access,**
Such crews in rout **herd to her,** and her court
So passing near lies, their way sweet and short;
But before Virtue[d] do the Gods rain sweat,

of confusion, as well in their deformed mixture as in the ruin
that inseparably follows it. But his confidence here, that
whosoever will do justice freely, and without respect of riches,
God will enrich him, and that the worse-inclined will feel it
in the hell of his conscience, the other's seed prospering
beyond himself, is truly religious and right Christian.

[d] Τῆς δ' ἀρετῆς, ante virtutem. His argument to persuade

Through which, with toil and half-dissolved feet,
You must wade to her; her path long and steep,
And at your entry 'tis so sharp and deep,
But scaling once her height, the joy is more
Than all the pain she put you to before. 460
The pain at first, then, both to love and know
Justice and Virtue, and those few that go
Their rugged way, is cause 'tis follow'd lest.
e Of all men, therefore, he is always best
That, not depending on the mightiest, 465
Nor on the most, hath of himself descried
All things becoming; and goes fortified
In his own knowledge so far as t' intend

to Virtue here is taken both from her own natural fate and the divine disposition of God; for as she hath a body, being supposed the virtue of man, and through the worthily exercised and instructed organs of that body her soul receives her excitation to all her expressible knowledge (for *dati sunt sensus ad excitandum intellectum*), so to the love and habit of knowledge and Virtue there is first necessarily required a laborious and painful conflict, fought through the knowledge and hate of the miseries and beastliness of Vice; and this painful passage to Virtue Virgil imitated in his translation of the Pythagorean letter Y. ἰδρὼς, or *sudor*, is to be understood of sweat, *ex labore et fatigatione orto*.

⁴⁶⁴ *c Οὗτος μὲν πανάριστος.* He tells here who is at all parts the best and happiest man, which Virgil even to a word almost recites, and therefore more than imitates, in this, *Felix qui potuit rerum cognoscere causas, &c.* wherein our divine and all-teaching poet since describes three sorts of men; one that loves virtue out of knowledge acquired and elaborate, which the philosopher calls *scientiam acquisitam*; the second, that loves her out of admonitions, which he calls *infusam scientiam*; the third is he that hath neither of those two knowledges, nor is capable of either, having both these ignorances in him, viz. *ignorantiam pravæ dispositionis* and *puræ negationis*. Livy, as well as Virgil, recites this place almost *ad verbum in Fabio et Minutio*, in these words, *Sæpe ego audivi, milites, eum primum esse virum qui ipse consulat quid in rem sit; secundum eum qui bene monenti obediat; qui nec ipse consulere nec alteri parere scit eum extremi ingenii esse.*

What now is best, and will be best at th' end.
Yet he is good, too, and enough doth know,
That only follows, being admonish'd how.
But he that neither of himself can tell
What fits a man, nor being admonish'd well
Will give his mind to learn, but flat refuse,
That man cast out from every human use.
  Do thou, then, ever in thy memory place
My precepts, Perses, sprung of sacred race,
And work out what thou know'st not, that with hate
Famine may prosecute thy full estate,
And rich-wreath'd Ceres (reverenc'd of all)
Love thee as much, and make her festival
Amids thy granaries.   Famine evermore
Is natural consort of the idle boor.
Whoever idly lives, both Gods and men
Pursue with hateful and still-punishing spleen.
The slothful man is like the stingless drone,
That all his power and disposition
Employs to rob the labours of the bee,
And with his sloth devours her industry
Do thou repose thy special pleasure, then,
In still being conversant with temperate pain,
That to thee still the Seasons may send home
Their utmost store.   With labour men become
Herdful and rich ; with labour thou shalt prove
Great both in human and the Deities' love.
One with another, all combin'd in one,
Hate with infernal horror th' idle drone.
Labour, and thrive, and th' idle 'twill inflame.
No shame to Labour ; Sloth is yok'd with shame.
Glory and Virtue into consort fall

With wealth; wealth, Godlike, wins the grace of all;
Since which yet springs out of the root of pain,
ᶠ Pain hath precedence, so thou dost maintain
The temper fitting, and the foolish vein
Of striving for the wealth of other men   505
Thou giv'st no vent, but on thine own affairs
Convert'st thy mind, and thereon lay'st thy cares.
And then put on with all the spirit you can;
Shame is not good in any needy man.
Shame much obscures, and makes as much to fame;
Wealth loves audacity; Want favours shame.   511
Riches, not ravish'd, but divinely sent
For virtuous labour, are most permanent.
If any stand on force, and get wealth so,
Or with the tongue spoil, as a number do,   515
When gain, or craft, doth overgo the soul,
And impudence doth honest shame controul,
God easily can the so-made-great disgrace,
And his house, rais'd so, can as easily race.
Riches bear date but of a little space.   520

ᵍ Who wrongs an humble suppliant, doth offend
As much as he that wrongs a guest, or friend.

⁵⁰³ ᶠ 'Εργάζεσθαι, *laborare autem melius.* Notwithstanding he hath no other way to persuade his unwise brother to follow his business, and leave his strife in law for other men's goods, but to propose wealth and honour for the fruits of it, yet he prefers labour alone, joined with love of virtue and justice, and the good expence of a man's time, before wealth and honour with covetousness and contention.

⁵²¹ ᵍ ⁺Ισον δ' ὃς, *par est delictum.* He says it is as great a sin to wrong a poor suppliant as to wrong a man's best friend or guest, which was then held one of the greatest impieties; and to deceive an orphan of his dead parent's gift he affirms to be nothing less an offence than to ascend to the bed of his brother; not that he makes all sins alike, but shows how horrible those sins are with which we are most familiar.

Who for his brother's wife's **love** doth ascend
His brother's bed, and **hath his** vicious end,
Offends no more than **he that doth deceive**   525
An orphan of the goods his parents leave;
Or he that **in the** wretched bounds of age
Reviles his father. All these Jove enrage,
And shall receive of him revenge at last,
Inflicting all pains that till then **they past.**   530

   From all these, therefore, turn thy striving mind,
And to thy utmost see the Gods assign'd
Chastely and purely, all their holy **dues.**
Burn fattest thighs to them; and sometimes **use**
Off'rings of wine; sometimes serve their delights   535
With burning incense; both **when** bed-time cites
And when from bed the sacred morning **calls;**
That thou may'st render the Celestials
All ways propitious; and so none else gather
Thy fortunes strow'd, but thou reap others rather.   540

   Suffer thy foe thy table; call thy friend
In chief one near, for if occasion send
Thy **household** use of neighbours, they undrest
Will **haste to thee**, where thy allies will rest
Till they **be ready.** An ill neighbour is   545
A curse; a good **one is as** great a bliss.
He hath a treasure, by **his** fortune sign'd,
That hath a neighbour of an **honest mind.**
No loss of ox, or horse, a man shall bear,
Unless a wicked neighbour dwell too near.   550
Just measure take of neighbours, just repay,
The same receiv'd, and more, if more thou may,
That after needing, thou may'st after find
Thy wants' supplier of as free a mind.

^h Take no ill gain ; ill gain brings loss as ill.   555
Aid quit with aid ; good-will pay with good-will.
Give him that hath given ; him that hath not give not ;
Givers men give ; gifts to no givers thrive not.
Giving is good, rapine is deadly ill.
Who freely gives, though much, rejoiceth still ;   560
Who ravines is so wretched, that, though small
His first gift be, he grieves as if 'twere all.
Little to little added, if oft done,
In small time makes a great possession.
Who adds to what is got, needs never fear   565
That ⁱ swarth-cheek'd hunger will devour his cheer ;
^k Nor will it hurt a man though something more
Than serves mere need he lays at home in store ;
And best at home, it may go less abroad.
If cause call forth, at home provide thy rode,   570
Enough for all needs, for free spirits die
To want, being absent from their own supply.
Which note, I charge thee. At thy purse's height,^l

⁵⁵⁵ ^h **Κακὰ** κερδ., *mala lucra æqualia in damnis*. According to this of the Scripture, *Male partam male disperit ; et de male quæsitis non gaudet tertius hæres*.

⁵⁶⁶ ⁱ Αἴθοπα λιμὸν, *atram famem*. **Black** or **swarth** he calls famine or hunger ; *ab effectu quod nigrum aut lucidum colorem inducat*.

⁵⁶⁷ ^k Οὐδὲ. He says it will not hurt a man to have a little more than needs merely laid up at home ; as we say, it will eat a man no meat, and prefers keeping a man's store at home to putting it forth, for it may go less so, as often it doth.

⁵⁷³ ^l Ἀρχομενου, *incipiente dolio*. At the beginning or height of a man's store he adviseth liberality, and at the bottom ; in the midst frugality ; admonishing therein not to be prodigal nor sordid or wretched ; but, as at the top of the cask wine is the weakest and thinnest, because it is most near the air, and therefore may there be best spent, at the bottom full of lees, and so may there be best spared, in the midst neatest and briskest, and should be then most made of or husbanded, so in the midst of a man's purse he adviseth parsimony.

And when it fights low, **give** thy use his freight ;
When in the midst **thou art,** then check **the blood ;** 575
Frugality at bottom is not good.
Even with thy brother think a ᵐwitness by,
When **thou** would'st laugh, or converse liberally ;
Despair hurts none beyond credulity.

 Let never ⁿneat-girt dame, that all her wealth   580
Lays on her waist, make profit of her stealth
On thy true judgment ; nor be heard to feign
With her **fork'd** tongue, so far forth as to gain
Thy candle rent (she calls it). He that gives
A woman trust doth trust a den of **thieves.**   585
º One only son preserves a family,
As feeding it with only fit supply.
And that house to all height his riches rears
Whose sire dies old, and leaves a son **of years.**
To many children, too, God easily **spares**   590

⁵⁷⁷ ᵐ Ἐπὶ μάρτυρα θέσθαι, **testem** adhibeto. The critics expound it as if a man, talking privately and liberally with his brother, should confer so securely that he must ever bring a witness with him of what words passed him ; and the critics intend it personally, where the word θέσθαι signifies here only *suppuita, cogita,* hypothetically, or by way of supposition ; θέσθαι coming of τίθημι, i. e. θέσιν et ὑπόθεσιν, *facio, esto ut ita sit:* suppose there were a witness by, and be as circumspect in speeches with your brother, **even** in your most private and free discourse, as if you supposed **a** third man heard you. The other exposition is to be exploded.

⁵⁸⁰ ⁿ Ἰσχιόστολος, *qui vel quæ clunes* **exornat.**

⁵⁸⁶ º Μουνογενής, *unigenitus.* He says one only son preserves his father's house, and adds most ingeniously, φέρβεμεν, i. e. *pascendo seu nutriendo;* intending that he adds only necessary vital fuel, as it were, to his father's decaying fire; where many sons oftentimes rather famish or extinguish a family than nourish or fuel it ; and yet he adds, most gravely and piously, that God can easily give store of goods fit for the greatest store of children ; but yet the more children the more care; and speaking to the happiest state of a family, he prefers one supplier to many.

GEORGICS OF HESIOD.

Wealth store; but still, more children the more cares,
And to the house the more access is made.
If, then, the hearty love of wealth invade
Thy thrifty mind, perform what follows here,
ᵖ And, one work done, with others serve the year.   595

⁵⁹⁵ ᵖ"Ερδειν, *sic facito*. A general conclusion, and transition to his doctrine of the next book.

THE END OF THE FIRST BOOK.

THE SECOND BOOK OF THE GEORGICS OF HESIOD.

HEN, Atlas' birth, the Pleiades arise,
Harvest begin, plow when they leave
  the skies.
Twice twenty days and nights these
  hide their heads;
The year then turning, leave again their beds,
And show when first to whet the harvest steel.   5
This likewise is the law the fields must feel,
Both with sea-dwellers, near and high, and those
Whose winding valleys Neptune overflows,
That ᵃfenny grounds and marshes dwell upon,
Along the fat and fruitful region.   10
But, wheresoever thou inhabit'st, ply
The fields before fierce winter's cruelty

---

[1] He begins his Works, to which immediately before he prepares his brother; this whole book containing precepts of husbandry, both for field and family. By the ascent and set of the Pleiades is shown the harvest and seed season, as well for ground near the seas as the far distant. The Pleiades, called the daughters of Atlas, are the seven stars in the back of the Bull, which the Latins called *Vergilias;* when which are seen near the sun rising, which is in June, he appoints entry on harvest affairs; when in the morning they leave this hemisphere, which is in November, he designs seed-time.

ᵃ Ἄγκεα, *palustrem terram significat.*

Oppress thy pains, when thou may'st naked plow,
Naked cast in thy seed, and naked mow,
If timely thou wilt bear into thy barn   15
The works of Ceres; and to that end learn
As timely to prepare thy whole increase,
Lest, in the meantime, thy necessities
Importune thee at others' doors to stand,
And beg supplies to thy unthrifty hand;   20
As now thou com'st to me, but I no more
Will give, or lend thee, what thou may'st restore
By equal measure, nor will trust thee so.
Labour, vain Perses, and those labours do,
That, by the certain sign of beggary   25
^b Demonstrated in idle drones, thine eye
May learn the work that equal Deity
Imposeth of necessity on men;
Lest with thy wife, and wanting childeren,
(Thy mind much griev'd) thou seek'st of neighbours food,
Thine own means failing. Men grow cold in good.   31
Some twice, or thrice, perhaps, thy neighbour will
Supply thy wants; whom if thou troubl'st still,
Thou com'st off empty, and to air dost strain
A world of words; words store make wanting men.   35
I charge thee, therefore, see thy thoughts employ'd
To pay thy debts, and how thou may'st avoid
Deserved famine. To which end, first see
Thy wife well order'd, and thy family;
Thy plow-drawn ox; thy ^c maid, without her spouse, 40

---

^{26 b} Διατεκμαίρομαι, *per signum demonstro ita ut conjectare sit facile.*

^{40 c} Κτητὴν, *famulam considerate acquisitam.* He would have her likewise unmarried, οὐ γαμετὴν, *non nuptam;* his reason he shows after.

And wisely hir'd, that business in thy house
May first work off, and then to tillage come.
To both which offices make fit at home
Everything needful, lest abroad thou send
To ask another, and he will not lend;
Meantime thou want'st them, time flies fast away,
Thy work undone, which not from day to day
Thou should'st defer; the ^d work-deferrer never
Sees full his barn; nor he that leaves work ever,
And still is gadding out. ^e Care-flying ease
Gives labour ever competent increase.
^f He that with doubt his needful business crosses
Is ever wrastling with his certain losses.
When, therefore, of the ^g swift-sharp-sighted sun
The chief force faints, and ^h sweating heat is done,
Autumn grown old, and ⁱ opening his last vein,
And great Jove steeping all things in his rain,
Man's body chang'd, and made more lightsome far,
(For then but small time shines the Sirian star
Above the heads of ^k hard-fate-foster'd man,
Rising near day, and his beams Austrian
Enjoy'd in night most),—when, I say, all this
Follows the season, and the forest is

⁴⁵ d 'Ετωσιοεργὸς, non assiduus in opere.
⁵⁰ e Μελέτη, cura cum industriâ et exercitatione.
⁵² f 'Αμβολιεργὸς, qui opus de die in diem rejicit et procrastinat.
⁵⁴ g 'Οξέος ἠελίοιο, metaphoricè accipitur pro acumine et visus celeritate.
⁵⁵ h 'Ιδάλιμος, sudorificus humidus calor does not express the word, being so turned in the verbal translation.
⁵⁶ i Μετοπωρινὸς, qui extremi et senescentis Autumni est.
⁵⁸ k Κηριτρεφῆς, qui unà cum lethifero fato alitur, vel qui educatur inter multas duræ sortis miserias, the most fit epithet of man.
⁶² Pro sylvâ.

Sound, being fell'd, his leaves upon the ground
Before let fall, and leaving what they crown'd 65
Then constantly take time to fell thy wood;
Of husbandry the time kept is the blood.

    Cut then your three-foot [1]quern; whose pestle cut
Three cubits long; your axletree seven foot.
If it be eight foot, cut your mallet thence; 70
The felfs, that make your cart's circumference,
Cut three spans long. Many crook'd pieces more,
Ten palms in length, fell for your wagons' store.
All which poor rules a rich convenience yield.

    If thou shalt find a culter in the field, 75
Or on the mountain, either elm or oak,
Convey it home, since, for thy beasts of yoke
To plow withal, 'twill most his strength maintain;
And, chiefly, if [m]Athenian Ceres' swain
It fixing to the draught-tree, lest it fails, 80
Shall fit it to the handles' stay with nails.

    Two plows compose, to find thee work at home,
One with a share that of itself doth come
From forth the plow's whole piece, and one set on;
Since so 'tis better much, for, either gone, 85
With th' other thou may'st instantly impose
Work on thy oxen. On the laurel grows,
And on the elm, your best plow-handles ever;
Of oak your draught-tree; from the maple never
Go for your culter; for your oxen chuse 90
Two males of nine years' old, for then their use

---

[68] Ἴ"Ολμον. A kind of mortar to bray corn in, which the ancients used for a little mill or quern.

[79] m 'Αθηναίης δμῶος, *Atticæ Cereris servus;* a periphrasis of a plowman; she being called Attic Ceres, *quod ipsa Athenienses, adeoque omnes homines, de frugibus docuerit.*

Is most available, since their strengths are then
Not of the weakest, and the youthful mean
Sticks in their nerves still; nor will these contend
With skittish tricks, when they the stitch should end, 95
To break their plow, and leave their work undone.
These let a youth of ⁿforty wait upon,
Whose **bread** at meals in four good shivers cut,
Eight **bits in** every shive; for º that man, put
To **his fit** task, will see it done past talk   100
With any fellow, **nor** will ever balk
In any stitch he **makes,** but give his mind
With care t' his labour. **And this man no hind**
(Though much his younger) **shall his** better be
At sowing seed, and, shunning skilfully,   105
Need to go over his whole work again.
Your younger man feeds still a flying vein
From his set task, to hold his equals chat,
And trifles works he should be serious at.   109

    Take notice, then, when thou the crane shalt hear
Aloft out of the clouds her clanges rear,
That then **he** gives thee signal when to sow,
And Winter's wrathful season doth foreshow;

---

97 ⁿ Τετράτρυφον, ὀκτάβλωμον, *quadrifidum, octo morsuum.*
He commends a man of forty for a most fit servant; and therefore prescribes allowance of bread to his meals something extraordinary, saying he would have allowed four shives of bread at a meal to his meat, every shive containing eight bits or morsels; not that the whole four shives should contain but eight morsels, as the critics expound it; for how absurd is it to imagine a shive of bread but two bits? and how pinching a diet it were for an able plow-man?
99 º"Ὃς κ ἔργου. *Qui quidem opus curans, et ætatis quam in* **nervo** *requirit* (says Melancthon) *rationes addit admodum graves, sentitque multum situm esse in maturitate ætatis.* Forty years then being but a youth's age.

And then the man, that can no oxen get,
Or wants the season's work, his heart doth eat. 115
Then feed thy oxen in the house with hay;
Which he that wants with ease enough will say,
"Let me, alike, thy wain and oxen use."
Which 'tis as easy for thee to refuse,
And say thy oxwork then importunes much. 120
He that is rich in brain will answer such:
"Work up thyself a wagon of thine own;
For to the foolish borrower is not known
That each wain asks a hundred joints of wood;
These things ask forecast, and thou shouldst make good
At home before thy need so instant stood." 126

When, therefore, first fit plow-time doth disclose,
Put on thy spirit; all, as one, dispose
Thy servants and thyself; plow wet and dry;
And when Aurora first affords her eye, 130
In Spring-time, turn the earth up; which see done
Again, past all fail, by the Summer's sun.
Hasten thy labours, that thy crowned fields
May load themselves to thee, and rack their yields.
The tilth-field sow on earth's most light foundations; 135
The ᵖ tilth-field, banisher of execrations,
Pleaser of sons and daughters; which, t' improve
With all wish'd profits, pray to earthly Jove,
And virtuous Ceres, that on all such suits
Her sacred gift bestows in blessing fruits. 140

[136] ᵖ Νειὸς ἀλεξιάρη, *novalis imprecationum expultrix.* The tilth-field he calls banisher of execrations, and pleaser of sons and daughters; first, because rude husbandmen use to curse when their crops answer not their expectations; and next, it pleases sons and daughters, since it helps add to their portions.

When first thou enter'st foot to plow thy land,
And on thy plow-staff's top hast laid thy hand,
Thy oxen's backs, that next thee by a chain
Thy oaken draught-tree draw, put to the pain
Thy goad imposes; and thy boy behind,   145
That with his iron rake thou hast design'd
To hide thy seed, let from his labour drive
The birds that offer on thy sweat to live.
The best thing that in human needs doth fall
Is Industry, and Sloth the worst of all.   150
With one, thy corn-ears shall with fruit abound,
And bow their thankful foreheads to the ground;
With th' other, scarce thy seed again redound.

When Jove, then, gives this good end to thy pain,
Amids the vessels that preserve thy grain   155
No spiders then shall need t' usurp their room,
But thou, I think, rejoice, and rest at home,
Provision inn'd enough of everything
To give thee glad heart till the neighbour Spring,
Not go to others to supply thy store,   160
But others need to come to thee for more.

If at the sun's conversion thou shalt sow
The sacred earth, thou then may'st ⁹sit and mow
Or reap in harvest; such a little pain
Will serve thy use to sell thy thin-grown grain,   165
And reaps so scanty will take up thy hand;
Thou hid in dust, not comforted a sand,
But gather 'gainst the grain. Thou should'st be then

---

[163] ⁹ Ἥμενος, *sedens*. He disproves sowing at the winter solstice, and says he that doth sow then may sit and reap for any labour his crop will require; a reap they call as much as at once the reaper grasps in his hand.

Coop'd in a basket up; for wordly men
Admire no unthrifts, Honour goes by gain. 170
As times still change, so changeth Jove his mind,
Whose seasons mortal men can hardly find.
  But if thou shouldst sow late, this well may be,
In all thy slackness, an excuse for thee:
When in the oak's green arms the cuckoo sings, 175
And first delights men in the lovely springs,
If much rain fall, 'tis fit then to defer
Thy sowing work; but how much rain to bear,
And let no labour to that much give ear
Past intermission, let Jove steep the grass 180
Three days together, so he do not pass
An ox's hoof in depth, and never stay
To strow thy seed in; but if deeper way
Jove with his rain makes, then forbear the field,
For late-sown then will past the foremost yield. 185
  Mind well all this; nor let it fly thy pow'rs
To know what fits the white Spring's early flow'rs;
Nor when rains timely fall; nor, when sharp cold
In Winter's wrath doth men from work withhold,
Sit by smiths' forges,ʳ nor warm taverns* haunt, 190*
Nor let the bitterest of the season daunt
Thy thrift-arm'd pains, like idle Poverty;
For then the time is when th' industrious thigh
Upholds, with all increase, his family.

  ¹⁹⁰ ʳ Χάλκειον θῶκον, *æneam sedem.* By which he understands smiths' forges, where the poorer sort of Greece used to sit, as they do still in the winter amongst us, and as amongst the Romans, *in tonstrinis,* or barbers' shops.
  ¹⁹⁰ ˢ Ἐπαλέα λέσχην, *calidam tabernam.* These λέσχαι were of old said to hold the meetings of philosophers; and after, because amongst them mixed idle talkers over cups, they were called λέσχαι, *nugæ,* λεσχηνία, *loquacitas* or *garrulitas.*

With whose rich hardness **spirited**, do thou
Poor Delicacy fly, lest, **frost and** snow
Fled from her love, Hunger sit both them out,
And make thee, with the beggar's lazy gout,
Sit stooping to the pain, still pointing to 't,
And with a ^{t} lean hand stroke a foggy foot.   200

   The slothful man expecting many things,
With his vain hope that cannot stretch her wings
Past need of necessaries for his kind,
Turns,^{u} like **a** whirlpit, over in his mind
All means that rapine prompts to th' idle hind ;   205
Sits in the tavern, and finds means to spend
Ill got, and ever doth to **worse contend.**

   When Summer, therefore, in her tropic sits,
Make thou thy servants wear their winter **wits,**
And tell them this, ere that warm season wast   210
Make nests, for Summer will not ever last.
The month of ^{x}January's all-ill days,
For oxen's good, shun now by **July's** rays.

  200 ^{t} Λεπτῇ δέ, *macilentâ vero crassum pedem manu premas*. Aristotle in his problems, as out of this place, affirms that daily and continual hunger makes men's feet and ankles swell ; and by the same reason *superiores partes extenuantur et macrescunt*, for which Hesiod uses this ingenious allusion to his bother, advising him to take heed *ne pedem tumefactum tenui manu demulcere oporteat ;* πιέζω, signifying here *demulceo*, not *stringendo crucio*, or *premo*, as it is usually rendered. But (for the pain) stroke or touch it softly, **for** some ease to it, though it doth little good to it, but only **makes** good the proverb, *Ubi dolor ibi digitus.*

  204 ^{u} Κακὰ προσελέξατο, *mala intra animum versat*. And therefore, says Melancthon, out of Columella, *homines nihil agendo male agere discunt ;* but προςελέξατο signifies not only *versat*, but *instar undarum flurii vel voraginis versat.*

  212 ^{x} Μῆνα δὲ Ληναιῶνα, *mensis in quo festum in honorem Lenei celebratur.* Bacchus being called Ληναῖος, *quoniam torcularibus et vini expressioni præest ;* and because his feast used to be solemnized in January, Ληναιών is called *Januarium.*

When air's chill ʸ North his noisome frosts shall blow
All over earth, and all the wide sea throw   215
At heaven in hills, from cold horse-breeding Thrace ;
The beaten earth, and all her sylvan race,
Roaring and bellowing with his bitter strokes ;
Plumps of thick fir-trees and high-crested oaks
Torn up in vallies, all air's flood let fly   220
In him at Earth, sad nurse of all that die ;
Wild beasts abhor him, and run clapping close
Their sterns betwixt their thighs ; and even all those
Whose hides their fleeces line with highest proof,
Even ox-hides also want expulsive stuff,   225
And bristled goats, against his bitter gale,
He blows so cold he beats quite through them all.
Only with silly sheep it fares not so ;
For they each summer fleec'd, their fells to grow,
They shield all winter, crush'd into his wind.   230
He makes the old man trudge for life to find
Shelter against him ; but he cannot blast
The tender and the delicately-grac't
Flesh of the virgin, she is kept within
Close by her mother, careful of her skin,   235
Since yet she never knew how to enfold
The force of Venus swimming all in gold ;
Whose snowy bosom, choicely wash'd and balm'd
With wealthy oils, she keeps the house becalm'd
All winter's spite. When in his fireless shed   240
And miserable roof still hiding head,

---

[214] ʸ Πνεύσαντος Βορέαο, *flante Borea hiemis tempus, et mensem Boreali frigore gravissimum copiose et eleganter descripsit*, says Melancthon.

The ᵃboneless fish doth eat his feet for cold,
To whom the sun doth never food unfold,
But turns above the black men's populous towers,
On whom he more bestows his radiant hours   245
Than on th' ᵃHellenians, then all beasts of horn,
And smooth-brow'd, that in beds of wood are born,
About the oaken dales that north-wind fly,
Gnashing their teeth with restless misery;
And everywhere that care solicits all   250
That, out of shelter, to their coverts fall,
And caverns eaten into rocks; and then
Those wild beasts shrink, like tame ᵇthree-footed men
Whose backs are broke with age, and foreheads driven
To stoop to earth, though born to look on heaven;   255
Even like to these those tough-bred rude ones go,
Flying the white drifts of the northern snow.
Then put thy body's best munition on,
Soft waistcoats, weeds that th' ankles trail upon;
And with a little linen weave much wool   260
In forewov'n webs, and make thy garments full.
And these put on thee, lest thy harsh-grown hair
Tremble **upon** thee, and into the air
Start, as affrighted; all that breast of thine
Pointed with ᶜ bristles like a **porcupine**.   265
About thy feet see fitted shoes be tied,

---

²⁴¹ ᵃ'Ἀνόστεος, exossis. He intends the Polypus, that hath no bones, but a gristle for his back-bone.
²⁴⁶ ᵃ Πανελλήνεσσι. Hellen was son to Deucalion, of whom, as being author of that nation, Ἕλλην, *dicitur Græcus, ut testatur* Plinius, lib 4, cap. 7. The sun being in Sagittarius is longer with the Æthiops, which are meridional, than with the Græcians.
²⁵³ ᵇ Τρίποδι βροτοὶ ἶσοι, *tripodi homini similes*. He calls old men helped with staves in their gait three-footed.
²⁶⁵ ᶜ Ἀείρειν, *pennarum in more in altum erigere*.

Made of a strongly-dying ox's hide,
Lin'd with ᵈ wool socks; besides, when those winds blow
Thy first-fall'n kid-skins sure together sow
With ox's sinews, and about thee throw,   270·
To be thy refuge 'gainst the soaking rain.
Upon thy head a quilted hat sustain,
That from thy ears may all air's spite expell.
When north-winds blow the air is sharp and fell;
But morning air, that ᵉ brings a warmth withal   275·
Down from the stars, and on the earth doth fall,
Expires a breath that, all things cheering then,
Is fit to crown the works of blessed men.
Which drawing out of floods that ever flow,
Wind-storms are rais'd on earth, that roughly blow;   280·
And then sometimes a shower falls towards even,
And sometimes air in empty blasts is driven,
Which from the north-wind rising out of Thrace,
And gloomy clouds, rais'd, haste thee home apace,
Thy work for that day done, th' event forseen,   285·
Lest out of Heaven a dark cloud hide thee clean,
Thy weeds wet through, and steep thee to the skin;
But shun it, for when this cold month comes in
Extreme it is for sheep, extreme for men.
Take from thy oxen half their commons ᶠ then,   290·
But mend thy servants', for ingenious Night,

²⁶⁸ ᵈ Πίλοις, not *pilis*, as it is usually translated, but *soculis laneis*
²⁷⁵ ᵉ 'Aὴρ πυροφόρος, *aer ignifer*, not *frugifer*, though fruits are the chief effects of it, but air that brings a comfortable fire with it, and he says, ἀπ' οὐρανοῦ ἀστερόεντος, *à cœlo stellifero*.
²⁹⁰ ᶠ Τῆμος, *tum*, &c. Then sharpen thy oxen's stomachs with taking away half their allowance, but give more to thy servants; his reason is, because the days being shorter by half then than in summer, and so take away half the work of the ox, therefore half their fother should be in equal husbandry

Then great in length, affects the appetite
With all contention, and alacrity
To all invention, and the scrutiny
Of all **our** objects, and must therefore feast
To make the spirits run high in their inquest.
These **well** observing all the year's remain,
The days and nights grow equal ; till again
Earth, that of all things is the Mother Queen,
All fruits promiscuously brings forth for men.
When, after sixty turnings of the sun,
By Jove's decrees, all Winter's **hours are run,**
Then does the evening-star, g Arcturus, rise,
And leave the unmeasur'd ocean ; all men's eyes,
First noting then his beams ; and after **him,**
Before the clear morn's light hath chac'd the dim,
Pandion's Swallow breaks out with her **moan,**h
Made to the light, the Spring but new put on.
Preventing which, cut vines, for then 'tis best ;
But when the horn'd house-bearer leaves his rest,

abated ; but since servants must work in night as well, and that the nights are much longer, he would have their commons increased, allowing even those bodily labourers, in a kind of proportion, the same that is fit for mental painstakers, students, &c., for the word εὔφροναι, taken here for nights, is usurped for the effects of night, εὐφρονέων signifying *prudentiâ valens*, and εὐφρόνη is called night, *quod putaretur multum conferre ad inventionem eorum quæ quæruntur*, intending in studies and labours of the soul, especially the epithet ἐπίῤῥοθοι, signifying *auxilium seu inspirationem ferentes magnâ cum alacritate et contentione.* All that since therefore the words containing, a man may observe how verbal expositors slubber up these divine expressions with their contractions and going the next way.

305 g Ἀρκτοῦρος, *Arcturus* is a star *sub zonâ Bootæ ; oritur vespere, initio Veris.*

307 h Ὀρθρογόη, *ante lucano tempore quiritans.* The construction should be, not *prorumpit ad lucem*, but *lugens ad lucem,* since it came not soon enough to prevent the night's tyranny in *Tereus ;* the fiction of which is too common to be repeated.

GEORGICS OF HESIOD. 189

And climbs the plants, the Seven Stars then in flight,
Nowhere dig vines, but scythes whet, and excite
Servants to work; fly shady tavern bow'rs,
And beds, as soon as light salutes the flow'rs.

  In harvest, when the sun the body dries,   315
Then haste and fetch the fields home; early rise,
That plenty may thy household wants suffice;
The morn the third part of thy work doth gain;
The morn makes short thy way, makes short thy pain;
The morn being once up fills the ways with all,   320
And yokes the ox, herself up, in his stall.

  When once the thistle doth his flower prefer,
And on the tree the garrulous grashopper,
Beneath her wings, all day and all night long
Sits pouring out her derisory song,   325
When Labour drinks, his boiling sweat to thrive,
Then goats grow fat, then best wine choose, then strive
Women for work most, and men least can do;
For then the Dog-star burns his drought into
Their brains and knees, and all the body dries.   330
But then betake thee to the shade that lies
In shield of rocks; drink ⁱ Biblian wine, and eat
The creamy wafer, goats' milk that the teat
Gives newly free and nurses kids no more,
Flesh of bough-browsing beeves that never bore,   335
And tender kids; and, to these, taste black wine,
The ^k third part water of the crystalline

---

  332 ⁱ Βίβλινος, *Biblinum vinum dicitur a Biblia regione Thraciæ, ubi nobilissima vina sunt.*
  337 ^k Τρεῖς ὕδατος, *tertiam aquæ partem infunde.* The Greeks never drunk *merum*, but *dilutum vinum*, wine allay'd with water. Athenæus says that to two cups of wine sometimes they put five cups of water, and sometimes to four of wine

Still-flowing fount that feeds a stream beneath ;
And sit in shades where temp'rate gales may **breath**
On thy oppos'd cheeks, when Orion's **rays** 340
His influence in first ascent assays.
 Then to thy labouring servants give command
To dight the sacred gift of Ceres' hand,
In some place windy, on a well-plan'd floor,
Which all by measure into vessels pour. 345
Make then thy man-swain one that hath no house,
Thy handmaid one that hath nor child nor spouse,
Handmaids that children have are ravenous.
A mastiff likewise **nourish** still at home,
Whose [1] teeth are sharp and close as any comb, 350
And meat him well, to keep with stronger guard
The [m] day-sleep-wake-night **man** from forth thy yard,
That else thy goods into his caves will bear.
Inn hay and chaff enough **for all the** year
To serve thy oxen and thy mules, and then 355
Loose them, and ease the dear knees of thy men.
 When Sirius and Orion aspire
To heaven's steep height, and bright Arcturus' fire
The rosy-finger'd Morning sees arise,
O Perses, then **thy** vineyard faculties 360
See gather'd **and got** home ; which twice five days
And nights, no less, **expose to Phœbus'** rays ;
Then five days inn them, **and in** vessels close
The gift the gladness-causing God bestows.
 But after that the Seven-stars and the Five 365

but two of water, which they order according to the strength
or weakness of their wine.
 350 1 Καρχαρόδους, *dentes inter se pectinatim coëuntes habens.*
 352 m'Ἡμερόκοιτος ἀνήρ, *die dormiens vir.* A periphrasis of
a thief.

That 'twixt the Bull's horns at their set arrive,
Together with the great Orion's force,
Then ply thy plow as fits the season's course.
  If of a ⁿchance-complaining man at seas
The humour take thee, when the Pleiades   370
Hide head and fly the fierce Orion's chace,
And the dark-deep Oceanus embrace,
Then diverse gusts of violent winds arise;
And then attempt no naval enterprise,
But ply thy land-affairs, and draw ashore   375
Thy ship, and fence her round with stonage store,
To shield her ribs against the humourous gales;
Her pump exhausted, lest Jove's rainy falls
Breed putrefaction; all tools fit for her,
And all her tacklings, to thy house confer;   380
Contracting orderly all needful things
That imp a water-treading vessel's wings;
Her well-wrought stern hang in the smoke at home,
Attending time till fit sea-seasons come;
And then thy swift sail launch, conveying in   385
Burthen that richly may that trade begin,
As did our father who a voyage went
For want of an estate so competent
As free life ask'd; and long since landed here
When he had measur'd the unmeasur'd sphere   390
Of all the sea, Æolian Cumas leaving,
Not ⁰flying wealth, (revenues great receiving,

---

  ³⁶⁹ ⁿ Δυσπέμφελος, *qui de sorte suâ queritur.*
  ³⁹² ⁰ Οὐκ ἄφενος φεύγων, *non redditus seu divitias fugiens.*
He blames those that having richly enough of their own,
which they freely and safely possess ashore, will yet, with
insatiate desire of more, venture the loss of all; which his
father, he says, was not to be blamed for, in going to sea,

And bliss itself possess'd in all fit **store**,
If wisely us'd; yet selling that t' explore
Strange countries, madly covetous of more,)   395
But only shunning loathsome poverty,
Which yet Jove sends, and men should never fly.
The seat that **he** was left to dwell upon
Was **set in** Ascra, near to Helicon,
Amids a miserable village there,   400
In winter vile, in summer noisomer,
And profitable **never.** Note thou, then,
To do all works the proper season when,
In sea-works chiefly; for whose use **allow**
A little ship, but **in her** bulk bestow   405
A great big burthen—the more ships sustain
The surer sail they, and heap gain on gain,
If seas run smooth and rugged gusts abstain.
When thy vain mind, then, would sea-ventures try,
In love the land-rocks of loath'd Debt to fly,   410
And ᵖHunger's ever harsh-to-hear-of cry,
I'll set before thee all the trim and dress
Of those still-roaring-noise-resounding seas,
Though ᵠneither skill'd in either ship or sail,
Nor ever was at **sea**; or, lest I fail,   415
But for Eubœa once from **Aulis,** where
The Greeks, with tempest driv'n, for shore did stere
Their mighty navy, gather'd **to** employ

---

who only took that course to avoid poverty, his means by land not enough to live withal freely.

⁴¹¹ ᵖ Ἀτερπέα λιμόν, *famem auditu insuavem.*

⁴¹⁴ ᵠ Οὔτε τι, *etsi neque navigandi peritus.* Melancthon, in this free confession of his unskilfulness in what he intended to teach, gives this note: *Removet se reprehensionem ob imperitiam; hic videmus, σοφίζειν, primo usurpatum fuisse, cum laude, pro docere et tradere aliquid eruditius præ aliis.*

For sacred Greece 'gainst fair-dame-breeding Troy;
To Chalcis there I made by sea my pass,
And to the Games of great ʳAmphidamas,
Where many a fore-studied exercise
Was instituted, with exciteful prize,
For great-and-good and able-minded men;
And where I won, at the Pierian pen,
A three-ear'd tripod, which I offer'd on
The altars of the Maids of Helicon;
Where first their loves initiated me
In skill of their unworldly harmony.
But no more practice have my travails swet
In many-a-nail-composed ships; and yet
I'll sing what Jove's mind will suggest in mine,
Whose Daughters taught my verse the rage divine.

Fifty days after heaven's converted heat,
When Summer's land-works are dissolv'd with sweat,
Then grows the navigable season fit,
For then no storms rise that thy sail may split,
Nor spoil thy sailors; if the God that sways
Th' earth-shaking trident do not overpaise,
With any counsel beforehand decreed,
The season's natural grace to thy good speed,
Nor Jove consent with his revengeful will,
In whom are fixt the bounds of good and ill.
But in the usual temper of the year,

---

⁴²¹ ʳ'Αμφίδαμας, king of Euboea, was slain in battle against the Erythræans; at whose funerals his sons instituted Games. And from hence Melancthon gathers, by that time in which the king died, Hesiod then living, that Homer lived a hundred years before him, and so could not be the man from whom our author is affirmed by some historians to win the prize he now speaks of.

Easy to judge of, and distinguish clear, 445
Are both the winds and seas, none rude, none cross,
Nor misaffected with the love of loss;
And therefore put to sea; trust even the wind
Then with thy swift ship; but when thou shalt find
Fit freight for her, as fitly stow it straight, 450
And all haste home make. For no new wine wait,
Nor aged Autumn's showers, nor Winter's falls
Then fast approaching, nor the noisome gales
The humorous South breathes, that incense the seas,
And * raise together in one series 455
Jove's Autumn dashes, that come smoking down,
And with his roughest brows make th' ocean frown.

But there's another season for the seas,
That in the first Spring others' choices please;
When, look how much the crow takes at a stride, 460
So much put forth the young leaf is descried
On fig-tree tops; but then the gusts so fall,
That oft the sea becomes impervial.
And **yet** this vernal season many use
For sea affairs; which yet I would not chuse, 465
Nor give it my mind any grateful taste,
Since then steals out so many a ravenous blast;
Nor but with much scath thou canst 'scape thy bane,
Which yet men's greedy follies dare maintain.
Money is soul to miserable men, 470
And to it many men their souls bequeath.
To die in dark-seas is a dreadful death.

All this I charge thee, need to note no more;
Nor in one vessel venture all thy store,

---

[455] * Ὀμοβρόας, cœlestem imbrem vocutus; intending a following of those things quæ serie quâdam continuâ sequuntur.

But most part leave out, and impose the less, 475
For 'tis a wretched thing t' endure distress
Incurr'd at sea; and 'tis as ill, ashore
To use adventures, covetous of more
Than safety warrants, as upon thy wain
To lay on more load than it can sustain; 480
For then thy axle breaks, thy goods diminish,
And thrift's mean means in violent av'rice vanish.
The mean observ'd makes an exceeding state;
Occasion took at all times equals Fate.

Thyself if well in years, thy wife take home 485
Not much past thirty, nor have much to come;
But being young thyself, nuptials that seize
The times' best season in their acts are these:
At ᵗ fourteen years a woman grows mature,
At fifteen wed her, and best means inure 490
To marry her a maid, to teach her then
Respect to thee and chasteness t' other men.
In chief, choose one whose life is ᵘ near thee bred,
That her condition circularly weigh'd,
(And that with care, too,) in thy neighbours' eyes, 495
Thou wedd'st not for a maid their mockeries.
No purchase passes a good wife, no loss
Is than a bad wife a more cursed cross,
That must a gossip be at every feast,
And private cates provide, too, for her guest, 500
And bear her husband ne'er so bold a breast,

---

⁴⁸⁹ ᵗ Τέτορ. Pollux expounds this word, which is usually taken for four, fourteen. Plato and Aristotle appoint the best time of women's marriages at eighteen.
⁴⁹³ ᵘ 'Εγγύθι ναίει, quæ prope te habitat. His counsel is, to marry a maid bred near a man, whose breeding and behaviour he hath still taken into note. Counsel of gold, but not respected in this iron age.

¹ Without **a fire burns** in him even to rage,
And in his youth pours **grief on him** in age.
 The Gods' ʸ forewarnings, and pursuits of men
Of impious **lives** with unavoided pain,   505
Their sight, their rule of all, their love, their fear.
 Watching and sitting up give all thy care.
 Give ᵃ never to thy friend an even respect
With thy born brother, for in his neglect
Thyself thou touchest first with that defect.   510
 If thou shalt take thy friend with an offence
By word, or deed, twice only, try what **sense**
He hath of thy abuse **by** making plain
The wrong **he did thee**; and if then again
He will turn friend, confess and pay all pain   515
Due for his forfeit, take him **into** grace;
The shameless man shifts friends still with his place.
But keep thou friends, forgive, and so convert
That **not thy look** may reprehend thy heart.

⁵⁰² ˣ Εὕει ἄτερ δαλοῦ, *torret sine face et crudæ senectæ tradit ὠμῷ γήραϊ, senecta ante tempus adveniens*, which place Boetius imitates in his book *De Consolatione* in this distich:
 Intempestivi funduntur vertice cani,
  Et dolor ætatem jussit inesse suam.
 [Chapman has misquoted these lines. They **are** not a distich. The whole passage is as follows:
  Venit enim properata malis inopina senectus,
   Et dolor ætatem jussit inesse suam.
  Intempestivi funduntur vertice cani,
   Et tremit effæto corpore laxa cutis.—ED.]
 ⁵⁰⁴ ʸ Ὤπις, in God, signifies insight and government in all things, and his just indignation against the impious; in man, respect to the fear of God, and his reverence. *Melancthon*.
 ⁵⁰⁷ ᶻ Πεφυλαγμένος, *vigiliis et excubiis positis.*
 ⁵⁰⁸ ᵃ Μηδέ. This precept of preferring a man's own brother to his friend is full of humanity, and savours of the true taste of a trueborn man; the neglect of which in these days shows children either utterly misbegotten, or got by unnatural fathers, of whom children must taste, in disposition, as a poison of degeneracy poured into them both, and **a** just plague for both.

GEORGICS OF HESIOD.

 Be not a common host for guests, nor one   520
That can abide the kind receipt of none.
Consort none ill though rais'd to any state,
Nor leave one good though ne'er so ruinate.
Abhor all taking pleasure to upbraid
A forlorn poverty, which God hath laid   525
On any man in so severe a kind
As quite disheartens and dissolves his mind.
Amongst men on the earth there never sprung
An ampler treasure than a sparing tongue;
Which yet most grace gains when it sings the mean. 530
Ill-speakers ever hear as ill again.
Make not thyself at any public feast
A troublesome or over-curious guest;
'Tis common cheer, nor touches thee at all;
Besides, thy grace is much, thy cost is small.   535
Do not thy tongue's grace the disgrace to lie,
Nor mend a true-spoke mind with policy,
But all things use with first simplicity.
 To Jove nor no God pour out morning wine
With unwash'd hand; for, know, the Powers Divine 540
Avert their ears, and prayers impure reject.
 Put not thy urine out, with face erect,
Against [b] the Sun, but, sitting, let it fall,
Or turn thee to some undiscovering wall;

---

[543] [b] Μηδ' ἀντ' ἠελίου, *neque contra solem versus erectus meito.*
He would have no contempt against the Sun; either directly,
or allegorically, intending by the Sun great and reverend men,
against whom *nihil proterve et irreverenter agendum.* If in the
plain sense, which he makes serious, he would not have a man
make water turning purposely against the Sun, nor standing,
but sitting, as at this day even amongst the rude Turks it is
abhorred, *quibus religiosum est ut sedentes mingant, et ingens fla-
gitium designari credunt siquis in publico cacaret aut mingeret.*

And, after the great Sun is in descent, 545
Remember, till he greet the Orient,
That, in way or without, thou still forbear,
Nor ope thy nakedness while thou art there
The nights the Gods' are, and the godly man
And wife will shun by all means to profane 550
The Gods' appropriates. ᶜ Make no access,
Thy wife new left, to sacred mysteries,
Or coming from an ominous funeral feast;
But, from a banquet that the Gods have blest
In men whose spirits are frolicly inclin'd, 555
Perform those rites that propagate thy kind.

Never the fair waves of eternal floods
Pass with thy feet, but first invoke the Gods,
Thine eyes cast on their streams; which those **that wade,**
Their hands unwash'd, those Deities invade 560
With future plagues and even then angry are.

Of thy ᵈ five branches see thou never pare
The dry from off the green at solemn feasts;
Nor on the quaffing mazers of thy guests
Bestow the bowl vow'd to the Powers Divine, 565
For harmful fate is swallow'd with the wine.

When thou hast once begun to build a house,
Leav't not unfinish'd, lest **the ominous**

---

⁵⁵¹ ᶜ Μηδ' αἰδοῖα. Melancthon expounds this place, *a congressu uxoris ne sacra accedas*, whom I have followed; δύσφημος signifies here *infaustus*, and τάφος, *funebre epulum*.

⁵⁶² ᵈ Μηδ' ἀπὸ πεντόζοιο. He says a man must **not** pare his nails at the table; in which our reverend author is so respectful and moral in his setting down, that he nameth not nails, but calls what is to be pared away, *αὖον, siccum* or *aridum*, and the nail itself, χλωρὸν, *viridum*, because it is still growing; he calls likewise the hande πεντόζος, *quæ in quinos ramos dispergitur*, because it puts out five fingers like branches.

⁵⁶⁴ [*Mazers*—cups. See RICHARDSON.]

Ill-spoken crow encounter thee abroad,
And from her bough thy means outgone explode.   570
    From three-foot pots of meat set on the fire
To serve thy house; serve not thy taste's desire
With ravine of the meat till on the board
Thou seest it set, and sacrifice afford,
Not if thou wash first, and the Gods wouldst please   575
With that respect to them; for even for these
Pains are impos'd, being all impieties.
    On tombstones, or fix'd seats, no boy permit,
That's grown to twelve years old, to idly sit;
For 'tis not good, but makes a slothful man.   580
    In baths, whose waters women first began
To wash their bodies in, should bathe no man;
For in their time even these parts have their pain
Grievous enough. If any homely place,
Sylvan or other, thou seest vow'd to grace   585
Of any God, by fire made for the weal
Of any poor soul mov'd with simplest zeal,
Mock not the mysteries, for God disdains
Those impious parts, and pays them certain pains.
    Never in channels of those streams that pay   590
The ocean tribute give thy urine way;
Nor into ᵉfountains; but, past all neglect,
See thou avoid it; for the grave respect
Given to these secrets meets with blest effect.
    Do this, and fly the people's ᶠ bitter fame,   595

---

⁵⁹² ᵉ *Hi rectè in fontes immingere dicuntur, qui sacram doctrinam commaculant.*

⁵⁹⁵ ᶠ Δεινὴν, *gravem* or *terribilem famam* he adviseth a man to avoid: intending with deserving a good and honest fame amongst men, which known to himself impartially and betwixt God and him, every worthy man should despise the contrary

For fame is **ill, 'tis light and** rais'd like flame;
The burthen **heavy yet,** and hard **to cast.**
No fame doth wholly perish, when **her blest**
Echo resounds in all the people's cries,
For she herself is of the Deities. 600

conceit of the world; according to that of Quintilian, writing to Seneca, affirming he cared no more what the misjudging **world** vented against him, *quàm de ventre redditi crepitus.*

THE END OF THE SECOND BOOK OF WORKS.

HESIOD'S BOOK OF DAYS.

HE Days that for thy works are good or ill,
According to the influence they instil,
Of Jove with all care learn, and give
them then,
For their discharge, in precept to thy men.
The Thirtieth day of every month is best,   5
With diligent inspection to digest
The next month's works, and part thy household foods;
That being the day when all litigious goods
Are justly sentenc'd by the people's voices.
And till that day next month give these days' choices,   10
For they are mark'd out by most-knowing Jove.

---

⁶ Ἐπόπτομαι, *diligenti inspectione digero, seu secerno et eligo.*
He begins with the last day of the month, which he names
not a day of any good or bad influence, but being, as it were,
their term day, in which their business in law was attended;
and that not lasting all the day, he adviseth to spend the rest
of it in disposing the next month's labours. Of the rest he
makes difference, showing which are unfortunate, and which
auspicious, and are so far to be observed as natural cause is to
be given for them; for it were madness not to ascribe reason
to Nature, or to make that reason so far above us, that we
cannot know by it what is daily in use with us, all being for
our cause created of God; and therefore the differences of
days arise in some part from the aspects, *quibus luna intuetur
solem, nam quadrati aspectus cient pugam naturæ cum morbo.*

First, the First day in which the moon doth move
With radiance renew'd; and then the Fourth;
The Seventh day next, being first in sacred worth,
For that day did Latona bring to light   15
The gold-sword-wearing Sun; next then the Eighth
And Ninth are good, being both days that retain
The moon's prime strength t' instruct the works of men.
The 'Leventh and Twelfth are likewise both good days;
The **Twelfth** yet far exceeds the 'Leventh's repair,   20
For that day hangs the spinner in the air,
And weaves up her web; so the spinster all
Her rock then ends, exposing it to sale.
So Earth's third housewife, the ingenious ant,
On that day ends her mole-hills' cure of want.   25
The day herself in their example then
Tasking her fire, and bounds her length to men.

The Thirteenth day take care thou sow no seed,
To plant yet 'tis a day of special speed.
The Sixteenth day plants set prove fruitless still,   30
To get **a son** 'tis good, a daughter ill,
Nor **good to get,** nor give in nuptials.

[12] Ἡρῶτον ἔνη, *primum novilunium,* which is called sacred, *nam omnia initia sacra;* the fourth likewise he calls sacred, *quia eo die prodit a coitu Luna, primumque tum conspicitur.*

[18] Ὀγδοάτη. The second and fifth day let pass, and sixth, *ut mediis,* he comes to the eighth and ninth, which in their increasing he terms truly profitable, *nam humores alit crescentia lunæ.*

[19] Ἐνδεκάτη. The tenth let pass, the eleventh and twelfth he praises diversely, because the moon beholds the sun then in a triangular aspect, which is ever called benevolent.

[32] Οὔτ' ἄρ γάμον, *neque nuptiis tradendis.* The sixteenth day, he says, is neither good to get a daughter, nor to wed her, *quia à plenilunio cœpit jam humor defecere;* he says it is good to get a son in, *nam ex humido semine fœmellæ, ex sicciore puelli nascuntur.*

HESIOD'S BOOK OF DAYS. 203

Nor in the Sixth day any influence falls
To fashion her begetting confluence,
But to geld kids and lambs, and sheep-cotes fence, 35
It is a day of much benevolence;
To get a son it good effects affords,
And loves to cut one's heart with bitter words;
And yet it likes fair speeches, too, and lies,
And whispering out detractive obloquies. 40

The Eighth the bellowing bullock lib and goat;
The Twelfth the labouring mule. But if of note
For wisdom, and to make a judge of laws,
To estimate and arbitrate a cause.
Thou wouldst a son get, the great Twentieth day 45
Consort thy wife, when full the morn's broad ray
Shines through thy windows; for that day is fit
To form a great and honourable wit.
The Tenth is likewise good to get a son;
Fourteenth a daughter; then lay hand upon 50
The colt, the mule, and horn-retorted steer,
And sore-bit mastiff, and their forces rear
To useful services. Be careful, then,
The Four-and-twentieth day (the bane of men,

---

[38] Κέρτομος, cor *alicui scindens*.

[41] [*Lib*—castrate.]

[43] Ἴστορα φῶτα, *prudentum* **virum** *judicem, seu arbitrum, quod eos cognaros esse oporteat rei de quâ agitur.* He calls it the great twentieth, because it is the last μηνὸς μεσοῦντος, which is of the middle decad of the month; *diebus τοῦ φθίνοντος*, or days of the dying moon immediately following.

[50] Τετράς. The fourteenth is good to get a daughter, because the **moon then** abounds in humours, and her light is more **gelid and cold**, her heat more temperate; and therefore **he** says **it is good** likewise to tame beasts in, since then, by the abundance of humours, they **are made** more gentle, and consequently easier tamed.

[54] Τετράδ. He calls **this day so baneful, because of the**

Hurling amongst them) to make safe thy state,
Tor 'tis a day of death **insatiate**.
The Fourth day celebrate thy nuptial-feast,
All birds observ'd that fit a bridal best.
All Fifth days to effect affairs in fly,
Being all of harsh and horrid quality;
For then all vengeful spirits walk their round,
And **haunt** men like their handmaids, to confound
Their faithless peace, whose plague Contention got.
The Seventeenth **day** what Ceres did allot
Thy barns in harvest (since then view'd with **care**)
Upon a smooth floor let the vinnoware
Dight and expose to the opposed **gale**;
Then let thy forest-feller cut thee **all**
Thy chamber fuel, and the numerous parts
Of naval timber apt for shipwrights' arts.
The Four-and-twentieth day begin to close
Thy ships of leak. The Ninth day never blows
Least ill at all on men. The Nineteenth day
Yields (after noon yet) a more gentle ray,
Auspicious both to plant, and generate

---

opposition of sun and the **moon, and the time** then being, that is, between the old and new moon, **are** hurtful for bodies; such as labour with choleric diseases, most languish then; those with phlegmatic, contrary.

[59] Πέμπτας. He warns men to fly all fifth days, that is the fifth, the fifteenth, and the five-and-twentieth, because all vengeful spirits he affirms then to be most busy with men.

[64] The seventeenth day he thinketh best to winnow, or dight corn, à plenilunio, because about that time winds are stirred up and the air is drier.

[66] [*Vinnoware*—winnower.]

[72] Πρωΐστη εἰνὰς, *prima nona*. That is from the beginning of the month, he calls harmless, *propter geminum aspectum, cum sol abest a signis.*

Both sons and daughters; ill to no estate.
But the Thrice-Nine day's goodness few men know,
Being best day of the whole month to make flow
Both wine and corn-tuns, and to curb the force
Of mules and oxen and the swift-hoov'd horse; 80
And then the well-built ship launch. But few men
Know truth in anything, or where or when
To do, or order, what they must do, needs,
Days differencing with no more care than deeds.
The Twice-Seventh day for sacred worth exceeds. 85
But few men when the Twentieth day is past,
Which is the best day (while the morn doth last
In her increasing power, though after noon
Her grace grows faint) approve or end that moon
With any care; man's life most priz'd is least, 90
Though lengthless spent as endless, fowl and beast
Far passing it for date. For all the store
Of years man boasts, the prating crow hath more
By thrice three lives; the long-liv'd stag four parts
Exceeds the crow's time; the raven's age the hart's 95
Triples in durance; all the raven's long date
The phœnix ninefold doth reduplicate;
Yet Nymphs (the blest Seed of the Thunderer)
Ten lives outlasts the phœnix. But prefer

---

[76] Proverb, *nullus dies omnino malus.*
[81] Παῦροι. He says few observe these differences of days, and as few know or make any difference betwixt one day and another.
[89] He says few approve those days, because these cause most change of tempests and men's bodies in the beginning of the last quarter.
[90] All this, and the lives of fowls, is cited out of this author by Plutarch, not being extant in the common copy.

Good life to long life; and observe these days 100
That must direct it, being to all men's ways
Of excellent conduct; all the rest but sounds
That follow falls, mere vain and have no grounds;
But one doth one day praise, another other,
Few knowing the truth. This day becomes a mother,
The **next a** stepdame. But, be **man still one,** 106
That man a happy angel **waits upon,**
Makes rich **and blessed,** that through all these days
Is knowingly employ'd; **in all his** ways
(Betwixt him and **the Gods) goes still** unblam'd; 110
All their forewarnings **and** suggestions fram'd
To their obedience, being directly view'd;
All good endeavour'd and all ill eschew'd.

[102] Αἱ δὲ μὲν ἡμέραι, *et hæ quidem dies hominibus sunt magno commodo*. The epilogue of the teacher; in all days is to be considered what religion commands, and then what riseth out of natural **causes.**

THE END OF HESIOD'S WORKS AND DAYS.

MUSÆUS.

THE
DIVINE
POEM OF
MUSÆUS.

Firſt of all BOOKES.

TRANSLATED
According to the Ori-
ginall

By GEO: CHAPMAN.

LONDON
¶ Printed by *Iſaac
Iaggard.* 1616.

TO THE MOST GENERALLY INGENIOUS, AND OUR ONLY LEARNED ARCHITECT, MY EXCEEDING GOOD FRIEND,

INIGO JONES ESQUIRE,

SURVEYOR OF HIS MAJESTY'S WORKS.

NCIENT Poesy, and ancient Architecture, requiring to their excellence a like creating and proportionable rapture, and being alike overtopt by the monstrous Babels of our modern barbarism, their unjust obscurity letting no glance of their truth and dignity appear but to passing few, to passing few is their least appearance to be presented. Yourself then being a chief of that few by whom both are apprehended, and their beams worthily measured and valued, this little light of the one I could not but object, and publish to your choice apprehension; especially for your most ingenuous love to all works in which the ancient Greek Souls have appeared to you. No less esteeming this worth the presenting to any Greatest, for the smallness of the work, than the Author himself hath been held therefore of the less estimation; having obtained as much preservation and honor as the greatest of others;

the smallness being supplied with so greatly-excellent invention and elocution. Nor lacks even the most youngly-enamoured affection it contains a temper grave enough to become both the sight and acceptance of the Gravest. And therefore, howsoever the mistaking world takes 'it (whose left hand ever received what I gave with my right) if you freely and nobly entertain it, I obtain my end; your judicious love's continuance being my only object. To which I at all parts commend

Your ancient poor friend,

GEORGE CHAPMAN.

TO THE COMMUNE READER.

HEN you see *Leander* and *Hero*, the subjects of this Pamphlet, I persuade myself your prejudice will increase to the contempt of it; either headlong presupposing it all one, or at no part matchable, with that partly excellent Poem of Maister Marloe's. For your all one, the Works are in nothing alike; a different character being held through both the style, matter, and invention. For the match of it, let but your eyes be matches, and it will in many parts overmatch it. In the Original, it being by all most learned the incomparable Love-Poem of the world. And I would be something sorry you could justly tax me with doing it any wrong in our English; though perhaps it will not so amble under your seisures and censures, as the before published.

Let the great comprehenders and unable utterers of the Greek elocution in other language drop under their unloadings, how humbly soever they please, and the rather disclaim their own strength, that my weakness may seem the more presumptuous; it can impose no scruple the more burthen on my shoulders, that I will feel; unless *Reason* chance to join arbiter with

Will, and appear to me; to whom I am ever prostrately subject. And if envious Misconstruction could once leave tyrannizing over my infortunate Innocence, **both** the Charity it **argued** would **render** them that use it the more Christian, and **me** industrious, to **hale** out of them the discharge of their own duties.

OF MUSÆUS.

OUT OF THE WORTHY D. GAGER'S COLLECTIONS.

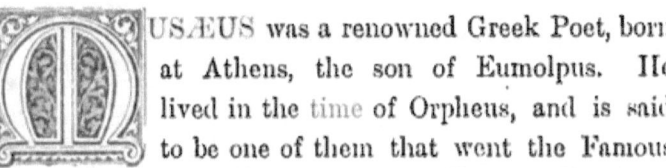USÆUS was a renowned Greek Poet, born at Athens, the son of Eumolpus. He lived in the time of Orpheus, and is said to be one of them that went the Famous Voyage to Colchos for the Golden Fleece. He wrote of the Gods' Genealogy before any other; and invented the Sphere. Whose opinion was, that all things were made of one Matter, and resolved into one again. Of whose works only this one Poem of *Hero* and *Leander* is extant. Of himself, in his Sixth Book of Æne. Virgil makes memorable mention, where in Elysium he makes Sibylla speak this of him—

> Musæum ante omnes; medium nam plurima turba
> Hunc habet, atque humeris extantem suspicit altis.

He was born in Falerum, a town in the middle of Tuscia, or the famous country of Tuscany in Italy, called also Hetruria.

OF ABYDUS AND SESTUS.

ABYDUS and Sestus were two ancient Towns; one in Europe; another in Asia; East and West, opposite; on both the shores of the Hellespont. **Their** names are extant **in Maps** to this day. But in their places are two Castles built, which the Turks call Bogazossas, that is, Castles situate by the sea-side. Seamen now call the place where Sestus stood *Malido.* It was likewise called *Possidonium.* But Abydus is called *Auco.* They are both renowned in all writers for nothing so much as the Love of Leander and Hero.

OF THE HELLESPONT.

HELLESPONT, the straits of the two seas, Propontis and Egeum, running betwixt Abydus and Sestus. Over which Xerxes built a bridge, **and joined these two towns** together, conveying over his army **of seven** hundred thousand men. It is now called by some *The Straits of Gallipolis;* but by Frenchmen, Flemings, and **others,** *The* **Arm** *of Saint George.* It had his name Hellespont, because *Helle* the daughter of *Athamas* K. *of Thebes* was drowned in it. And therefore of one it **is** called *The Virgin-killing Sea;* of another *The Virgin-Sea.* It is but seven *Italian* furlongs broad, which is one of our miles lacking a furlong.

MUSÆUS,

OF HERO AND LEANDER.

ODDESS, relate the witness-bearing light
   Of Loves, that would not bear a human
      sight;
   The Sea-man that transported marriages,
Shipt in the night, his bosom plowing th' seas;
The love joys that in gloomy clouds did fly   5
The clear beams of th' immortal Morning's eye;
Abydus and fair Sestus, where I hear
The night-hid Nuptials of young Hero were;
Leander's swimming to her; and a Light,
A Light that was administress of sight   10
To cloudy Venus, and did serve ᵃ t' address
Night-wedding Hero's nuptial offices;
A Light that took the very form of Love;
Which had been justice in ethereal Jove,
When the nocturnal duty had been done,   15
T' advance amongst the consort of the Sun,
And call the ᵇ Star that Nuptial Loves did guide,
And to the Bridegroom gave and grac'd the Bride,
Because it was ᶜ companion to the death
Of Loves, ᵈ whose kind cares cost their dearest breath; 20
And that ᵉ fame-freighted ship from shipwrack kept

That such sweep nuptials brought they never slept,
Till air ᶠ was with a bitter flood inflate,
That bore their firm loves as infixt a hate.
But, Goddess, forth, and both one issue sing,   25
The Light extinct, Leander perishing.

   Two towns there were, that with one sea were wall'd,
Built near, **and** opposite; this Sestus call'd,
Abydus **that**; the Love his bow bent high,
And at both Cities let one arrow fly,   30
That two (a Virgin and a Youth) inflam'd :
The youth was sweetly-grac'd Leander nam'd,
The virgin Hero ; Sestus she renowns,
Abydus he, in birth ; of both which towns
Both were the beauty-circled stars : and both   35
Grac'd with like looks, as with one love and troth.

   If that way lie thy course, seek for my sake
A Tower, that Sestian Hero once did make
Her watch-tower, and a torch stood holding there,
By which Leander his sea-course did steer.   40
Seek, likewise, of Abydus ancient tow'rs,
The roaring sea lamenting to these hours
Leander's Love and Death. But say, how came
He (at Abydus born) to feel the flame
Of Hero's love at Sestus, and to bind   45
In chains of equal fire bright Hero's **mind**?

   The graceful Hero, born of gentle blood,
Was Venus' Priest; and since she understood
No nuptial language, from her parents she
Dwelt in a tow'r that over-look'd the sea,   50
For shamefastness and chastity, she reign'd
Another Goddess ; nor was ever train'd

   ²⁹ **The** Love—Cupid. Perhaps we should read *then* Love.

In women's companies; nor learn'd to tread
A graceful dance, to which such years are bred.
The envious spites of women she did fly, 55
(Women for beauty their own sex envy)
All her devotion was to Venus done,
And to his heavenly Mother her great Son
Would reconcile with sacrifices ever,
And ever trembled at his flaming quiver. 60
Yet scap'd not so his fiery shafts her breast;
For now the popular Venerean Feast,
Which to Adonis, and great Cypria's State,
The Sestians yearly us'd to celebrate,
Was come; and to that holy day came all 65
That in the bordering isles the sea did wall.
To it in flocks they flew; from Cyprus these,
Environ'd with the rough Carpathian seas;
These from Hæmonia; nor remain'd a man
Of all the towns in th' isles Cytherean; 70
Not one was left, that us'd to dance upon
The tops of odoriferous Libanon;
Not one of Phrygia, not one of all
The neighbours seated near the Festival;
Nor one of opposite Abydus' shore; 75
None of all these, that virgin's favours wore,
Were absent; all such fill the flowing way,
When Fame proclaims a solemn holy day,
Not bent so much to offer holy flames,
As to the beauties of assembled dames. 80

 The virgin Hero enter'd th' holy place,
And graceful beams cast round about her face,
Like to the bright orb of the rising Moon.
The top-spheres of her snowy cheeks put on

A glowing redness, like the two-hued rose
Her odorous bud beginning to disclose.
You would have said, in all her lineaments
A meadow full of roses she presents.
All over her she⁵ blush'd; which (putting on   90
Her white robe, reaching to her ankles) shone
(While she in passing did her feet dispose)
As she had wholly been a moving rose.
Graces in numbers from her parts did flow.
The Ancients therefore (since they did not know   95
Hero's unbounded beauties) falsely feign'd
Only three Graces; for, when Hero strain'd
Into a smile her priestly modesty,
A hundred Graces grew from either eye.
A fit one, sure, the Cyprian Goddess found
To be her ministress; and so highly crown'd   100
With worth her grace was, past all other dames,
That, of a priest made to the Queen of Flames,
A new Queen of them she in all eyes shin'd;
And did so undermine each tender mind
Of all the young men; and there was not one   105
But wish'd fair Hero was his wife, or none.
Nor could she stir about the well-built Fane,
This way or that, but every way she wan
A following mind in all men; which their eyes,
Lighted with all their inmost faculties,   110
Clearly confirmed; and one (admiring) said,
"All Sparta I have travell'd, and survey'd
The City Lacedæmon, where we hear
All Beauties' labors and contentions were,
A woman, yet, so wise and delicate   115
I never saw. It may be Venus gat

One of the younger Graces to supply
The place of priest-hood to her Deity.
Ev'n tir'd I am with sight, yet doth not find
A satisfaction by my sight my mind.   120
O could I once ascend sweet Hero's bed,
Let me be straight found in her bosom dead!
I would not wish to be in heaven a God,
Were Hero here my wife. But, if forbod
To lay profane hands on thy holy priest,   125
O Venus, with another such assist
My nuptial longings." Thus pray'd all that spake;
The rest their wounds hid, and in frenzies brake;
Her beauty's fire, being so suppress'd, so rag'd.
But thou, Leander, more than all engag'd,   130
Wouldst not, when thou hadst view'd th' amazing Maid,
Waste with close stings, and seek no open aid,
But, with the flaming arrows of her eyes
Wounded unwares, thou wouldst in sacrifice
Vent th' inflammation thy burnt blood did prove,   135
Or live with sacred med'cine of her love.
   But now the love-brand in his eye-beams burn'd,
And with unconquered fire his heart was turn'd
Into a coal; together wrought the flame.
The virtuous beauty of a spotless dame   140
Sharper to men is than the swiftest shaft;
His eye the way by which his heart is caught,
And, from the stroke his eye sustains, the wound
Opens within, and doth his entrails sound.
Amaze then took him, Impudence and Shame   145
Made earthquakes in him with their frost and flame.
His heart betwixt them toss'd, till Reverence
Took all these prisoners in him; and from thence

Her matchless beauty, with astonishment,
Increas'd his bands; till aguish Love, that lent
Shame and Observance, licens'd their remove;
And, wisely liking impudence in love,
Silent he went, and stood against the Maid,
And in side glances faintly he convey'd
His crafty **eyes** about her; with dumb shows
Tempting **her** mind to error. And now grows
She **to conceive** his subtle flame, and joy'd
Since he **was** graceful. Then herself employ'd
Her womanish cunning, turning from him quite
Her lovely count'nance; giving yet some light,
Even by her dark signs, of her kindling fire,
With up and down-looks whetting his desire.
He joy'd at heart to see Love's sense in **her,**
And no contempt of what he did prefer.
And while he wish'd unseen to urge the rest,
The day shrunk down her beams to lowest West,
And East; [h] the Even-Star took vantage of her shade.
Then boldly he his kind approaches made,
And as he saw the russet clouds increase,
He strain'd her rosy hand, and held his peace,
But sigh'd as silence had his bosom broke.
When she, as silent, put on anger's cloke,
And drew her hand back. He, discerning well
Her [i] would and would not, to her boldlier fell;
And her elaborate robe, with much cost wrought,
About her waist embracing, on he brought
His love to th' in-parts of the reverend Fane;
She (as her love-sparks more and more did wane)
Went slowly on, and, with a woman's words
Threat'ning Leander, thus his boldness bords:

"Why Stranger, are you ^k mad? Ill-fated man,
Why hale you thus a virgin Sestian?
Keep on your way.   Let go, fear to offend
The noblesse of my birth-right's either friend.
It ill becomes you to solicit thus   185
The priest of Venus. Hopeless, dangerous,
The ^l barr'd up way is to a virgin's bed."
Thus, for the maiden form, she menaced.
But he well-knew, that when these female ^m mines
Break out in fury, they are certain signs   190
Of their persuasions. Women's threats once shown,
Shows in it only all you wish your own.
And therefore of the rubi-colour'd maid
The odorous neck he with a kiss assay'd,
And, stricken with the sting of love, he pray'd: 195
"Dear Venus, next to Venus you must go;
And next Minerva, trace Minerva too;
Your like with earthy dames no light can show;
To Jove's Great Daughters I must liken you.
Blest was thy great begetter; blest was she   200
Whose womb did bear thee; but most blessedly
The womb itself fare that thy throes did prove.
O! hear my prayer! Pity the need of Love.
As priest of Venus, practice Venus' rites.
Come, and instruct me in her bed's-delights.   205
It fits not you, a virgin, to vow aids
To Venus' service; Venus loves no maids.
If Venus' institutions you prefer,
And faithful ceremonies vow to her,
Nuptials and beds they be. If her love binds, 210
Love Love's sweet laws, that soften human minds.

¹⁸⁴ *My birth-right's either friend*—i. e. both my parents.

Make me your servant; husband, if you pleas'd;
Whom Cupid with his burning shafts has seiz'd,
And hunted to you, as swift Hermes drave
With his gold-rod Jove's bold son **to be slave** 215
To Lydia's sov'reign Virgin; but for me,
Venus insulting forc'd my feet to thee,
I was not guided by wise Mercury.
Virgin, **you** know, when Atalanta fled,
Out of Arcadia, kind Melanion's bed, 220
Affecting virgin-life, your angry Queen,
Whom first she us'd with a malignant spleen,
At last possest him of her **complete** heart.
And you, dear love, because I would avert
Your Goddess' anger, I would fain persuade." 225
With these [n] love-luring words conform'd he made
The maid recusant to his blood's desire,
And set her soft mind on an erring fire.
Dumb she was strook; and down to earth she threw
Her rosy eyes, hid in vermilion hue, 230
Made red with shame. Oft with her foot she rac'd
Earth's upper part; and oft (as quite ungrac'd)
About her shoulders gather'd up her weed.
All these fore-tokens are that men should speed.
Of a persuaded virgin, to her bed 235
Promise is most given when the least is said.
And now she took in Love's sweet-bitter sting,
Burn'd in a fire that cool'd her surfeiting.
Her beauties likewise strook her friend amaz'd:
For, while her eyes fixt on the pavement gaz'd, 240
Love on Leander's looks shew'd fury seiz'd.
Never enough his greedy eyes were pleas'd
To view [o] the fair gloss of her tender neck.

At last this voice past, and out did break
A ruddy moisture from her bashful eyes: 245
" Stranger, perhaps thy words might exercise
Motion in flints, as well as my soft breast.
Who taught thee words,ᵖ that err from East to West
In their wild liberty ?   O woe is me !
To this my native soil who guided thee ?   250
All thou hast said is vain; for how canst thou
(Not to be trusted ; one I do not know)
Hope to excite in me a mixed love ?
'Tis clear, that Law by no means will approve
Nuptials with us ; for thou canst never gain   255
My parents' graces.   If thou wouldst remain
Close on my shore, as outcast from thine own,
Venus will be in darkest corners known.
Man's tongue is loose to scandal ; loose acts done
In surest secret, in the open sun   260
And every market place will burn thine ears.
But say, What name sustainst thou ?   What soil bears
Name of thy country ?   Mine I cannot hide.
My far-spread name is Hero; I abide
Hous'd in an all-seen tow'r, whose topsᵠ touch heaven,
Built on a steep shore, that to sea is driven   266
Before the City Sestus ; one sole maid
Attending.   And this irksome life is laid
By my austere friends' wills on one so young ;
No like-year'd virgins near, no youthful throng,   270
To meet in some delights, dances, or so ;
But day and night the windy sea doth throw
Wild murmuring cuffs about our deaf'ned ears."
This said, her white robe hid her cheeks like spheres.
And then (with shame affected, since she us'd   275

Words that desir'd youths, and her friends accus'd)
She blam'd herself for them, and them for her.
Mean space Leander felt Love's arrow err
Thro' all his thoughts; devising how he might
Encounter Love, that dar'd him so to fight. 280
Mind-changing Love wounds men and cures again.
Those mortals over whom he lists to reign,
Th' All-tamer stoops to, in advising how
They may **with** some ease bear the yoke, his **bow.**
So our Leander, whom he hurt, he heal'd. 285
Who having long his hidden fire conceal'd,
And vex'd with thoughts he thirsted to impart,
His stay he quitted with this quickest art:
"Virgin, for thy love I **will swim a wave**
That ships denies; and though with fire it rave, 290
In way to thy bed, all the seas in one
I would despise; the Hellespont were none.
All nights to swim to one ʳsweet bed with thee
Were nothing, if when Love had landed me,
All **hid** in weeds and in Venerean foam, 295
I brought withal bright Hero's husband home.
Not far from hence, and just against thy town,
Abydus **stands,** that my birth calls mine own.
Hold but a torch then in thyˢ heaven-high **tow'r,**
(Which I beholding, **to** that starry pow'r 300
May plow the dark seas, **as the** Ship of Love)
I will not care to see Bootes move
Down to the sea, nor sharp Orion trail
His never-wet car, but arrive my sail,
Against my country, at thy pleasing shore. 305
But (dear) take heed that no ungentle blore
The torch extinguish, bearing all the light

By which my life sails, lest I lose thee quite.
Wouldst thou my name know (as thou dost my house)
It is Leander, lovely Hero's spouse." 310
Thus this kind couple their close marriage made,
And friendship ever to be held in shade
(Only by witness of one nuptial light)
Both vow'd; agreed that Hero every night
Should hold her torch out; every night her love 315
The tedious passage of the seas should prove.
The whole even of the watchful nuptials spent,
Against their wills the stern power of constraint
Enforc'd their parting. Hero to her tow'r;
Leander (minding his returning hour) 320
Took of the turret marks, for fear he fail'd,
And to well-founded broad Abydus sail'd.
All night both thirsted for the secret strife
Of each young-married lovely man and wife;
And all day after no desire shot home, 325
But that the chamber-decking night were come.
And now Night's sooty clouds clapp'd all sail on,
Fraught all with sleep; yet took Leander none,
But on th' oppos'd shore of the noisefull seas
The messenger of glitt'ring marriages 330
Look'd wishly for; or rather long'd to see
The witness of their Light to misery,
Far off discover'd in their covert bed.
When Hero saw the blackest curtain spred
That veil'd the dark night, her bright torch she shew'd.
Whose light no sooner th' eager Lover view'd, 335
But Love his blood set on as bright a fire;
Together burn'd the torch and his desire.
But hearing of the sea the horrid roar,

With which the tender air the mad waves tore, 340
At first he trembled; but **at last he** rear'd
High as the storm his spirit, and thus **cheer'd**
(Using these words to it) his resolute mind:
"Love dreadful is; the Sea with nought inclin'd;
But Sea is water, outward all his ire; 345
When Love lights his fear with an inward **fire.**
Take fire, my heart, fear nought that flits and raves,
Be Love himself to me, despise these waves.
Art thou to **know that** Venus' birth was here?
Commands the sea, and all that grieves us there?" 350
This said, his fair limbs of his weed he stript;
Which, at his head with both hands bound, he shipt,
Leapt from the shore, and cast into the sea
His lovely body; thrusting all his way
Up to the torch, that still he thought **did call;** 355
He oars, he steerer, he the **ship and all.**
Hero advanc'd upon a tow'r so high,
As soon would lose on it the fixedst eye;
And, **like** her Goddess Star, with her light shining,
The winds, that always (as at her repining) 360
Would blast her pleasures, with her veil she checkt,
And **from** their envies did her torch protect.
And this she never left, till she had brought
Leander to the havenful shore he **sought.**
When down she ran, and up she lighted then, 365
To her tow'r's top, the weariest **of men.**
First at the gates (without a syllable us'd)
She hugg'd her panting husband, all diffus'd
With foamy drops still stilling from his hair.
Then brought she him into the inmost fair 370
Of all, her virgin-chamber, that (at best)

Was with her beauties ten times better drest.
His body then she cleans'd; his body oil'd
With rosy odours, and his bosom (soil'd
With the unsavoury sea) she render'd sweet
Then, in the high-made bed (ev'n panting yet)
Herself she pour'd about her husband's breast,
And these words utter'd: "With too much unrest,
O husband, you have bought this little peace!
Husband! No other man hath paid th' increase
Of that huge sum of pains you took for me.
And yet I know, it is enough for thee
To suffer for my love the fishy savours
The working sea breaths. Come lay all thy labors
On my all-thankful bosom." All this said,
He straight ungirdled her; and both parts paid
To Venus what her gentle statutes bound.
Here weddings were, but not a musical sound;
Here bed-rites offer'd, but no hymns of praise,
Nor poet sacred wedlock's worth did raise.
No torches gilt the honor'd nuptial bed,
Nor any youths much-moving dances led.
No father, nor no reverend mother, sung
Hymen, O Hymen, blessing loves so young.
But when the consummating hours had crown'd
The down-right nuptials, a calm bed was found;
Silence the room fixt; Darkness deckt the bride;
But hymns and such rites far were laid aside.
Night was sole gracer of this nuptial house;
Cheerful Aurora never saw the spouse
In any beds that were too broadly known,
Away he fled still to his region,
And breath'd insatiate of the absent Sun.

Hero kept all this from her parents still,
Her priestly weed was large, and would not fill, 405
A maid by day she was, a wife by night;
Which both so lov'd they wish'd it never light.
And thus both, hiding the strong need of love,
In Venus' secret sphere rejoic'd to move.
But soon their joy died; and that still-toss'd state 410
Of **their** stol'n nuptials drew but little date.
For when the frosty Winter kept his justs,
Rousing together all the horrid gusts
That from the ever-whirling pits arise,
And those weak deeps that drive up to the skies, 415
Against the drench'd foundations making knock
Their curled foreheads; then with many a shock
The winds and seas met, made the storms aloud
Beat all the rough sea with a pitchy cloud.
And then the black bark, buffeted with gales, 420
Earth checks so rudely that in two it falls;
The seaman flying winter's faithless sea.
Yet, brave Leander, all this bent at thee
Could not compell in thee one fit of fear;
But when the cruel faithless messenger 425
(The tow'r) appear'd and shew'd th' accustom'd light,
It stung thee on, secure of all the spite
The raging sea spit. But since Winter came,
Unhappy Hero should have cool'd her flame,
And lie without Leander, no more lighting 430
Her short-liv'd bed-star; but strange Fate exciting
As well as Love, and both their pow'rs combin'd
Enticing her, in her hand never shin'd
The fatal Love-torch, but this one hour, more.
Night came. And now the Sea against the shore 435

Muster'd her winds up; from whose wint'ry jaws
They belch'd their rude breaths out in bitt'rest flaws.
In midst of which Leander, with the pride
Of his dear hope to bord his matchless bride,
Up on the rough back of the high sea leaps;   440
And then waves thrust up waves; the watry heaps
Tumbled together; sea and sky were mixt;
The fighting Winds the frame of Earth unfixt;
Zephyr and Eurus flew in either's face,
Notus and Boreas wrastler-like embrace,   445
And toss each other with their bristled backs.
Inevitable were the horrid cracks
The shaken Sea gave; ruthful were the wracks
Leander suffer'd in the savage gale
Th' inexorable whirlpits did exhale.   450
Often he pray'd to Venus born of seas,
Neptune their King; and Boreas, that t' would please
His Godhead, for the Nymph Atthea's sake,
Not to forget the like stealth he did make
For her dear love, touch't then with his sad state.   455
But none would help him; Love compels not Fate.
Every way toss'd with waves and Air's rude breath
Justling together, he was crush'd to death.
No more his youthful force his feet commands,
Unmov'd lay now his late all-moving hands.   460
His throat was turn'd free channel to the flood,
And drink went down that did him far from good.
No more the false light for the curst wind burn'd,
That of Leander ever-to-be-mourn'd
Blew out the love and soul. When Hero still   465
Had watchful eyes, and a most constant will
To guide the voyage; and the morning shin'd,

Yet not by her light she her love could find.
She stood distract with miserable woes,
And round about the sea's broad shoulders throws   470
Her eye, to second the extinguish'd light;
And tried if any way her husband's sight
Erring in any part she could descry.
When at her turret's foot she saw him lie
Mangl'd with rocks, and all-embrued, she tore   475
About her breast the curious weed she wore;
And with a shriek from off her turret's height
Cast her fair body headlong, that fell right
On her dead husband, spent with him her breath;
And each won other in the worst of death.   480

ANNOTATIONS UPON THIS POEM OF MUSÆUS.

Ver. 11. ^a Γαμοστόλος signifies one *qui nuptias apparat vel instruit*.

17. ^b Νυμφοστόλον ἄστρον ἐρώτων. Νυμφοστόλος *est qui sponsam sponso adducit seu conciliat*.

19. ^c Συνέριθος, *socius in aliquo opere*.

20. ^d Ἐρωμανέων ὀδυνάων. Ἐρωμανὴς signifies *perditè amans*, and therefore I enlarge the verbal translation.

21. ^e Ἀγγελίην δ' ἐφύλαξεν ἀκοιμήτων, κ. τ. λ. Ἀγγελία, besides what is translated in the Latin *res est nuntiata, item mandatum a nuntio perlatum, item fama*, and therefore I translate it *fame-freighted ship*, because Leander calls himself ὁλκὸς ἔρωτος, which is translated *navis amoris*, though ὁλκὸς properly signifies *sulcus*, or *tractus navis, vel serpentis, vel æthereæ sagittæ, &c.*

23. ^f Ἐχθρὸν ἀήτην. Ἔχθος, Ἔχθρα, and Ἐχθρὸς are of one signification, or have their deduction one; and seem to be deduced ἀπὸ τοῦ ἔχεσθαι, I. *hærere. Ut sit odium quod animo infixum hæret*. For *odium* is by Cicero defined *ira inveterata*. I have therefore translated it according to this deduction, because it expresses better; and taking the wind for the fate of the wind; which conceived and appointed before, makes it as inveterate or infixed.

89. ^g Χροιὴν γὰρ μελέων ἐρυθαίνετο, *colore enim membrorum rubebat*. A most excellent hyperbole, being to be understood *she blushed all over her*. Or, then follows another elegancy, as strange and hard to conceive. The mere verbal translation of the Latin being in the sense either imperfect, or utterly in-

elegant, which I **must** yet leave to your judgment, **for your** own satisfaction. **The** words are,—

Νισσομένης δὲ
Καὶ ῥόδα λευκοχίτωνος ὑπὸ σφυρὰ λάμπετο κούρης.

*Euntis vero
Etiam rosæ candidâ indutæ tunicâ sub talis splendebant puellæ.*

To understand which, that her white weed was all underlined with **roses,** and that they shined out of it as she went, is passing poor and absurd ; and as gross to have her stuck all over with roses. And therefore to make the sense answerable in heighth **and** elegancy to the former, she seemed (blushing all over her white robe, even below her ankles as she went) a moving rose, as having the blush of many roses about her.

167. ʰ *Ἀνέφαινε βαθύσκιος ἕσπερος ἀστήρ. Apparuit umbrosa Hesperus stella. E regione* is before ; which I English "*And east ; the Even-star took vantage of her shade,* viz. of the evening shade, which is the cause that stars appear.

174. ⁱ Χαλίφρονα νεύματα κ. *instabilis nutus puellæ.* I English *her would and would not.* Χαλίφρων, ὁ χάλις τὰς φρένας, signifying *cui mens laxata est et enerva ;* and of extremity therein *amens, demens.* Χαλιφρονέω, *sum χαλίφρων.*

181. ᵏ *Demens sum*—she calls him δύσμορε, which signifies *cui difficile fatum obtingit ;* according to which I English it, *infelix* (being the word in the Latin) not expressing so particularly, because the *unhappy* in our language hath divers understandings, as *waggish* or *subtle, &c.* And the other well expressing an ill abodement in Hero of his ill or hard fate ; imagining straight the strange and sudden alteration in her to be fatal.

187. ˡ Λέκτρον ἀμήχανον. Παρθενικῆς going before, it is Latined, *virginus ad lectum difficile* **est ire ;** but ἀμήχανος signifies *nullis machinis expugnabilis : the way unto a virgin's bed is utterly-barred.*

189. ᵐ Κυπριδίων ὀάρων αὐτάγγελοί εἰσιν ἀπειλαί. *Venerearum consuetudinum per se nuntiæ sunt minæ ;* exceeding **elegant.** Αὐτάγγελος signifying *qui sibi nuntius est, id est, qui sine aliorum opera sua ipse nuntiat ;* according to which I have Englished it. Ὄαρες, *lusus veneres.* Ἀπειλαί also, which signifies *minæ,* having a reciprocal signification in our tongue, being Englished *mines.* Mines, as it is privileged amongst us, being English, signifying mines made under the earth. I

have passed it with that word, being fit for this place in that understanding.

226. ⁿ Ἐρωτοτόκοισι μύθοις, ἐρωτοτόκος σάρξ, *corpus amorem pariens et alliciens*, according to which I have turned it.

243. º Ἀπαλόχροον αὐχένα. Ἀπαλόχροος signifies *qui tenerâ et delicatâ est cute ; tenerum* therefore not enough expressing, I have enlarged the expression as in his place.

248. ᴾ Πολυπλανέων ἐπέων is turned *variorum verborum*, πολυπλανής signifying *multivagus, erroneus*, or *errorum plenus*, intending that sort of error that is in the planets ; of whose wandering they are called πλανῆτες ἀστέρες, *sidera errantia*. So that Hero taxed him for so bold a liberty in words, as erred *toto cœlo* from what was fit, or became the youth of one so graceful; which made her break into the admiring exclamation, that one so young and gracious should put on so experienced and licentious a boldness, as in that holy temple encouraged him to make love to her.

265. ᑫ Δόμος οὐρανομήλης. It is translated *domo altissimâ ;* but because it is a compound, and hath a grace superior to the others in his more near and verbal conversion, οὐρανομήκης signifying *cœlum proceritate tangens*, I have so rendered it.

293. ʳ Ὑγρὸς ἀκοίτης, translated *madidus maritus*, when as ἀκοίτης is taken here for ὁμοκοίτης, signifying *unum et idem cubile habens*, which is more particular and true.

299. ˢ Ἠλιβάτον σέο πύργου, &c. Ἠλίβατος signifies *jam altus aut profundus ut ab ejus accessu aberres*, intending the tower upon which Hero stood.

FINIS.

JUVENAL.

A JUST REPROOFE

OF A

Romane Smell-Feaſt:

BEING THE FIFTH SATYRE OF

JUVENAL.

Translated by George Chapman.

Imprinted at London by Tho. Harper
M D C. X X I X.

TO THE RIGHT VIRTUOUS AND WORTHILY
HONOURED GENTLEMAN,
RICHARD HUBERT, ESQUIRE.

SIR,

REAT works get little regard; little and light are most affected with height; *omne leve sursum, grave deorsum*, you know; for which, and because custom or fashion is another nature, and that it is now the fashion to justify strange actions, I (utterly against mine own fashion) followed the vulgar, and assaid what might be said for the justification of a strange action of Nero in burying with a solemn funeral one of the cast hairs of his mistress Poppea. And not to make little labours altogether unworthy the sight of the great, I say with the great defender of little labours, *In tenui labor est, at tenuis non gloria.* Howsoever, as seamen seeing the approaches of whales, cast out empty vessels, to serve their harmful pleasures, and divert them from everting their main adventure (for in the vast and immane power of any thing, nothing is distinguished; great and precious things, basest and vilest, serve alike their wild and unwildy swings); so myself, having yet once more some worthier work than this oration, and following translation,

to pass this sea of the land, expose to the land and vulgar Leviathan these slight adventures. **The** rather, because the translation containing in two or three instances a preparation to the justification of my ensuing intended* translations, lest some should account them, as they have my former conversions in some places, licenses, bold ones, and utterly redundant. Though your judicial **self (as** I have heard) hath taken those liberal redundances rather **as** the necessary overflowings of Nilus, than rude or harmful torrents swoln with headstrong showers. To whose judgement and merit submits these, and all his other, services

GEORGE CHAPMAN.

---

* It would seem from this that Chapman intended other translations. None, however, have been printed.

TO THE READER.

BECAUSE, in most opinions of translation, a most asinine error hath gotten ear and head, that men must attempt it as a mastery in rendering any original into other language, to do it in as few words, and the like order, I thought it not amiss in this poor portion of translation to pick out, like the rotten out of apples if you please so to repute it, a poor instance or two that endeavour to demonstrate a right in the contrary; and the rather I take this course, ocularily to present you with example of what I esteem fit to save the liberty and dialect of mine own language, because there are many valetudinaries that never know the goodness of their stomach till they see meat afore them.

Where, therefore, the most worthy Satirist describes the differences of pages that attend the lord and the guests at the table, and expresses the disdain of the lord's page to attend his guest, bespeaks for his pride thus:—

——sed forma sed ætas
Digna supercilio.

Which I take out with this bold one: *And to say truth his form and prime beside may well allow him some few grains of pride.* To speak truth is too much, you say; I confess it in policy, but not in force and honest poesy.

In the other, the words are utterly altered. **It should** be so, to avoid verbal servitude; but the sense **I** might wish my betters could render no worse. It follows, where he sets down the difference betwixt the lord's bread and **the** guests'; where he hath played upon the coarseness and mustiness of the guests' pantry, he differences **his lord's** thus :—

> Sed tener et niveus, mollique siligine factus,
> Servatur domino.

Which **I** thus :—

> But for his bread, the pride of appetite,
> Tenderly soft, incomparably white,
> The first flow'r of fine meal subdu'd in paste,
> That's a peculiar for my lord's own taste.

O this, you will say, **is a** bold **one;** which **I am too** bashful to answer otherwise than thus, that here the purest bread affects a full description; which I amplifying no more than is needful **for** the full facture of it, if I be overflowing, my author is arid; but who would not greedily here have fallen upon *snowy*, it lying so fair for him? put *soft* faithfully in his proper place; and would ever have dreamed of *subdued in paste*, because **it** was **not put** in his mouth? And I hope it will seem no over-broad bold one, to enter where the purest bread out of industry should make his expected apparance. A number more out of this of no number I could instance, that would trouble men made of greatest number to imitate. But all mastery hath his end, to get great men to commend. It is the outward not the inward virtue that prevails. The candlestick more than the candle is the learning with which blind Fortune useth to prefer her favourites. And who, but the spawns of candlesticks (men of most lucubration for name) win the day from such dormice as wake sleeping; and rest only in those unprofitable and abhorred knowledges, that no man either praises or acknowledges.

> Me dulcis saturet quies.   Leni perfruar ocio.
> Ignotus omnibus.   Cognitus egomet mihi.

Quite opposite to your admired and known learned man: *Qui notus nimis omnibus, Ignotus moritur sibi.* And so shall know nothing either in life or death when every truly learned man's knowledge especially begins. Your servant.

D. JUNII JUVENALIS.

LIB. I. SAT. V.

TO TREBIUS. LABOURING TO BRING HIM IN DISLIKE OF HIS CONTINUED COURSE OF FREQUENTING THE TABLE OF VIRRO, A GREAT LORD OF ROME.

IF, of thy purpose yet, thou tak'st no shame,
But keep'st thy mind, immutably, the same,
That thou esteem'st it as a good in chief
At others' trenchers to relieve thy life;
If those things thou can'st find a back to bear,   5
That not Sarmentus nor vile Galba were
So base to put in patience of a guest,
No, not for Cæsar's far-exceeding feast;
Fear will affect me to believe thy troth
In any witness, though produc'd by oath;   10
For nothing in my knowledge falls that is
More frugal than the belly. But say this,
That not enough food all thy means can find,
To keep thy gut from emptiness and wind,
Is no creek void? No bridge? No piece of shed   15
Half, or not half? Would thy not being fed
At Virro's table be so foul a shame?

Does hunger blow in thee so false a flame,
As not to taste it nobler in as poor
And vile a place as hath been nam'd before ?   20
To quake for cold, and gnaw the mustiest grounds
Of barley-griest, bak'd purposely for hounds?
First, take it for a rule, that if my lord
Shall once be pleas'd to grace thee with his board,
The whole revenues that thy hopes inherit,   25
Rising from services of ancient merit,
In this requital amply paid will prove.
O 'tis the fruit of a transcendent love
To give one victuals; that thy table-king
Lays in thy dish though ne'er so thin a thing,   30
Yet that reproach still in thine ears shall ring.
If, therefore, after two months' due neglect,
He deigns his poor dependant to respect,
And lest the third bench fail to fill the rank,
He shall take thee up to supply the blank.   35
'Let's sit together Trebius,' says my lord;
Sees all thy wishes summ'd up in a word.
What canst thou ask at Jove's hand after this?
This grace to Trebius enough ample is
To make him start from sleep before the lark,   40
Posting abroad untruss'd, and in the dark,
Perplex'd with fear, lest all the servile-rout
Of his saluters have the round run-out
Before he come; while yet the fixed star
Shows his ambiguous head, and heaven's cold car   45
The slow Bootes wheel about the Bear.
And yet, for all this, what may be the cheer?
To such vile wine thy throat is made the sink,
As greasy wool would not endure to drink,

And we must shortly look to see our guest   50
Transform'd into a Berecynthian priest.
Words make the prologue to prepare the fray,
And in the next scene pots are taught to play
The parts of weapons; thy red napkin now
Descends to tell thee of thy broken brow;   55
And such events do evermore ensue
When you poor guests and Virro's serving crew
Grow to the heat of such uncivil wars,
The vile wine made the bellows to your jars.
For Virro's self, the wine he drinks was born   60
When consuls (Phœbus-like) appear'd unshorn;
A grape that long since in the wars was prest
By our confederate Marsians, and the rest;
Of which no drop his longing friend can get
Though blown in fume up with a cardiack fit.   65
Next day he likes to taste another field,
The Alban hills', or else the Setine yield,
Whose race and rich succession if you ask,
Age hath decay'd, and sickness of the cask;
Such Thrasea and Helvidius quaff'd, still crown'd, 70
When Brutus' birth, and Cassius' they renown'd.
Virro himself in solemn bowls is serv'd,
Of amber and disparent beryl kerv'd;
But to thy trust no such cup they commit,
Or, if they do, a spy is fix'd to it,   75
To tell the stones; whose firm eye never fails
To watch the close walks of thy vulturous nails.
'Give leave,' says Virro, and then takes the cup,
The famous jasper in it lifting up
In glorious praises; for 'tis now the guise   80
Of him and others to transfer such prize

Off from his fingers to his bowls that were
Wont to grace swords, and our young Trojan peer
That made Iarbus jealous (since in love
Preferr'd past him by Dido) us'd t' improve 85
By setting them in fore-front of his sheath.
But thy bowl stands an infinite beneath,
And bears the Beneventane cobbler's name,
Whose gallon drunk-off must thy blood enflame,
And is so craz'd, that they would let it pass 90
To them that matches give for broken glass.
Now, if by fumes of wine, or fiery meat,
His lordship's stomach over-boil with heat,
There's a cold liquor brought that's made t' outvie
The chill impressions of the north-east sky. 95
I formerly affirm'd, that you and he
Were serv'd with wines of a distinct degree,
But now remember, it belongs to you
To keep your distance in your water too.
And (in his page's place) thy cups are brought 100
By a swarth foot man, from Getulia bought,
Or some sterv'd negro, whose affrightful sight
Thou wouldst abhor to meet in dead of night
Passing the monuments of Latia.
In his eye waits the flower of Asia, 105
A jewel purchas'd at a higher rate
Than martial Ancus', or king Tullus', state,
(Not to stand long) than all the idle things
That grac'd the courts of all our Roman kings.
If then thy bowl his nectar's store shall need, 110
Address thee to his Indian Ganymed.
Think not his page, worth such a world, can skill,
Or does not scorn, for thread-bare coats to fill,

And, to say truth, his form and pride beside
May well allow him some few grains of pride.   115
But when does he to what thou want'st descend,
Or thy entreaties not contemn t' attend,
Supply of water craving, hot or cold?
No, he, **I tell** you, in high scorn doth hold
To **stir at** every stale dependant's call;   120
Or that thou call'st for anything at all,
Or sitt'st where he's forc'd stand, his pride depraves.
Houses of state abound with stately slaves.
And see, another's proud disdains resist
His hand to set thee bread; and yet what is't   125
But hoary cantles of unboulted **grist,**
That would a jaw-tooth rouse, and not admit,
Though ne'er so base, thy baser throat a bit?
But for his bread, the pride of appetite,
Tenderly soft, incomparably white,   130
The first flow'r of fine meal subdu'd in paste,
That's a peculiar for my lord's own taste.
See then thou keep'st thy fingers from offence,
And give the pantler his due reverence.
Or **say thou shouldst** be (malapertly) bold,   135
Seest **thou** not slaves enough, to force thy hold
From thy attempted prize, with taunts like these,
'Hands off, forward companion, will **you** please
With your familiar crible to be **fed,**
And understand the colour of your bread?'   140
    Then grumbles thy disgrace: 'And is it this
For which so oft I have forborne the bliss

---

[131] See Batrachomyomachia, 53.
[134] *Pantler*—the servant who kept the bread, the pantry.
[139] *Crible*—a finer sort of bran; seconds' bread.

Of my fair wife, to post with earliest speed
Up to Mount Esquiline, where agues breed?
When my repair did vernal Jove provoke   145
To drive his weather through my winter cloke,
And in his bitter'st hails his murmurs broke?'
But let us to our cates our course address:
Observe that lobster serv'd to Virro's mess,
How with the length of his extended limbs   150
He does surcharge the charger; how the brims
With lust-full 'sperage are all over-stor'd;
With what a tail he over-tops the board,
In service first borne-up betwixt the hands
Of that vast yeoman! But, for thee, there stands   155
A puny cray-fish, pent in half a shell,
The dish not feast enough for one in hell.
The fish he tastes swims in an oil that grew
In Campany, and drank Venafrian dew.
But, for the worts, poor snake, presented thee,   160
Whose pale aspect shows their infirmity,
They drink an oil much of the curriers' stamp,
Exquisite stuff, that savours of the lamp.
For know, that for your board is billetted
An oil that from the Lybian cane is shed,   165
The burthen of a sharp Numidian prow;
An oil, for whose strength Romans disavow
To bathe with Boccharis; an oil whose smell
'Gainst serpents doth an amulet excell.
   Next, for my lord, a mullet see serv'd in,   170
Sent from the Corsic-shore, or of a fin
Bred in Sicilia's Taurominian rocks;
All our seas being exhausted, all our flocks

         [160] *Worts*—vegetables, cole-worts.

Spent and destroy'd, while **our** luxurious diet
Makes havock, and **our kitchens** never quiet
Still with unwearied nets, that no truce keep,
Ransack the entrails of th' adjoining deep;
Nor respite our Etrurian fry to grow.
And **now our** markets their chief purveyance owe
To some remote and ditionary coast;
Thence come the dainties that our kitchens **boast**;
Such as to buy the vulture Lenas deigns,
Such as to sell Aurelia entertains.
In mess with that, behold for Virro lies
A lamprey of an exemplary size,
That for dimension bears the prize from all
Which gulphs Sicilian sent his festivall;
For while the South contains himself, while he
Lies close, and dries his feathers in his lee,
Our greedy pursenets for their gain despise
The danger that in mid Charybdis lies.

 Now, for his lamprey, thou art glad to take
An eel, near cousin to a hideous snake,
Or **else a** freckled Tiberine, bit with frost,
And he **the** poorest slave of all the coast,
Fed **with the torrent** of the common sewer,
And swims the town ditch where 'tis most impure.
Here would I on himself a word have spent,
So he inclin'd an ear benevolent.
Nor do we such benevolences crave,
As Seneca his mean acquaintance gave;
Such as good Piso; such as Cotta made
To deal for largess; a familiar trade;
For times have been, that in the world's account
The title of munificence did mount

Above triumphant or imperial bays.
But our desire in this due limit stays,
That you will make, when you entreat a guest,
Civil respect the steward of your feast.
Do this, and be, as many lords are more, 210
Rich to yourself, and to your followers poor.
   Before him see a huge goose-liver set ;
A capon cramm'd, even with that goose ; for great
A whole wild boar, hid in his smoking heat,
That gold-lock'd Meleager's dart deserv'd ; 215
And after all this, Virro's self is serv'd
With pure dress'd mushrooms, be the spring then freed,
And wished thunders make his meals exceed.
And then the gully-gut (Aledius) cries
O Lybia, keep with thee thy wheats and ryes, 220
And ease thy oxen, sending these supplies.
And that no indignation want to thee,
(As bound t' observe) the carver thou must see
Dancing about his business ; and he
That teaches him the laws to the true life 225
Of carving comely, with his flying knife
Touching at every joint he carves, before
He dares th' attempt, till not a gesture more
In all his dictates can deserve offence.
Nor must your note fail, how huge difference 230
There is 'twixt the unlacing of your hare,
And hen's dissection. 'Gainst which if you dare
But whisper, like a three-nam'd noble man,
Like Cacus, struck by hands-Herculean,
Thou shalt be by the heels dragg'd forth the place. 235
But when doth Virro then vouchsafe the grace
To drink to thee ? Or touch the cup that thou

Hast with thy lips profan'd? Or which of you
So desperate is, so lost, to bid the king
'Drink to me, sir?' No. There is many a thing   240
That thread-bare coats dare not for fear bring forth.
But if some God, or God-like man, or worth
Better than fate, would wealth bestow on thee,
Fit to maintain a knight of Rome's degree,
How huge a piece of man shouldst thou ascend   245
Rais'd out of nothing! **How** much Virro's friend!
'Give **Trebius.**' 'Set to Trebius.' 'Brother (now)
Please you these **puddings'** taste?' O moneys, you
He gives this honour, you these brother are.
Yet notwithstanding, if thou please to share   250
His lordship with him, or become his king,
You must to court no young Æneas **bring,**
Nor daughter, though his daintier, **to be**
Play-peers with Virro's daintiest progeny,
But childless be. A pleasing and dear friend   255
A barren wife makes. But suppose she lend
Thy lap much issue (even at one birth three)
So thou be rich, Virro will join with thee
In joy of that thy prating progeny;
And ever when the infant parasite   260
Comes to the table, asking his delight,
Virro commands it all his appetite.
To all his cheap priz'd friends, they serve the board
With dangerous toad-stools; mushrooms for my lord,
But such as Claudius pleas'd to taste, before   265
His wife's gift came that made him taste no more.
  Virro commands for him, and all the rest
Of the Virronian rank, fruit of such feast
As thou shalt only in their odour **eat,**

Such as Phæacia's endless autumns sweat, 270
Or thou wouldst think got from the golden trees
That grew in guard of the Atlantides;
Where thou eat'st spaky fruit, of that sour sort
That fresh-train'd soldiers feed on in their fort,
Bestow'd on them in practise of their art 275
At a stuff'd goat-skin to bestow a dart,
Fearing for their default the scourge's smart.
Perhaps, for saving cost, thou may'st conceive
That Virro feeds thee so? No, 'tis to grieve
Thy greedy liquorous appetite, because 280
There is no comedy of more applause,
Nor any excellentest Zany can
More than a weeping-gut delight a man.
All is then done (if we must teach thine ears)
To make thee purge thy choler by thy tears, 285
And live still gnashing of thy great-eye-teeth.
Thou think'st, he thinks thee free, and not beneath
Guests for his love and grace; but he knows well
Thee only taken with his kitchen's smell.
Nor thinks amiss; for who so naked lives, 290
That twice on his entreats attendance gives?
Vain hope of supping well deceives you all
'But see' (say you) 'that half-eat hare will fall
In his gift to our shares; or of that boar
Some little fragments, that his haunches wore; 295
Or sure that cap'net.' When, for all prepar'd,
Your musty bread par'd clean, and no bit shar'd
Of all those meats of mark, and long'd-for dishes,
Your vain hopes vanish, and y' are mute as fishes.

²⁷³ *Spaky*—specky, rotten.
²⁹⁶ *Cap'net*—caponet, little capon.

He's wise that serves thee so ; **for if** thou can 300
Bear all, thou should'st, and he's no unjust man
That lays all on thee, even to stoop thy head
To the fool's razor, and be buffeted ;
Which if thou do'st, nor let'st thy **forage fear**
Besides **to suffer** Virro's whipping cheer, 305
With **all** the sharp sauce that he can extend,
Thou'rt worthy such a feast, and such a friend.

FINIS

A GLOSSARIAL INDEX

TO

THE WHOLE OF CHAPMAN'S CLASSICAL
TRANSLATIONS.

THE Editor gives this Index as a valuable adjunct to the five volumes of the Translations. Explanations are only affixed to such words as seem to need them. Many words are noted as early instances of their use, and as not occurring in the ordinary dictionaries. This, it is hoped, will be of some philological value. One or two references have been thought sufficient.

The abbreviations are—Il. for Iliad; Od. for Odyssey; Bat. for Batrachomyomachia; H. A. for Hymn to Apollo; H. H. for Hymn to Hermes; H. V. for Hymn to Venus; and the smaller Hymns are generally cited by the page; Hes. for Hesiod; Mus. for Musæus; and Juv. for Juvenal.

INDEX.

A.

Able (to). Il. xxiii. 724
Ablesse. Il. v. 248
Abodes = prognostications. Il. xiii. 145
Abodes = stays. Od. iii. 471; iv. 201
Acceptant (n. s.) Il. vii. arg. 3.
Accited = summoned, roused. Il. xi. 595
Accost (to) = approach, draw near. Il. x. 461; Od. iv. 418
Addictions = inclinations. Il. ii. 60
Address (to) = **prepare.** Il. ii. 24; Od. ii. 586
Addression. Il. vi. 371; Od. i. 438
Administress. Mus. 10
Admiration = astonishment. Il. ix. 194
Admired = wonderful. Il. iii. 138
Adviceful Il. ix. 87
Advise (to) = notify. Od. xx. 334
Affair = endeavour. Il. v. 503
Affects = passions, inclinations. Il. i. 209; Od. ii. 54
Affect (to) = **act** upon, **move.** Il. v. 180
Affected = **made show of.** Il. iii. 210.
Affected = loved. Il. iii. 368; viii. 318.
Affrightful. Juv. 102
Aidful. Il. i. 483
Allowance = approbation. Il. ii. 5; vii. 43
Allowed = **approved.** Il. iii. 12
Amazeful. Il. xvii. 658
Ambassadress. Il. iii. 126
Ambassage. Il. ix. 655

Ambassy. Il. v. 806; Od. v. 42
Ambuscadoes. Il. xviii. 479
Amelled = enamelled. Il. xvi. 123
Amendsful. Il. iii. 383
Amiable = lovely. Il. v. 214
Amorous = ardently desiring. Il. ii. 690
Angel = messenger, *passim.*
Anger (to), **v. a.** Il. vii. arg. 9; Od. xviii. 33.
Annoy (n. s.) = trouble. Od. iv. 131
Apaid (or appaid) = satisfied. Il. v. 143; Od. i. 134
Aped = imitated. Bat. 218
Appall (n. **s.**) = fear. Bat. 440
Apposed = placed. Il. ii. 371; ix. 95
Appropriates (n. s.) Bat. 184
Approve = prove. Il. iii. 110
Apt = ready, fit. Il. xvi. 470; Od. vi. 122
Arbitrement. Il. xviii. 456
Arbitry. Od. xi. 738
Areeds = counsels, advises. Il. viii. 85
Arew = on **a row.** Il. vi. 259
Argument = example. Il. vi. 55
Arras. Il. x. 139
Arrasted = carpeted. Il. v. 199
Arrive (to) = to cause to arrive. Il xxiv. 299; H. A. 684
Arrive = arrival. Od. ii. 379
Arted well = well-made, jointed. Il. xviii. 356
Artfully = dexterously, **skilfully.** Il. xxiv. 557; Od. v. 342
Aspire (to) = to aspire to. Il. x. 399
Assay (to) = endeavour. Il. ii. 58; Od. ii. 512

260   INDEX.

Assistful. Il. v. 119
Assume (to) = take up. Od. xi. 159
Assumpt (n. s.) = that which is assumed. Od. xvi. 252
Asteep = steeped. Od. viii. 237
Atone (to) = make at one. Il. xiv. 257
Attained = touched, hit. Il. xi. 175, 512
Augurous. Il. xviii. 191
Authentic = trusty. Il. viii. 74
Author (to) = cause. Il. v. 70; xi. 441; H. A. 99
Avail (n. s.). Il. ii. 672
Aversively. H. H. 398
Ayles = beards of corn. Il. xx. 211

B.

Bace (to) = to run by. Od. x. 527
Bain = bath. Od. x. 567
Bane = destruction. Il. iii. 111
Banquet (to), v. a. Il. xviii. 343
Banquetants. Od. xx. 280
Barbed = caparisoned with armour, Il. xx. 152
Bastardice. Il. iii. 319
Battalia. Il. xi. 49
Bavins. Il. xxi. 344
Beamy. Od. xviii. 300
Beastly = of the nature of beasts. Il. iv. 259
Bedfere = **bed-companion**. Od. iii. 542
Behave (n. s.) = behaviour. **Od. xxii. 545**
Beldame. Il. iii. 404
Belluine. H. V. 5.
Bent = nod. Il. ii. 95
Beray (to) = foul. Il. xxi. 379
Bereaven. H. V. 348
Besogne = beggar. Od. Ep. Ded. p. 1.
Better (to). Il. xxii. 288
Bever. Od. xvii. 795 (where see note).
Bevy. Od. vi. 115 (where see note); xviii. 284; H. A. 312; H. V. 71
Bewray (to) = betray. Il. xviii. 262; Od. i 555
Bid = challenge. Il. i. 155
Billeted = placed, disposed. **Juv. 164**

Blanch (to) = put a fair appearance on, disguise. Il. xii. 223; Od. xi. 492
Blame-too. Od. iii. 365 (see note); xxii. 624
Blames. Od. xxiii. 38
Blood = disposition. Il. iii. 229; v. 516
Bloody **(to).** Il. xviii. 293
Blore = **blast.** Il. ii. 122; xiv. 330, &c.
Blore = simply air. **Od.** iv. 1138
Board (to) = to accost. Od. xv. 500; xxiv. 191; Mus. 439
Boggle (to) = to start. Il. x. 420
Bossy. Il. xii. 161
Boot = booty. Il. xi. 597; Od. ix. 630
Boot-haling = foraging for booty. Bat. 187
Boulted = sifted. **Bat. 53.** Unboulted. **Juv.** 126
Bracks = tatters. Od. xvii. 249, 765
Brast. **Il.** xvii. 425 (see note)
Brave (to) = to boast. Il. v. 111
Brave (to) = to challenge. Il. xvii. 171
Brave (n. s.) = challenge, boasting speech Il. iii. arg. **3**; xi. 319
Braver = boaster. Il. xi. 342
Brawn = muscle. Il. v. 90
Brawn = hog. Od. xiv. 527; xx. 253
Bray (to) = yell. Il. v. 280 (n.s.); H. to Diana, p. 113
Bray (to) = beat. Il. xxiii. 586
Breach of air. Il. x. 159
Breeze = gad-fly. Od. xxii. 387
Broches = spits. H. H. 227
Burgonet. H. to Sun, 13, p. 118
Burly = boisterous. Il. xxi. 123
Burthen = birth. Il. iii. 258
Butleress. Od. xvii. 346

C.

Caddesses = daws. Il. xvi. 541
Cantles = portions. Od. iii. 625; Juv. 126
Caponet = little capon. Juv. 296
Carcanet = chain of jewels. H. A. 150
Careful = anxious. Il. vi. 275
Carriages = burdens. Il. xxiii. 115

INDEX. 261

Casqued. Il. iv. 291. Casque. Od. xxiv. 305
Cassocks = outward coats. Od. xiv. 654
Castrell = kestrel. Pref. to Il. p. xc.
Cates = delicacies. Il. xxiv. 71; Od. x. 312
Cautelous = wily. H. H. 626
Cease (to) = to make to cease. Il. vi. 318; xxii. 71
Censure = opinion. Il. xiii. 655; Od. ii. 106
Chace (n. s.) = enclosure. H. H. 435
Champian = level country. Il. xii. 29; xxi. 376
Changeling = waverer. Il. v. 883
Cheat = seconds-bread. Bat. 52
Check = reproof. Il. ii. 213; iii. 37; Od. ii. 155
Check, to take = hesitate. Il. xiii. 500
Choleric. Od. xviii. 473
Circular = always returning, vehement. H. H. 874
Circumscription. H. V. 425
Clange. Il. iii. 5; x. 244
Claver-grass = clover. H. to Earth, 26, p. 117
Cloddy. Il. v. 49
Clossets = closes. H. to Pan, 27
Closure = union. Il. viii. 283
Clottered. Il. iv. 231; v. 801
Clout (to) = beat. Od. xviii. 43
Coach. Il. iii. 325; Od. vii. 5
Coloquintidas = pumpkins. Bat. 88
Commixtion. Od. x. 640
Commons = allowance of food. Hes. Bk. ii. 290
Compact. Il. vi. 435
Compell = collect. Il. v. 650
Complotting. Il. iv. 24
Comprehend = contain. Il. xxiii. 58
Comprobation = approbation. Il. i. Com. p. 25
Concave = heaven. Il. ii. 507
Conceit = thought. Il. viii. 438; ix. 80
Conceited = designed. Il. ix. 184
Conceiting = thinking. Bat. 214
Conduct = convoy. Il. i. 18. 143
Confect (to) = make up. Il. xi. 556

Confer (to) = give. Il. ii. 307; iii. 7
Confer (to) = talk together. Od. vi. 444
Confine (to) = bound. Il. ii. 365
Confine (to) = terminate. Od. v. 365; xv. 443
Confirmance. Od. iii. 497
Confluence = flowing together. Il. xvii. 654
Confluent = affluent. Il. ix. 157
Confluent = water. Bat. 24
Consolate (to). Od. viii. arg. 2
Consorts = companions. Il. xxiii. 231
Consorts = companionships. Il. vi. 215
Consort = a concert. H. H. 834
Consort (to) v. a. Od. i. 429; ii. 9; viii. 54
Consorted = associated with. Il. viii. 385
Conspicuity. Od. xxiv. 120
Constrain = draw together. Il. viii. 17
Consults = deliberations. Il. x. 281
Contained = restrained. Il. iii. 198
Contendress. H. V. 112
Continent = possession. Il. i. 170
Continent = that which contains. Od. xii. 323
Continuate = continuous. Od. iv. 962; x. 119
Convent = convene. Il. ii. 8; vii. 291
Conversant = employed in. Il. v. 791; Od. xiv. 97
Converted = turned towards. Il. x. 164
Convince (to) = overcome. Il. vi. 182
Cookly. Il. xxiv. 556
Co-partner. Il. ii. 572
Cope = match. Il. v. 472
Cope = concave of heaven. Il. v. 573
Core = heart (cœur). Od. viii. 281
Cormorand. Od. xvii. 508 (see note)
Cotes = sheep-cotes, shepherds' houses. Il. xviii. 535
Cote (to) = to pass by. Il. xxiii. 324 (see note), 456; Od. xiii. 421
Couched = laid close together. Il. xiii. 719; xvii. 235
Counterbraves. Il. xvi. 580
Counterprise. H. V. 301

Covert. **Od.** xxiv. 204
Coward. Od. xviii. 106 (see note)
Coy. Il. xx. 158
Crased = stunned. Il. xv. arg. 5
Cressets. Od. xviii. 496
Crible = seconds-bread. Juv. 139
Crown = sovereign. Il. **i.** 274
Crown = circle. Il. **xv. 7**
Crown = end, fulfilment. Il. ii. 286
Crowning = fulfilment. Il. ii. 304
Crows = crow-bars. Il. xii. 273
Cuff (to) = buffet. Il. xxii. 124
Cuffs (n. **s.**) = buffets. Il. xxiii. 208
Cunningly = skilfully. Il. ii. 373
Curace = cuirass. Il. vii. 222; **viii.** 163. (Plural xi. 387)
Curets = shirt of mail. Il. iii. 343; iv. 153; x. 63. The same word as above
Curious = careful. Il. xxiv. **162**
Curiously = carefully Il. ii. **225**; vi. 413
Currie = quarry. Il. xvi. 145, 693
Cyper's-grass = galingale. Od. iv. 802 (see Il. xxi. 333)

D.

DAINTY. Il. ii. **680**
Damask and damasked = inlaid. **Il.** x. 63; iii. 345
Dancery. Od. viii. **504**
Dare (to) = to venture. Il. **i. 228**
Dare (to) = to provoke (pain). Il. **xi.** 406
Dare = defiance. Il. xx. 196
Darksome. Il. xi. 318, 402
Deaded. Od. xviii. 372
Deathful. Il. i. 93
Deathless. Il. ii. 420
Deathsman. Il. xxiv. 457
Declined = turned aside. Il. **v. 807**; Od. iv. 295
Deduction = leading away, conveyance home. Od. viii. 39, 202
Deedless = inactive. Il. iv. **351**
Deedless = causing inaction. **Od. xii.** 480
Deepsome. **Od. iv. 769**

Deface (n. s.) Il. vi. 298
Defame = disgrace. Il. vii. 81; **xvii.** 474
Defamed = disgraced. Od. i. 386
Defect = fault. Il. xiii. 102
Deft. Il. i. 580
Deject = hurl-down. Bat. 228.
Delayful. Od. iv. 1041
Delicious = delicate. Il. v. 413; Od. xxiv. 370
Delightsome. Il. xii. 313; H. A. 322
Delightsomely. Il. ii. 235
Den = herd or pack. Il. xi. 417
Den (to) = dwell. H. A. 112
Deny = say nay. Il. vi. 166; vii. 303
Depeople (to). Il. xix. 146; Od. ix. **75**
Depopulacy. Bat. 405
Depopulate. Il. ii. 611
Depose (to) = lay down. Il. xix. 34
Deposition = laying-down. H. A. 710
Deprave (to) = to defame, dishonour. Il. vi. 564; Bat. 106
Deprave (n. s.) = defamation. Od. xxii. 585
Deprehended = caught in the act. Il. vi. 358
Derisory = mocking. Hes. Bk. ii. 325
Desertful = meritorious. Pref. to Il. p. lxix.
Designment. Il. ii. 454
Desire = regret. Il. xvii. 380; Od. v. 277
Deviceful. Od. i. 206
Difference (to) v. a. Il. v. 130
Dight (to) = to winnow (really to prepare.) Hes. Bk. ii. 343; Bk. of Days, 67
Dignified = rendered worthy. Od. xiii. 84
Disanimates = discourages. Il. xvi. 603
Disclosed = discovered, looked upon Il. xxi. 467
Discoloured = divers-coloured. Il. xvi. 160
Discovery = declaration. Il. i. 70
Discrepance = difference. Il. xi. 442

INDEX. 263

Disease (to) = disturb, arouse. Il. x. 45; Od. v. 68
Disease (n. s.) = unrest, uneasiness. Od. iv. 188
Disfurnished. Il. ii. 525
Disgrace = disfavour. Il. ix. 20
Disgrace (to) = to disfavour, be unkind to. Od. i. 365
Dishelm (to). Od. xiv. 383
Disherit (to). Od. ix. 3
Dishonoured = dishonourable. Il. iv. arg. 10
Disinflamed. Il. xii. 400
Disjunctions. Il. i. 253
Dislived = deprived of life. Od. xxii 355
Disperpled = sprinkled. Il. xi. 466; Od. x. 473
Display (to) = to show. Il. v. 693
Display (to) = to view. Il. xi. 74; xvii. 90; Od. v. 350
Disposure. Od. iii. 71
Dispraise (to) = to blame. Od. ii. 214
Dispread. Il. iv. 490
Dissentiously. Il. ii. 22, 54
Dissite = distant, sundered apart. Od. vii. 270
Dissolved = let loose. Il. v. 353
Dissundered. Od. i. 36
Distain. Il. v. 33; xxii. 349
Distempering = disturbing, discouraging. Il. xiv. 35
Disterminate = divided, separated by bounds. Od. x. 106
Distinguished = varied. Il. v. 758
Distract = distracted. Il. xi. 475
Distrustful. Od. iv. 1022
Diters = winnowers. Il. v. 499
Dites = winnows. Il. v. 498. (See note on this passage in our second edition. The word seems usually applied to *winnow*, and is found in an old political squib of the time of Richard II. in Disraeli's Amenities of Literature (chap. xii.), "Let Piers the Plowman dwell at home, and *dyght* us corn.")
Ditionary = provincial, contributory. Juv. 180

Diversly. Il. ii. 347
Diversory = way-side inn. Od. xiv. 536
Diverted = turned away. Il. xxiii. 47
Dooms = decisions. Il. iii. 78, 337; xviii. 457
Dop-chick = dab-chick. Od. xv. 636
Dorp = village. Il. xi. 587
Doubt = redoubt, battlement. Il. xii. 286
Doubtless (n. a.) = undoubting. Od. iv. 344
Down (to) = keep down. Il. xxi. 56; Od. xix. 702
Downright = plain, without ceremony. Il. xxiv 637; Mus. 396
Dreadless. Il. x. 261
Drifts = designs. Il. ix. 26; x. 88
Dubbed = stuck on, loaded. Il. i. 448; ii. 369; Od. iii. 619
Duke = leader. Il. ii. 470; Od. iii. 532
Durance. Bat. 21
Dusted = thumped. Il. xxi. 377 (see note)
Dwarfy. Od. ix. 692

E

Eager = sharp. Il. x. 150; xi. 231
Eagerly = sourly, sharply. Il. i. 99
Eared = ploughed. Il. xviii. 492
Effeminacies. Il. vi. 347
Egression. Od x. 33
Eld = old age. Il. xxiii 688
Elephant = ivory. Od. xix. 77; xxiii. 308
Elusive = mocking. Il. xi. 319
Embattelling. Il. iv. 308; xvi. 155
Embossed = foaming at the mouth. Il. iv. 258; Od. vi. 510 (see note)
Embrodery. Od. xvii. 39
Embrued = imbued with moisture. Od. vi. 185; xvii. 125; xix. 644 (see note)
Empery = sovereign authority. Il. i. 86; Od. iv. 233
Emprise = enterprise. Il. xi. 257
Enambushed. Il. x. 257

INDEX.

Enchased = enclosed. Il. **xv. 147**; xix. 346; Od. ii. 415
Encoached. H. A. 373
Endears. Od. xv. 30
Endless = immortal. H. **H. 411**
Endless = last. Il. xxiii. **125**
Endlessly = for ever. Il. **iv.** 565
Enflamed = set on fire. Od. iii. 17
Enflowered. Od. **v.** 96; xiii 286
Enforceful. H. **V.** 247
Enforcive. Il. viii. **212**; **x. 128**
Enfranchise **(to)** = set **free.** Il. **i. 96**; v. 374; Od. xi. **400**
Enfranchisement. Il. v. 375
Enginous = ingenious. Od. i. 452
Engored. Il. xxi. 22
Engrailed = variegated. Il. xxiii. 761
Engrost = made thick, large. Il. xvii. 640; Od. v. 374
Enranked. Il. iii. 339
Enslumbered = put to sleep. Il. **xxiv.** 399
Ensphere (to). Od. iii. 78; xiii. 271
Ensue (to) = to follow upon. Il. xi. 463; H. A. 719
Entoiled = entangled, **surrounded.** Il. ii. 455
Envy = grudge. Il. xiii. 477 (see note); xxiii. 478
Equalize = to render equal. Il. xi. 297. (See Pref. Poem to Reader, 17)
Erring = wandering. Il. ii. 402 *et passim*
Escape = transgression of **female** virtue. Il. ii. 312; v. 358
Escheat = plunder. Il. viii. 439
Eternified. Od. i. 162
Events = issue. Il. xxii. 44
Eversion = overthrow. Il. ix. 48
Evicke = ibex. Il. iv. 122
Evulsion. Il. xxi. 174
Example (to), v. a. Il. iv. 238; **v. 804**
Exanimate. Il. xvii. 598
Exciteful. Hes. Bk. ii. 423
Exemplary = as a specimen, sample. Juv. 185
Exempt = perfect. Il. ix. 604; **x. 214**
Exhale (to) = draw out. Il. xx. 195
Exhorts = exhortations. Il. **xi. 183**; xvi. 358

Exile (to) = banish. Il. xvi. 369
Expansion. Il. xvii. 320
Expect (to) = await. Il. iv. 359; Od. iv. 1061 *et passim*
Expectance. Od. xi. 475
Expert = skilful. Il. iv. 311. = free from. H. V. 358 (see note)
Expiscating = searching into. Il. x. 181
Explode (to) = drive out with disgrace. Hes. Bk. ii. 570
Explore (to) = search out. Il. **i. 543**; vi. 140
Expugn (to) = take by assault. Il. iv. arg. 2
Expulse (to) = drive out. Il. vi. 566; viii. 467
Expulsive. Il. xii. 187; Hes. Bk. ii. 225
Expulsure = driving forth. Il. xi. 339
Exquire (to) = search out. Od. iv. 520
Exsequies. Il. xxii. 446 (see Bk. xxiii. arg. 1)
Exspire (to) = breathe out. **Od.** ix. 554
Extenuate (to) = render less. Il. xvi. 673
Extremes = necessities. Il. ii. 300
Eveful = visible. Il. x. 396
Eyeshot = range of eye. Il. i. Com. p. 23, line 5
Eyne = eyes. Il. x. 487; Od. xvi. 217

F.

FADING. Il. **xxii. 194**
Falls. Il. **ii. 396**
Fame = report. **Od. iii. 126**
Fantasy. Il. **ii. 45**
Fat (to) = fatten. **Od. xiv.** 60
Fatal = destined. Il. viii. 344; Od. ii. 515
Faultful. Od. i. 47
Fausens = eels. Il. xxi. 190
Fautour = favourer, patron. Il. i. 441
Fautress = patroness. Il. xxiii. 671
Fawn (n. s.) = fawning. Od. x. 286
Fawn (to) = court, entice. Odd. xii. 71
Fearful = timid. Il. i. 290; xxiii. 740; Od. xx. 381

Fellowless = peerless. Il. ii. 434; xii. 108
Fells = skins. Il. ix. 630; Od. iii. 58
Feltred = matted, clotted. Il. iii. 219
Fenceful. Bat. 190
Fere = companion. Il. xviii. 339
Ferrary = art of working in iron. Il. xiv. 141
Fescue. H. A. 288 (see note)
Fetched = reached (a naval term). Od. xxiv. 219
Fictive = imaginary. Od. Ep. Ded., p. xlix line 9
Fight = bulwark. Il. xii. 271
Filed = defiled. Il. xvi. 733; xviii. 21
Filed = polished (filed-speech). Od. vi. 219; H. H. 568
Fistulary = like a pipe. H. H. 896
Flaw = gust of wind. Il. iv. 449
Fled = put off. Od. iv. 339
Fleer (to) = leer. Il. xi. 343
Fleet = float. Il. xix. 204
Flesh (to) = initiate. Il. xiii. 158
Flexure = turning of the goal. Il. xxiii. 409
Flies = transcends, escapes. Il. xvi. Com. p. 104, line 18; Od. xvii. 504
Flitting = floating. Od. viii. 789
Fluences = pourings forth. Il. xvi. 244
Fluent = a stream. H. A. 28
Fly (to) = pass over, avoid. Od. xvii. 423
Foil = defeat. Il. vi. 344-5, 372; viii. 478
Foody. Il. xi. 104; Od. ii. 558
Footmanship. Od. iv. 270
Forceful. Od. xv. 313
Forechace. Il. xvii. 637
Forefeels. Il. xiv. 113
Foregale. Od. iv. 485
Foregoes. Il. ii. 281
Forehead of the Morn. Il. ix. 347
Forepast. H. to Hercules, line 7, p. 104
Foreright. Od. iii. 244; H. A. 639
Foreseer. Il. vi. 385
Foresent. Od. iii. 245
Forespeak. Il. xvi. 792; xvii. 32; H. A. 307

Foreteams. Il. xvi. 352
Forewhile. Od. ii. 256
Forewinds. Od. ix. 130; xi. 866
Fountful. Il. xiv. 238
Franchisement = freedom. Il. v. 375
Frequent = numerous. Il. ii. 71
Fret (to) = to ornament with raised work. Il. ix. 184
Frets = stops of a lute. H. H. 87
Froes = frows, women. Il. vi. 129
Frontless = shameless. Il. i. 159; Od. i. 425
Fulsome = nasty. Od. xvii. 556
Fume = anger. Il. i. 100; Od. xvii. 281
Funeral = death. Il. viii. 309
Furrow = lair. Il. xi. 105
Futurely. Il. vi. 201; xxiv. 390

G.

GABARDINE = coarse cloak. Od. xiv. 742
Gables = cables. Od. vi. 415 et passim
Gadding. Od. vi. 430
Galingale = sweet cyperus. Il. xxi. 333
Gamed = played at games. Il. xxiii. 574
Gavel = sheaf of corn. Il. xxi. 328
Gaze (at-gaze) = staring. A stag was said to look *at-gaze* when it looked as it were full at you. Il. iii. 149; xx. 303; Od. vii. 181
Gaysome. Il. xi. 194
Giggots = slices. Il. i. 452; ii. 372
Girlond = garland, i.e. crown. Od. i. 619
Gladded. Od. xix. 88
Gleby. Il. iii. 81
Glew (to) = join together. Il. xviii. 540
Glibness = smoothness, slipperiness. Od. xii. 130
Glister = glitter. Od. xviii. 280
Glorious = boasting. Il. xiii. 738
Gloriously = boastingly. Il. iii. 20
Glose (to) = to deceive. Od. iii. 139. = flatter. Od. xv. 99, 344
Gloss = lustre. Il. i. 133
Gobbets = mouthfuls. Od. ix. 512
Grace = favour. Il. vi. 290
Gracious = graceful. Il. xviii. 23
Gratulate = confer favour. Il. xxi. 422
Grave = heavy. Il. v. 752

Grave (to) = to bury. Il. vii. arg. 7
Graved = put into the grave. Il. xxiv. 705
Green = fresh. Od. xi. 46
Guardfully. Il. i. 441
Guise = custom. Il. iii. 284
Gulfy. Il. x. 7 ; xiii. 33
Gulls = swallows. Il. **xxi. 132**

H.

HABILITY = power. **Il. xi. 673**
Hales = hauls, **drags**. · Il. v. **478** *et passim*
Halsers and halsters = hawsers. Od. ii. 609 ; v. 333
Harpsical = harpsichord. H. A. **293**
Hatched = inlaid. Il. xxiii. 700
Health = safety. Il. xv. 683
Hearten = encourage. Il. i. 444
Heartless = out-of-heart. Il. xv. 296
Heartquakes = fears. Il. vii. 188
Heat = courage. Il. ii. 323
Heaven = past tense of heave. Il. xxiii 299
Heavy = sad. Il. ii. 699 ; xvii. 30
Heired = inherited. Il. v. 296; xiv. 90
Helm = handle. Od. v. 312
Helpless = unaiding. Il. vi. 385
Helptire = assistance. Il. v. 253
Herby = grassy. Il. v. 39; Od. iv. 453
Herdful. Hes. Bk. i. 494
Hernshaw. Il. x. 243
Het = past tense of heat. **Od. xix. 594;** xxi. 246
Hind = servant. Hes. Bk. ii. 205
Hind = doe. Il. xi. 105
Hogherd. Il. xxi. 263
Hoice and hoise = hoist. Il. ix. **403** ; Od. ii. 609 *et passim*
Hollows = shouts, halloes. H. V. 24
Honorary (n. s.) = gift. Od. xiii. 16
Horror = bristling. Il. vii. 49 *et passim*
Housewifely. H. to Vesta, p. **111**, line 6
Humans = men, mortals. **Il. xii. 64** ; H. A. 298
Humorous = moist, watery. **Il. xxi.** 186 ; Od. iv. 1020

Hurls = hurlings. Il. A. 24
Husband (to) = cultivate. Od. xxiv 349

I.

IDOL = image. Od. xxiv. 19 *et alibi*
Illuded = mocked, deluded. Il. xiv. 302 ; H. H. 642
Illustrate = illustrious. **Il.** viii. 252 ; x. 251
Illustrated = brightened with light. · Od. v. 2
Immane = huge, cruel. Il. xxi. 296
Immartial = not warlike. Od. ii. 100
Immortalize = render deathless. Il. xvi. 416
Imp (to) = to insert a feather. **Hes.** Bk. ii. 382
Impair (n. s.) = detriment. Il. ix. 75 ; xi. 275
Impair (to) = depreciate. Il. x. 221
Impales = surrounds. Od. v. 308
Imperatory = governing. H. H. 807
Impervial = unpassable. Hes. Bk. ii. 463
Implied = enfolded. Il. iv. 521 ; Od. i. 509
Important = anxious. Il. vi. 560
Importuned = vexed. Il. v. 349 ; vii. 317
Impose = place upon, or in. Il. xviii. 28 ; Od xiii. 553
Impostorous = cheating. Od. Ep. Ded. p. 7
Improve = reprove. Il. x. 108
Impulsion. Il. ix 182 ; Od. xxiv. 316
Impurpled. Il. vi. 227 ; H. A. 482
Inaccessible = unapproachable. Il. i. 550 ; xx. 450
Incense (to) = feel angry. Il. xiii. 430. To rouse to anger. Il. iv arg. 12
Incense (to) = to set on fire. Il. xxiii. 164
Incensory = altar. Il. xi. 686
Incessancy. Od. i. 248
Inclose = harness. Od. iii. 658
Inclusions. Il. xvi. 291
Incontinent = immediate. Il. xxiv. 299

INDEX. 267

Incorrupted = uncorruptible. Il. xxi. 458
Inculpable. Il. iv. 103
Indecently = unbecomingly. Od. xvi. 140
Indevirginate = unmarried. H. V. 11
Indifferent = impartial. Il. vi. arg. 1; xiii. 9
Indistinguished = undistinguishable, plain. Il. ix. 301
Induction = entrance. Od. vi. 406
Inenarrable. Il. ii. 422
Inevitable = not to be avoided. Hes. Bk. i. 142
Inexpiate = implacable. Il. ix. 493
Inexpugnable. Il. xxi. 413
Infer (to) = to bring in. Il. vii. 183
Infestive = troublesome. Il. viii. 151
Inflamed = set in flames. Il. i. 312
Inflexive. H. to Mars, 35
Influent = attracting. Od. Ep. Ded. xlvi.
Informed = made. Il. vi. 122; H. A. 575, 779
Informs = animate. Il. xx. 52 (see note); xxii. 311
Infortunate. Il. xix. 125
Infortune Od. iii. 234; xx. 219
Infract. Il. ii. 419
Ingenerate = born. Il. xviii. 323
Ingression. Od. vii. 110
Inn (to) = to gather in. Hes. Bk. ii. 158, 364
Innative. Il. iv. 524; Od. v. 37
Inquest = search. Od. i. 146
Insea'd = inclosed by sea. Il. xi. 637
Insecution = pursuit. Il. xi. 524; xxiii. 448
Inspersion = sprinkling in. Il. xi. 452
Instruct = fitted. Od. iv. 755
Instructed = drawn-up. Il. v. 495
Insultance. Od. ix. 635
Insultation. Il. xiii. 556
Integuments. Il. xxii. 446; Od. xvi. 619
Intend = attend to. Il. vi. 98; viii. 80; Od. iii. 648
Intendments = intentions. Il. xvi. 356

Intentively = scrupulously. Od. viii. 772
Interested = placed among. Od. xv. 326
Interminate. Od. vii. 397
Interprease = interpose. Od. iv. 896
Intervent. Il. xi. 609
Inure = use, commit. Il. viii. 311; Hes. Bk. ii. 490
Invitement = invitation. Od. x. 345
Involved = rolled in. Il. ii. 179
Irrision = mocking. Il. ii. Com. p. lx. line 4.

J.

Jacks = jerkins. Il. xiii. 637 (see note); Bat. 188
Jar = quarrel. Il. i. 315; xiv. 176, 177
Jet (to) = to strut. Od. xiii. 227
Jetty = black. Il. ii. 629
Junkets. Od. vi. 106 (see note); Bat. 60
Justs = games, tournaments. Od. vii. 265; Mus. 412
Justled. Od. xix. 229

K.

Keels = ships. Od. xxiv. 400
Kels = cauls. Il. xxiii. 223
Kelsine = kelson. Il. i. 426
Kept = dwelt. Od. iv. 1077
Kerved = carved. Od. i. 182; iii. 59
Kitling = kitten. Od. xii. 137
Kymnels = household-tubs. Bat. 54

L.

Laboursome. Od. xxii. 634
Laced (strait-laced) = strict. Il. xii. 426
Lackey = go on foot. Il. xiv. 253; Od. v. 131
Landleapers. Od. xvii. 508 (see note)
Largess. Od. xvii. 350
Laterally. Il. xi. 216; Od. iii. 614
Laver = washing vessel. Od. iv. 63
Leaveless = leafless. Il. ii. 370
Leavy = leafy. Il. vi. 127. Leavy gates = folding doors. Il. vi. 86

Leech = physician. Il. iv. 232
Legacy = embassy. Il. vii. 349; ix. 220
Legacy = bequest. Il. iv. 373
Legate. Il. iii. 226; ix. arg. 3
Lengthful. Il. xi. 182
Leopard. Il. xvii. 15
Lets = hindrances. Od. xiii. 38
Lewd = dissolute. Od. vi. 318
Lib = castrate. Hes. Bk. of Days, 41
Libertine = a freeman. Il. xvi. 50
Lightsome. Il. xvii. 319; Hes. Bk. ii. 58
Likes = pleases. Il. vii. 29
Linne = flax. Il. ii. 459
Liquorous = lickerous, dainty. Juv. 280
List = wish. Od. iv. 799
Liveries = deliveries. Il. v. 529
Liverings = liver-puddings. Bat. 58
Loathes = creates disgust in. Il. xiv. 74
Look = appearance. Il. i. 200; v. 842
Loser = destroyer. Il. xviii. 109
Lucerns. Il. xi. 417, 421 (see note)
Lurch = deceit. H. H. 336
Lust = wish. Od. xiii. 503
Luster = den. Od. xvii. 159
Lybberds = leopards. H. V. 120

M.

MACERATE. Epigram, p. 130, line 36
Malapertly = saucily. Juv. 135
Mall = beat. Od. xviii. 44
Mandilion = a sort of cloak. Il. x. 120
Mankind = masculine. H. V. 119
Manless = cowardly. Il. iii. 39. = inhuman. Il. ix. 64
Manlessly = inhumanly. Il. xxii. 405
Marine. Od. xxiv. 67
Maritimal = sea-side. Il. xxiii. 50; Od. v. 91
Mask (v. n.) = disguise. Il. v. 187
Masterful. Il. ii. 410
Mate (to) = oppose. Od. iv. 218 (see note)
Maund = basket Od. vi. 105
Mazers = cups. Hes. Bk. ii. 564
Meated. Il. ii. 336; viii. 443
Mechanicals = mechanics. Od. vi. 422

Memorised = remembered. Il. iii. 488
Mere = entire, one's own. Il. vi. 183 et passim
Merit (v. a.) = to reward. Il. ix. 258
Met = measured. Il. iii. 327
Metalline. Od. xxiii. 233
Mettle = spirit. Il. xxiii. 561
Minion (in a bad sense). Od. xviii. 557; xix. 96
Ministress. Mus. 100
Misease. Il. xiii. 521; Od. xiii. 139
Miss = loss. Il. ii. 4; xiii. 683; Od. xiii. 325
Mittens = hedging-gloves. Od. xxiv. 304
Moil = toil. Il. xxiii. 637
Moists (v. a.). Il. xxii. 428
Monied = converted into money. Il. xi. 590
Monster = show. Il. iii. 42
Mows = stacks. Od. xviii. 47
Mulct = penalty. Il. iii. 485
Murrion. Il. x. 227
Muse = haunt of an animal. Il. xi. 368

N.

NATURAL = legitimate. Il. iii. 259; xiii. 166; xvi. 182
Neat = pure. Il. iv. 276
Neat = oxen. Il. xviii. 480
Neesing = sneezing. Od. xvii. 732
Neglective. Il. xiv. 356
Nephew = grandson. Od. xxiv. 690
Nervy. Il. xvii. 253
Netify = polish. Il. ii. Com. p. 56
Nock and nocked. Il. iv. 133, 138; viii. 281
Noiseful. Od. xxiv. 553; Mus. 329

O.

OBJECTED = presented. Od. xi. 501
Observed = preserved. Od. x. 505
Occurrents (n. s.). Il. xi. 751; xxiv. 172
Ocular = visible. Od. xxiii. 115
Odd = unequalled. Od. viii. 397; xxii. 251 (see Addenda).
Offend = strike. Il. xiii. 510

INDEX. 269

Ope (n. a.). Il. xii. 123
Opposed = opposite. Il. ii. 556
Opposite = in contest. Il. ii. 519
Opprobration. H. H. 605
Optimates. Il. ix. 322; Od. i. 386
Orby. Il. iii. 357
Ordure. Il. xxiii. 674
Ostent = prodigy. Il. ii. 277, 280; Od. ii. 249
Ostentful. Od. xv. 214
Ossifrage = osprey. Od. iii. 506
Osspringer = osprey. Il. xviii. 557
Otherwhere. Il. xviii. 450
Ought = owed. Il. xi. 608
Outray = to fly out. Il. v. 793
Outrays = outrageous. Il. xxiii. 506; Bat. 80
Outscape. Od. ix. 423
Outwrought. Il. xxii. 119
Overgo. Hes. Bk. i. 517
Overlaid = covered. Il. xxi. 379
Overpaise = overbalance. Hes. Bk. ii. 439
Overseen = deceived. Il. xiv. arg 2
Overthwart = adverse. Il. xxi. 255
Overthwarts (adv.). Il. xxiii. 107
Overture = opening. H. H. 41
Owe = own. Il. ii. 736; Od. ii. 190
Oxy. Il. iv. 139

P.

Paise = weight, balance. Il. xii. 375, 430
Palfrey. Od. vii. 2
Palisadoes. Il. vii. 366; viii. 297
Palm = deers' horns. Il. iv. 124
Palm = palm of hand. Il. v. 879
Pantler = pantry-servant. Juv. 134
Paramour. Il. xvi. 46
Parcel-gilt. Od. xxiii. 438 (see note)
Parley. Il. iii. 86
Parricide. Od. iii. 262
Pashed = crushed. Il. xiii. 299
Passages. Il. xxiii. 579 (see note)
Pass (to) = surpass. Il. ii. 594; iii. 174; Hes. Bk. ii. 497
Penury = in want of. Od. xvi. 45

Perfume (to) Il. ii. 349; Od. xxiii. 74
Pervially = in passing. Bk. ii. Com. p. 75; xiii. p. 31
Petulancy = wantonness. Bat. 264
Picked = piked, pointed. Il. iv. 126
Pile = point, or barb of arrow. Il. iv. 139, 488; xi. 205
Pile = heap. H. A. 40
Pinch (to) = press on like dogs. Il. v. 462; viii. 294; Od xix. 318
Pine (to), v. a. Il. iii. 194
Pined = worn out, withered. Il. v. 160
Pittance = small portion. Il. xi. 547
Plain = complain. Il. vi. 345
Plained = levelled. Il. xii. 42
Plaints = complaints. Il. xxiii. 32
Planky. Il. xii. 442
Plashing. H. H. 351 (see note)
Plumed = plucked the feathers. Od. xv. 697
Plumps = crowds. H. A. 213
Poitrils = pectorals. Il. v. 738; xix. 380
Policies = schemes, stratagems. Od. xxiii. 207
Polled-off = stripped off. Il. xvi. 113
Portly = grand. Od. iv. 487
Prease = press, *passim*
Prefixed = foredoomed. Il. xviii. 414
Prejudice = loss. Il. ix. 351
Premonitions = notice. Od. ii. 321
Preposterously. Il. v. 584 (see note)
Presence = demeanour. Il. iii. 186
Presents = represents. Il. xvii. 51
Prest = hired. Od. iv. 861 (see note)
Prest = ready, *passim*
Presumes = presumptions. Il. xi. 495
Pretermit. Il. xxiv. 79
Prevent (to) = anticipate. Il. v. 122; xvi. 793
Prey = booty. Il. ii. 205
Preyful. H. V. 115
Prise = booty. Il. i. 119 (see note)
Prise = grasp. Il. iv. 139
Procinct = girding. Il. xii. 89 (see note)
Profuse (to), v. a. = pour forth, waste. Od. xxi. 156

270 INDEX.

Profused = poured forth. **Il. xxiv.** 295
Proin (to) = to lop off. Il. x. **397**; Od. i. 302; xxiv. 300
Prollers = wanderers in quest of plunder. Od. xi. 490
Propensions = inclinations. **H.** to Earth, p. 117, line 12
Proper = its own. Od. vii 161
Proposing = **holding out.** Il. i. 14; v 471; xi. **554**
Proud. See Od. xx. 235 **(see note).** = luxuriant. Od. xxiii. **289**
Proyning = preening. **H.** to **Phœbus,** p. 110
Puft = puff. Od. v. 65; vi. 28
Pursenets. See Juv 190
Purveyed. Od. i. 180; iii. 646

Q.

QUAINT = pretty. Od. xiii. **327 (see note)**
Qualitied. Il. xiv. 104
Queach = thicket Od. xix. 610 (see note); H. A. 375; H. to Pan, p. 106
Quern = handmill. Od. vii. 139
Quick = alive, life. Il. vi. 296; **xxii.** 332
Quilt (to). Il. x. 230; **Bat. 190**
Quite (to) or quit = pay. **Il. i.** 95; v. 655; x. 23
Quitture = issue, **discharge. Il. xiv.** 7; xxiv. 374

R.

RACE = race, **scratch.** Il. iv. 158 et alibi
Raft = reft. Il xi. 332
Rage = power, inspiration. Il. i. **66**
Ramped = raged. Od. i. 291
Rampire = rampart. Il. iv. 361; **Od.** vii. 61
Ranch = wrench, tear. **Il. v. 856**
Randon. Od. v. 422
Rapeful. Il. i. 251
Rapinous. H. H. 692
Rapt = snatched. Od. xvii. 618

Rapting. Bat. 417
Rapture = seizure. Od. xiv. **428**
Rare = early. Od. vi. 422
Rate = estimation. Il. i. 109; xx. 287
Rates = qualifications. Il. iv. 275
Rates = consents, ratifications. **Il.** i. 509
Rate (to) = to ratify. **Il. iii.** 123
Ravelin. Il. vii. 289
Ravine = snatching. Hes. Bk. ii. 573
Ray = eye. H. H. 308
Rearfeast = latter portion of feast. Od. iv. 286
Reave (to) = take by violence. Od. Ep Ded. p. 10; Od. xvii. 106
Recoil = defeat. Il. xi. 666
Re-collect. Od. v. 617
Re-comfort. Il. xxii. 73; Od. xiv. **226**
Re-cure = recovery. Il. i. 436; v. **898**
Recured = recovered. Il. v. 896
Recureless. Il. xvi. 446
Recúsant. Mus. 227
Redemptory. Il. i. 94
Redition = return. Od. vi. **486**
Reddition = translation, explanation. Bk. ii. Com. pp. 56, 57
Reducers = bringers back. Od. xvi. 296
Refell = refute, repress. Il. ix. 36; Od. xxi. 120
Referred = gave back. Od. xviii. 221
Reflected = turned back. Il. iii. 358; vii. 229; ix. 180
Reflection = turning **back. Il.** xviii. 404
Regiment = rule. Il. xvi. 168
Remember = remind. **Il. xv. 31**; Od. x. 592
Remorse = **pity. Il. viii. 409**; Od. iv. 341
Remorseful = compassionate. Il. viii. 208; Od. iv. 388
Remove = removal. Il. ii. 134
Rendry = giving-up. Od. xxi. 26
Renown (to), v. a. Il. i. 484; viii. 133
Renowmed. Il. iv. 311
Repair = resort. Od. vi. 207
Repeat = repetition. Il. xvi. 57
Repercussions. H. to Pan, 39

INDEX.

Repercussive. **H. to Mother of Gods,** p. 104
Reposed = replaced. Il. **xiii. 591**
Repoured. Il. x. 175
Repressions. Il. xi. 472
Reprise. IL xvii. 130
Repulse (to) = repel. Il. xi. 514; Od. v. 570
Repulsive. Il. xvii. 233
Repurchased = regained. **IL xxii.** 343
Require = seek, enquire. **Od. xx.** 215
Reremouse = bat. **Od. xii. 610**
Resolved = informed. Il. **iv. 37**
Resound (n. s.). Il. **v. 47**
Respective = respectful. Il. **xi. 689**; xiii. 373
Respectless. Od. **iv. 390**
Resty = **restiff.** Il. **v. 234**
Retire (to) = withdraw. Il. **iii. 81**; viii. **381**
Retire (n. **s.**) = retreat. Il. **xi. 662**
Retreat = return. Il. ix. **143**
Retreatful. Bat. 96
Return (to), v. **a.** = give account of. Il. ix. 580
Return (to) = restore, bring back. Od. xxi. 269
Revoked = called back. Od. **xxiii. 5**
Revoluble. Il. ii. 256
Rew = row. Il. vi. 256
Rigging = tricking. **H. H 512**
Rock = distaff. Od. vi. 77, **479**
Room = place. Il. xii. **360**
Rout = rabble. Il. xv. **249**; **Od.** viii. 150
Roy. **Od. v.** 140
Rub = chance. Il. xv. 245
Rue = pity. Il. xxi. 72
Ruff = angry mood, huff. Il. **xxiii. 517**
Ruffinous. Il. vi. **457**
Ruin = **fall.** Il. xvi. 436
Ruinate (to) = subvert. Il. **iv. 42**; Hes. Bk. ii. 523
Rundled = rounded. Il. **vii.** 239
Rush (to), v. a. Il. **v. 18**
Ruts (v. a.) = routs. **Od.** xviii. 47
Ruth = pity. Il. ii. **20**; vi. 419

S.

Sackful = pillaging. Il. ii. 601
Sacring = consecrating. H. to Diana, 15
Sad = heavy. Il. iv. 526 (see note)
Saft = past tense of save. Il. v. 112; Od iv. 674
Saised = seised, filled **with. H. to Moon,** p. 119
Saker = falcon. Od. xv. 696
Sardinian = sardonic. Od. **xx. 457** (see note)
Sattled = settled. Od. xviii. **345**
Say to take. Il. xix. 246 (see **note)**
Scandalling. Od. xxiv. 616
Scape (see Escape). **H. to** Mercury, 14, p. 106
Seconded. Od. xxi. 320
Secure = careless. Il. x. 437
Secureful = protecting. Il. vii. 209
Security = carelessness. Il. xiii. 10
Seel (to) = sew up the eyes. Il. xvi. 314; Od. xiii. 118
Seemless = unseemly. **Od. xx. 397**
Seised of = in possession. Od. i. 340
Sence = seven. Od. xii. 518 (see note)
Scres = talons. Il. viii. 212; Od. ii. 238
Several = separate. Il. ii. 714
Severally = separately. IL viii. **348**
Sewer = carver. Il. xxiv. 558; **Od.** i. 221
Shame = modesty. **Hes. Bk. i. 122**
Shamefastness = modesty. **Mus. 51**
Shapeful. Od. **xvii.** 648
Shawms. Il. **x. 12**
Sheaf = bundle of **arrows.** Il. **iv.** 115
Sheath = shining **appearance?** Od. xviii. 231
Shent = disgrace. Od. xxiii. 341 (see note)
Shittle = shuttle. Od. v. 86
Shive and shivers = slices. Hes. Bk. ii. 98, 99
Shots = reckoning. Od. **i. 352**; xi. 545 (see note)
Showed = appeared. Od. **vi.** 381
Shrewd = mischievous. Il. viii. 233
Shrewish. Il. iv. 497

Shrikes = shrieks. Il. vii. 403
Shrowd = den. H. H. 695
Sieged = besieged. Il. xi. 367
Sincere = pure, unmixed. H. A. **178**
Skeane = a short sword. H. A. **819**
Skiff. Od. v. 48
Slaughterous. Il. xxi. 27; Od. xxiv. 600
Slick = smooth. Il. ii. 680
Slick (to). Il. xxiii. 2)9; Od. vi. **359**
Smalls = ankles. H. V. 143
Smoke (to) = discover. Od. iv. 338; xi. 712
Snaky = serpentine. Il. ii. 779
Snew = past tense of to snow. H. H. 884
Snore = **snort**. Il. x. 420
Solemn = ceremonial, sacred. **Il. xi** 641
Solicited = vexed. Il. xvi. 10
Solicitous = anxious. Il. xviii. **2**
Sooth = truth. Il. iv. 343
Sorcerous = containing enchantments. Od. x. 376
Sorrel = reddish colour. Il. xi. 590
Sort = number (or as we say *lot*). Il. iv. 460; v. 461
Sort = fate. Il. **xii.** 331
Sort (to) = happen. Il. xxiii. 294
Sorted = fated. Od. xvii. 203
Soundful. Od. viii. 359
Spakey = specky, rotten. Juv. 273
Sparseth = disperses. Il. xi. 268
Spelt = a kind of corn. Od. iv. 803
Spersed. Il. xi. 558
Spinster = a spinning woman. **Il. xii.** 426
Spiny = thin, thorny. Il. iii. **161 (see** Addenda to third edition)
Spiritful. Il. xii. 194
Spleen = anger. Il. iii. 103; viii. 420
Spleenless = kind. Od. xiii. 247
Spoil = spoiler. Il. iv. 467
Spoilful = destructive. Il. viii. **180**; Od. iii. 437
Spring = race. H. A. 554
Spring (to) = produce. Il. xxiv. **494**
Springall. Bat. 379
Sprout = shoot, offspring. Il. iii. **131**

Spurry. Il. xix. 367
Spurs = incitements. Il. x. 103
Stablish = settle. Il. xi. 93
Stale = stele, shaft of arrow. **Il. iv.** 173
Stares = starlings. Il. xv. 541
Start = past tense of to start. **Il.** xviii. 483; Od. ii. 581
States = princes. Il. ii. 69; Od. i. 329
Stead = place of a thing, such as homestead, navelstead, girdlestead, chamberstead
Stere = to stir. Od. **xxi. 324**
Stern-part = breast (στέρνον). Il. iv. 568
Sterved = starved. Il. xviii. 144
Sting = impulse. Il viii. 252; xiii. 233
Stitch = stich, furrow. Il. xviii. 495-7
Stomach = be angry, haughty. Il. **v.** 491
Stomach = courage. Il. ix. 335
Stonage. Hes. Bk. ii. 376
Stool-ball Od. vi. 139
Stoop (to), v. a. Il. vi. 408; xvii. 591
Strains = families, race. Od. i. **344**; H. A. 231
Strait-laced = constrained. Il. xii. 426
Straited = straitened. Il. xiv. 28
Strakes = iron with which wheels are bound. Il. xx. 347
Strappled = entangled. Il. xvi. **438**; H. H. 720
Streaked = stretched. Od. ix. 416; xii 148
Strip (to) = to pass **by** rapidly. H. A. 641
Stroy = destroy Il. xx. 37
Strouted = swelled. Il. **1.** 464
Stub = short stock. Il. xxiii. 305
Study = deep thought. H. H. 546
Stupid = astonished. Od. xiii. 247
Stupidity = astonishment. Od. vi. 252
Submitted = placed under. Il xix. 258
Substanced. Od. iv. 119
Subtile = fine. Il ix. 629
Sumpture = splendour, expense. **H. H.** 128
Suppliance = assistance. Il. viii 321. = supplication. Il. xviii. 402

INDEX. 273

Supply = compensation. Il. i. 116
Supportful. Od. xxiii. 182
Supposes = suppositions. Od. xvii. 769
Surcease. Il. vii. 45
Surcharged. Il. iv. 243
Surcuidrie = over-weening pride. Il. xvii. 20 (see note)
Surrebound. Il. xxi. 361
Survival. Od. xvii. 711
Suspect = suspicion. Il. i. 546; x. 210
Swathbands. H. A. 179, 190; H. H. 33
Sweet = suite. H. H. 244
Swet = past tense of sweat. Od. iv. 48; xi. 64

T.

Taint = blame. Il. xiii. 235
Taint = touch, attempt. Il. iii. 374 (see note); vii. 223
Taint (to) = to hit, touch. Il. viii. 259; xi. 478, 574; xiii. 449; Bat. 73
Take = overtake. Hes. Bk. ii. 511
Take-in (to) = conquer. Il. ii. 10, 54, 119
Tamrick = tamarisk. Il. x. 395
Tapish (to) = hide, seek cover. Il. xxii. 158
Tapistries = coverts, hiding-places. H. to Pan, 25
Targeteers = armed with target. Il. ii. 339; viii. 178
Tarriance = delay. Od. iv. 507
Taste (to) = to try, test. Od. xxi. 211
Temper (to) = to moderate. Od. vi. 497
Tendered = regard with kindness. Il. xxiv. 670
Tennis. Od. v. 431
Thankless = not grateful to. Il. iii. 12
Thirsted = desired. Il. v. 694; Od. iii. 393
Thirsty = desirous. Il. v. 850
Thrall = bond, subject. H. H. 924; H. V. 181
Threaves = numbers. Il. xi. 477
Throat = voices, noises. Il. ii. 396

Throated = uttered. Il. xiii. 135
Thrumbs = ends of weavers' threads. Il. xvi. 20
Tiller = bow. H. A. 13
Timeless = untimely. Il. v. 557; vi. 349
Tincture = colour. H. to Juno, p. 103
Touch = feeling. Il. xiii. 433
Transcended = climbed. Od. xvii. 377
Transcension = passing over. H. V. 487
Trebled = whined. H. H. 645
Tress = trace. Il. xxiii. 412
Trim = order, disposition. Il. v. 365
Trim = geer. Od. v. 233; xiii. 228; H. A. 245, 318, 639
Trim = dress. Od. vi. 233
Troublous. Il. xix. 328
Trundlebed. Od. vii. 48
Truss = accoutrement. Il. x. 19
Truss (to) = to seize and wound. Il. xxii. 124
Trussed = harassed. Il. xii. 237
Tumble (to), v. a. Il. xi. 282; xii. 23
Tutoress. H. H. 929
Twinks = twitters. Od. xxi. 548
Twybill = a kind of halberd. Il. xv. 656
Tyring. See note on Il. i. 422

U.

Unaltered = unalterable. Od. v. 148
Unbuild. Il. xiii. 561
Unconquered = invincible. Il. x. 425; xvi. 451
Uncontained = irrestrainable. Il. i. 93
Uncontrolled = uncontrollable. Il. iii. 257
Uncore = uncover. Od. xvii. 194 (see note)
Undeadly. Il. xi. 390
Underdive. Od. xi. 198
Undergore. Il. xiv. 408
Underput. Il. xxi. 342
Undifferencing. H. H. 1006
Undiked. Il. xv. 341

INDEX

Undisplaid = **not** to be discovered. H. H. 711
Unended = endless. Il. vi. 397
Unequal = unjust. Od. xiii. 28
Unexcogitable. H. H. 157
Unextinguished = inextinguishable. Il. xxii. 83
Unfiery. Il. vii. 84
Unfrighted = not **to be** frightened. Il. xvii. 286
Ungear (**to**). **Il. xi.** 536
Ungentle. **Il. i. 337**; Od. xi. 218
Unheired = without an heir. Il. v. 25
Unhorse. Il. **iv.** 325
Unimpeached = unimpeachable. **Il.** vii. 267 ; ix. 383
Unleft = not left. Il. ii. 622
Unlettered. Il. ii. 774
Unmatched = matchless. Od. xi. 617
Unmeasured = immeasurable. Il. ii. 78 *et alibi*
Unpassionate = impartial. Od. x. 242
Unpleased = implacable. Il. ix. 538
Unrecovered = irrecoverable. Il. ix. 247
Unreached = that cannot be reached. Il. xiii. 748
Unremorseful = unpitying. Il. ix. 597
Unremoved = firm, irremovable. Il. xvii. 379
Unreproved = irreproachable. **Il.** i. 87
Unresisted = irresistible. Il. **viii.** 122
Unrest. **Il. xi.** 340 ; **Od. i.** 641
Unruled = **not to** be **ruled**. **Il. ix.** 162 ; Od. iv. 925
Unsatisfying = unsatisfactory. **H. to** Pan, 71
Unsepulchred. Il. xxii. 331
Unsheath = pull out. Il. v. 705
Unsilenced = not to be silenced. Od. Ep. Ded. p. xlvi.
Unsuffered = insufferable. Il. iii. 6
Unsure. Od. xvi. 493
Untamed = not to be tamed. **Il. ii.** 133
Unthought-on. Il. xxii. 331
Outhrifts. Hes. Bk. ii. 170
Untrussed = with hose untied. Juv. 41

Unturned = not **to be** turned. Il. viii. 165
Unvalued = invaluable. Il. i. 12
Upbraids (n. s.). Il. vi. 389
Upland = country. Il. xiii. 523 ; Od. i. 315
Uplandish = rustical. Il. xxiii. 43
Ure = use. Il. xvii. 545
Usually = wontedly. Il. ix. 507
Utter = outer. Od. **iv.** 24

V.

VAIL = to lower. **Final** poem **to** Odyssey, 10
Vall = ditch. Il. iv. 479
Vanguard. Il. iv. 267 ; viii. 188
Vaunt (n. s.) = boast. Il. ii. 523
Vent (to) = to give birth to. Il. xix. 97
Vent (to) = to give way to. Il. **xix.** 406-7
Vinnoware = winnower. Hes. Bk. of Days, 66
Virtuous = valorous. Il. xiii. 148
Voiceful. Il. iii. 263
Voluntary = musical term. H. H. 851
Vulturous = voracious. Juv. 77

W.

WAGGONESS. Il. **v. 838**
Wan = wand. Od. **xi. 163-4**
Wavy. Il. ii. 446
Wayless = pathless. Od. ii. 547
Wealthy. Il. iii. 220 ; Od. iii. 478
Weed = dress. Il. ii. 33, &c., &c.
Well-rode = well-riding. Il. iii. 269
Wench = young woman. Il. i. 295 ; Od. iv. 977 (see note)
Whisking. Od. xxiv. 602
Whirlpits. Il. xx. 75
Whitleather. Il. xxii. 341 (see Addenda to third edition)

Whorlbats. Il. xxiii. 53 (see Addenda to third edition); Od. viii. 285
Whuling = howling. Od. xii. 135
Wishful. Od. ix. 55
Wishly. Il. xi. 522
Withdrawn-room. Od. xxiii. 8
Witty = wise. Il. v. 66
Wiving. H. V. 414
Wrackful. Od. xiii. 209
Wraths (plural). Il. iii. 354

Wreak = revenge (a common word). Il. iii. 25; Od. i. 583
Wreakful = revengeful. Il. vii. 184; Od. i. 396
Wreath = crown. Il. iii. arg. 8; xxiii. 578

Y.

Yare = ready, quick. Il. v. 727
Yet = while. Il. ix. 259
Yoted = soaked. Od. xix. 7

www.ingramcontent.com/pod-product-compliance
Lightning Source LLC
Chambersburg PA
CBHW022027240426
43667CB00042B/1219